THE STORYTELLER'S GUIDE

THE STORYTELLER'S GUIDE

STORYTELLERS SHARE ADVICE FOR THE CLASSROOM, BOARDROOM, SHOWROOM, PODIUM, PULPIT AND CENTER STAGE

WRITTEN AND EDITED BY
BILL MOONEY
AND DAVID HOLT

August House Publishers, Inc.
LITTLE ROCK

To all the storytellers

past

present

future,

who keep

the fires burning

© 1996 by Bill Mooney and David Holt.
All rights reserved. This book, or parts thereof,
may not be reproduced in any form without permission.
Published 1996 by August House, Inc.,
P.O. Box 3223, Little Rock, Arkansas, 72203,
501-372-5450.

Printed in the United States of America

10 9 8 7 6 5 4 3 2 1 PB

LIBRARY OF CONGRESS
CATALOGING-IN-PUBLICATION DATA
The storyteller's guide : storytellers share advice for the
classroom, boardroom, showroom, podium, pulpit, and
center stage / written and edited by Bill Mooney and
David Holt.
p. cm
Includes bibliographical references.
ISBN 0-87483-482-1 (alk. paper)
1. Storytelling —Philosophy. 2. Storytelling—Study and
teaching. 3. Storytellers—Interviews.
I. Mooney, William. II. Holt, David.
PN4061.S76   1996
808.5'43—dc20   96-9500

President and publisher: Ted Parkhurst
Executive editor: Liz Parkhurst
Project editor: Suzi Parker
Cover design: Wendell E. Hall
Production assistant: Ira L. Hocut
Assistant editor: Karen Martin
Editorial assistant: Brent Williams

The paper used in this publication meets the
minimum requirements
of the American National Standards for
Information Sciences—
permanence of Paper for Printed Library Materials,
ANSI.48-1984

CONTENTS

INTRODUCTION

♦ ♦ ♦ ♦

This is a guide for everyone, because everyone tells stories.

"Wait'll I tell you what I saw on the way to work …!"

"What's the story on that guy …?"

"The same thing happened to me when I was growing up …"

When we are asked to tell a story, however, many of us reply, "Oh, I don't know any stories! And even if I did, I wouldn't be able to tell them!"

Of course we can. We all tell stories every day of our lives about anything and everything that happens to us. That is how we communicate.

This book will guide you to be a better storyteller, no matter what your experience. It is for teachers, librarians, parents, grandparents, preachers, lawyers, all levels of storytellers, amateur and professional—in short, for everyone.

We interviewed more than fifty of America's best-known storytellers, asking them the major questions every storyteller needs answers to. As you read through the chapters, it will be like sitting around a table listening to good friends discussing interesting topics. Like any good conversation, you can enjoy it straight through or dip into it a little at a time.

We have also included two chapters directed toward the biggest group of storytellers in the world—teachers and librarians—entitled "How Can a Teacher Use Storytelling in the Classroom?" and "How can a Media Specialist Improve and Expand Storytelling in the Library?" We interviewed teachers and librarians from all regions of the country who are currently using storytelling in the classroom with great effectiveness and success. We think you will find these two chapters particularly informative and inspiring.

WHY IS STORYTELLING SO IMPORTANT?

Stories are how we learn. The progenitors of the world's religions understood this, handing down our great myths and legends from generation to generation. The Jewish and Hindu faiths are veritable treasuries of great stories. Christ taught by parable. The Muslim and Buddhist religions are equally story-rich. Families throughout the generations have used stories not only to teach moral and ethic behavior, but to preserve the memories and deeds of their forebears. Now, however, with the advent of so many single parent homes (or both parents working) and the fact that our grandparents aren't living with us any longer, fewer and fewer stories are being passed from one generation to the next, depriving our children of a basic human need. As Gay Ducey says, "Storytelling is the way we learn naturally. It's the way lessons and information get transmitted. I can't imagine how we'd communicate without it."

Television is now our big storyteller. But television is a passive storyteller. It doesn't care if we leave the room to raid the fridge. It doesn't care if we turn it off right at the crucial point of a story. It doesn't care about us. Worst of all, television does not allow us to use our imaginations. Add to that, many stories presented on commercial television have an underlying violence and consumerism. Television can never take the place of people telling each other stories. Storytelling is not passive, it is active. According to Mark Wagler, storytelling is our native language.

We humans have an innate desire to share experiences with others. Steve Sanfield believes, "There is a deep-seated need in the human spirit to tell stories, to hear stories, to share stories."

But why is it important to us? And particularly, why is it so important to us right now at the tag end of the twentieth and the beginning of the twenty-first centuries?

Penninah Schram answers, "Storytelling connects people. It connects hearts. It helps answer questions like: Who am I? Who are my people? With what values did they live? How should I live? How should I die? What are the legacies that I want to transmit to my children and to the next generation?

"The voice is the messenger of the heart," Penninah continues. "It's from my heart to your heart that I answer these questions best—through stories."

Doug Lipman adds, "The people in our society are hungry for community. There is something about being in a storytelling audience that creates community. Not only do you experience something, but you feel like you've constructed it together. It's like a barn-raising or a quilting bee."

"The importance of stories?" asks Kathryn Windham. "They give great pleasure. They divert if you're troubled. They stir memories. Stories make us laugh together. They make us aware of the shared experiences in life. Isn't that important?"

"I was telling stories at a prison for youthful offenders in Wisconsin," Kathryn continues. "I had one hundred seventy-five young felons sitting around me on the floor. Most of them came because they didn't have anything better to do, but they certainly didn't want to hear storytelling from a gray-haired woman who didn't even talk right. I started off by telling them some of my father's stories. They began to sit up and listen. I told them some ghost stories and they began to move in. I told them about growing up in the South. I told them stories for over an hour. When I had finished, so many of them came up and said, *'Nobody has ever told me a story before. Nobody ever told me a story!'*

"It has haunted me. You wonder what difference stories might have made to those boys. They may never have been behind those walls. If somebody had just taken the time to say, 'Come here and let me tell you this story.' It troubles me, and that is one reason why I keep telling stories. I ought to be home. Why am I gallivanting all over the country? I want people to tell stories. I want them to get to these children and teenagers. Everybody *needs* stories. Stories plainly say, 'I love you.' If you are going to tell stories really well, you have to care about the people you are telling stories to, even though you don't know their names, or anything about them. You need to realize that whoever is listening is looking for something. If you can provide some encouragement and some hope and laughter, and stir some memories, you have done a good day's work."

Bill Harley thinks that storytelling is more important for our culture right now than it has been for decades. "We understand ourselves through stories, by making stories out of our lives. Storytellers give people structure with which they can begin to look at their own lives and try to make sense of them. With all the noise we have in this culture, it's heartening that one person talking can still command attention."

Robin Moore believes that storytelling teaches people to dream again. "I don't mean dream in terms of getting a new boat or a bigger house or anything like that, but just the capacity to dream and imagine. Some tribal cultures feel that when you lose the ability to dream, you are no longer human; you cease to be a human being. Storytelling is what makes us most essentially human. Birds fly; fish swim; human beings dream."

Carol Birch agrees. "Storytelling strengthens the imagination. People frequently think of imagination in terms of children, but I think it is just as important for adults. To imagine is to envision, to see with the inward eye. This ability to imagine is the basis of all creativity. Creativity is being able to see beyond what is readily apparent. It is seeing a new answer to an old problem."

Laura Simms takes this one step further when she brings up the inner world "which is so belittled in our culture. The inner world is alive and functioning when one is telling a story. The mythic quality from the inside is set in vibration, so that there is a tremendous giving of joy, because the whole person is called upon.

"Storytelling brings us back to a more expansive awareness of being,"Simms adds."It inspires interdependence with the earth and with each other. It's like being wide awake in a dream, where instead of dominating the world, we are actually a part of the world. We create the world moment by moment inside the story, whether we are telling it or hearing it."

Heather Forest reminds us that storytelling harkens back to the oldest community experiences around the hearth fire. "Everywhere, every place on the planet, people have told stories."

Heather feels that by telling stories she helps keep an ancient tradition alive.

"In our society, printed words are respected more than spoken words. Written contracts carry more weight than oral ones. In American society, the electronic media is the storyteller. I suspect that if we changed the stories people hear every day, we could change the world.

"Old folktales have vast cultural knowledge embedded in the plot lines," Heather says. "The kind of cultural wisdom that has been passed down over the generations can inform, enlighten, entertain, and uplift the spirit of modern day listeners, just as these tales did in ancient times. As a storyteller, I have a responsibility to choose stories that are nourishing for my listeners, both emotionally and spiritually. I want to choose stories that will help them on life's journey."

Gayle Ross says, "The telling of stories, the desire to share our experiences, is what made us develop into a species with a spoken language. I think everybody has the capability of responding to a story on the deepest level. For that reason alone it's important."

History is nothing but a series of stories, whether it be world history or family history. Diane Ferlatte tells about her family: "I was born in New Orleans, but when I was nine, my father got a job in California and moved us all there. But every summer like clockwork, we went back to Louisiana. I would always ask,"How come we can't go somewhere else? How come we've got to drive in a hot car all the way back to Louisiana? Same old place!" But that's what Mom and Dad wanted to do. They wanted to go home. Home to Grandma and Grandpa.

"Now that I'm older and look back on it, my parents knew what they were doing taking me back to my roots, to Grandma, Grandpa, to the old things in the house. The old talk, the old songs, the old screened-in front porch, big old swings, bugs, crickets, country store around the corner. The storms, the lightning, the man across the street who wore a hat and tie all day, every day."

At the end of his adult storytelling sessions, Bill Mooney charges the audience to tell stories to their children, to their children's children, and especially to their children's children's children. "Tell them stories about how it was when you grew up. Tell them what was important to you then and why. Tell them about your triumphs, but also tell them about your failures, your missed chances. These small personal stories are so important to our children. They teach as much as the big stories. They enlighten. They help us to understand why people act the way they do. If we know the story behind an action, we are better able to understand and forgive it. Tell your children stories. If you don't, when you die your stories die with you." Remember, stories aren't stories until they are told. Everyone should tell stories.

As the old Celtic taleteller, William Butler Yeats, said, "Storytellers make us remember what mankind would have been like, had not fear and the failing will and the laws of nature tripped up its heels."

HOW DO I GET STARTED?

◆ ◆ ◆ ◆

The journey of a thousand miles begins with a first step, but that initial step is usually the hardest. You begin with a million questions. Where do I start? Which way do I head? Can I go the distance?

There is no reason to be a storyteller unless you feel the need and hear the call. But when something inside you says, "I need to try this," then it is time to take action. You can watch and listen to other storytellers and learn a lot, but at some point you have to take that first step and start telling. Of course, you have to learn and practice your story, but it is the act of telling your tale to another human being that brings it alive. At this point you will feel vulnerable, but as Bill Harley and Margaret Read MacDonald agree, you just have to do it. You will need a safe place to perform and a place to fail.

Jay O'Callahan tells how he started with his own children and built up from there. Jackie Torrence, Connie Regan-Blake, and Len Cabral say to learn a few stories and tell them everywhere, see how the audience reacts and how you react to the audience. Gayle Ross tells the beginner to build a reputation in his or her own community. Then, she adds, "Don't quit your day job." Pleasant DeSpain, however, knew he wanted to be a professional, so he set up his career with no easy exit. He made storytelling his job from the beginning. Robin Moore offers a detailed look at how he made the transition from amateur to professional.

When looking for material to tell, Jim May reminds us to look at what has moved us in our lives. Diane Wolkstein says we need to start with a passion for a tale and a need to tell it. Donald Davis begins by looking for stories in his own life, noting that originality is very important in the long run.

Milbre Burch starts by reading, Joseph Bruchac by listening, and Ed Stivender starts with a good strong cup of coffee.

What it all comes down to is this: You can find a story you like and run over it in your head endlessly or practice it in front of a mirror for hours, but only when you tell it to another person does it really start to become yours. You start by taking that first step. Find a story and tell it.

Bill Harley: There's no substitute for just doing it. I started by the seat of my pants. I decided I was a storyteller and told people, then I got put into situations where I had to do it. I think you can read and talk and think about it; but, ultimately, you just have to do it. One of the things that you should do first is find a safe place to fail—a place where you can work and try things out. Whenever you tell stories you are vulnerable—vulnerability is always a part of it—but you need to find a place like the library or your kid's classroom to start telling stories and find out what works and what doesn't. There's no substitute for simply doing it.

Beth Horner: These days there are so many festivals, classes, and workshops it's fairly easy to get introduced to storytelling. Take a class and get started. It was harder ten years ago, definitely twenty years ago, for the first generation, but now it's easier. Back then, you had to invent your own venues and try to figure out what stories worked best in them. You had to educate people about storytelling. Now beginning storytellers can follow the examples that have been set, and the paths that one can take to become a professional storyteller.

Margaret Read MacDonald: Just jump in. Storytelling is like swimming. You can't do it by sitting on the bank. You have to jump in and start dog paddling. You take a story that you love and think would be fun to tell, and you just start telling it. You keep on doing it until you get good at it. It's that simple, but you've got to start. You'll never do it sitting on the bank.

Ed Stivender: Every morning I rise just before dawn and sight the morning star. Then I make cowboy coffee and Quaker Oats. Then I read the "Deer's Cry," St. Patrick's word-armor prayer. By this time the oats and coffee are ready. On payday, I have an apple fritter from Rindelaub's, the perfect food, with no repetitions.

I watch the sun rise from my twelfth floor rook-nook overlooking Wissahickon Notch, and the seventeenth century village of Rittenhousetown and Penn Charter School, and the skyline of the City of Brotherly Love.

Two forty-minute sessions at the barre, then over to the Nautilus. And, of course, a swim in the heated pool Grace Kelly almost got thrown into in either *Philadelphia Story* or at the wedding reception held at the manor house just beyond the tipper from my building, the Kenilworth.

By this time I am ready to work in front of the mirror for an hour and then the first of my two hours of writing a day. I try to get to my old college chapel for noon mass if I'm not real hot on the keys. I spend the afternoon doing research, discussing stocks, and investments with my partner, Nancy Clancy, and waiting for Disney to call.

But it's the coffee that I would really say is how I get started in the morning.

Maggi Peirce: If you really want to get started, listen to people on stage. I know some people who make awfully bad tapes and records, but on stage they're magic. First of all, go and listen to people telling stories; if you have people in your family who tell good stories, listen to them. Listen. Don't stop them in the middle of the story. Watch them. Watch their every move. When people ask me, "Who taught you storytelling?" I say to them, "Nobody taught me storytelling. I imbibed it."

Some of the hand movements that I make are my father's. When I stop in astonishment, it's my aunt Aileen. When I whisper and tell something very confidential, it's my mother. I imbibed these because children were literally seen and not heard in Belfast when I was growing up. This meant that I kept my mouth shut. But boy, were my ears and eyes open!

Don't rush in too quickly. I remember one young lassie who came to my door asking for storytelling help. I gave her as much help as I possibly could. It must have lasted almost two hours, and then I discovered she was out telling stories in schools with a fancy brochure and all the rest of it. And do you know what her repertoire was? Six stories!

Now I'm sorry, but you should not have a brochure made and be ringing up schools and saying, "I'm a storyteller!" with six stories. And I feel that you also should choose stories that speak to you. Don't listen to a story and say, "Oh so-and-so tells that so well, therefore, I'll be able to do it as well." You maybe won't.

Always try to find stories that have action in them.

Start with action. Start with laughter. Start with ghost stories that go "BOO" at the end. Start easy, be easy on yourself at the beginning, and then you will grow within the whole idea of storytelling, slowly, slowly.

Donald Davis: Everybody has stories. The story process to me is one of finding the story inside you, rather than picking a story outside you. If there's a story told by someone else and you really love that story, I would ask what is it in that story that reminds you of your life? What time and place are you reminded of? Try to work very hard with your own original story. Because in the long term, originality is going to be a very important thing. It's good to start with it early.

Jim May: Work on stories. It's one of those things where the answer to the question is obvious. Get some stories together. Think about what stories have meant to you; think about the people who have told stories in your own life. It may be you have a whole bunch of aunts and uncles who are all good storytellers. It may be that they're literary people who have been moved by books and great stories. It really doesn't matter. This is what matters: what has really moved *you* in your life. Go to that. Start building stories within yourself, and keep in mind that there is a world of storytelling out there that will welcome that. Always start within yourself. Sherwood Anderson told William Faulkner, "Go back to Oxford, Mississippi, and write about something you know."

Len Cabral: Go to the library. Find stories that you enjoy reading. Start sharing them with youngsters. Volunteer at a day care center or Headstart. Work your way up to an elementary school. Find stories that you're comfortable with. Find out if storytelling is for you. It isn't for everyone. The way to find out is by testing the water.

Robin Moore: I think you need to begin by asking yourself some pretty elementary questions. First of all: Are you interested in doing this as a hobby or as a profession?

When I was a boy, my father gave storytelling performances at our local Boy Scout camp and at outdoor festivals in our little town. He never made much money at it, but he had a lot of fun and gave pleasure to a lot of people who heard his tales. There's nothing wrong with that approach.

On the other hand, if you want to do it as a profession, you need to ask yourself if you plan to tell stories as your sole activity or if you plan to combine storytelling with some other talents such as teaching or writing. The answers to these questions will determine a lot about how you proceed in the beginning.

> *You need lots of experience listening and lots of experience telling.*
> *— Peninnah Schram*

It is possible at this time to make a comfortable living by traveling around and telling stories. Thanks to the National Storytelling Association and the many people who have fueled the storytelling revival, storytelling is a viable career choice.

I began telling stories full-time in 1981, and since then I have made my living primarily by fees from storytelling engagements. I do between three and four hundred storytelling performances a year. Most of my clients are elementary schools. The educational world is very supportive of storytelling, and I have no problem getting enough work to pay the bills.

Heather Forest: Everyone is a storyteller. Any time a person answers the question, "What happened?" they are telling a tale. The long continuum of storytelling goes from personal communication, one on one, to the performing artist on stage, talking to hundreds or thousands. The styles of storytelling that exist right now in the American renaissance of storytelling are diverse. The only stylistic element that is common is that storytellers know their stories by heart. The first step in getting started is to know tales by heart and tell them even to one person. There is no shortcut to artistry … practice!

Penninah Schram: How do you get started? (You know, you ask storytellers a question and they answer with a story.)

There is a tradition of reading the Haggadah, the story of the exodus from Egypt at Passover time. The story of the exodus from Egypt focuses on Moses and the Jews who had to cross the Red Sea. When did the Red Sea part? Not as Moses raised his staff, but rather the Red Sea parted when the first person, a man by the name of Nahshon, jumped into the water and went in up to his chin.

You start by telling stories. By literally jumping in. I don't think there's any other way to do it.

You need lots of experience listening and lots of experience telling. You make occasions; you make opportunities to tell stories. Literally invite friends, sit around the table, ask each one to bring a story, and just tell stories to each other. Go to schools or organizations, especially where they would welcome storytellers but don't necessarily have the funds to pay them. Until you build a repertoire, until you build up the experience, until you trust yourself to know how to be there and enjoy and be flexible in the storytelling experience, you really need to take the time and make those opportunities. Tell the stories, find the place, build a repertoire.

Try telling the same story twenty times because until the twentieth time it's not yours. Allow for failure; allow for changing the way you tell it. Don't let it be memorized and set in stone. All of those things take years. I don't think anyone can instantly become a storyteller and say, "OK, here I am, a professional." No one can just put storyteller on the letterhead and go out and do it. I think people have to

allow time—sometimes years—to build those foundations before they can earn the name "storyteller."

Milbre Burch: My path to storytelling came first through reading. I came from a family of readers and writers. I was unaware of having heard oral stories until well into my adulthood. But the savoring of language itself and appreciation of the written word have been ingrained in my family for at least three generations. Also, I was a performer and a carport theatrical producer even as a child. It's not surprising to me now that the spoken word, the intersection of personal language and performance, has become my profession.

Jay O'Callahan: I started with a safe group. That's still helpful even now that this is my work. My safe group was, first of all, a brother and sister, and later it was as a parent with children who were two and four, then three and five. Those were great ages. No criticism at all, just sheer delight. If possible, get someone who is delighted that you're giving them some attention with a story. Find a group of friends and make a safe arena for yourself. I think you need to feel encouraged.

With a safe group, you can explore and find out, "Gosh, I'm pretty good with sounds," or "Oh, my golly, when I make up this rhythm, they really seem to light up," or "I made that face and they really were laughing," or "That whole group was so quiet." Then you have to take some of it seriously and try to be brave enough to say, "I really stank on that," or "I really did well on that," and then define it, so that you know what you're confident about.

Have some sense of what your strengths are; that's what is going to hold you up. I'm just mirroring my experience. Mine was growing bigger and bigger and bigger, starting with two children. Then it was a tiny little local library where I told stories to six or eight children. Then it was going into schools. I didn't do it for money. I would tell to twenty kids there and then I would tell, again for no money, to Cub Scout groups and to four or five hundred people at occasional community things. It was, "Come on over, Jay, and tell a story." They often forgot to say, "We'll throw in ten dollars, too." But that was fine. It enabled me to think, gosh, I can really be very good at this. Get the confidence to say, "I am finally going to take it seriously and do it."

Pleasant DeSpain: First find the stories that are right for you to tell. Then prepare to tell them. When you are ready, go out and find an audience that is willing to listen, be it in a school, a park, a library or a campground. Essentially, every program leads to at least one more program. I never know who's listening, but I know there is always someone listening who will help me get another program. I got started by doing it and finding an audience. I went to coffeehouses twenty-two years ago, put out a hat, said I was a storyteller, and told some stories. I started by not creating back doors, meaning: "Well, if I don't make it here, then I'll go do something else." I also got started by finding a way to support myself in order to do the important work—whatever it took.

Joseph Bruchac: Listening is at the heart of it. Listen to everything. If you don't listen, you'll never hear a story. All around you there is sound and motion and the circle of life, but many people walk through these with their ears and eyes closed. Unless you listen and observe, you are never going to learn. That's the most important thing for a young storyteller or a continuing storyteller to know.

Jon Spelman: You start telling stories by telling stories. I think it's that simple, and "story" is a simple concept: A story is some kind of narration; it has a beginning, middle, and end. When you start telling a story, you think about the beginning and tell it; then you think about the middle and the end and tell each of them.

Many jokes are a form of early developmental storytelling; so is the reporting of what you did during the day—the natural storytelling you do when you tell your spouse what happened at work. When you are answering a small child's questions, you're very often telling a story.

Carol Birch: You tell stories, and you don't expect to get paid. I know somebody who made up a brochure and he had four things listed. I said, "I didn't know you had four programs." It turned out this person didn't have four programs. He had four stories.

David Novak: My suggestion would be: Ask yourself, what stories do I know? What stories are important to me? Start where you feel comfortable. For example, many teachers who want to get started in storytelling feel much more comfortable telling stories to their students than telling stories to adults. Maybe later they'll branch out and do something in the library, where there are mostly children but perhaps a few adults. And then maybe, by virtue of those first efforts, there'll be a positive response—good word-of-mouth—that will start drawing them out farther and farther afield as people invite them to come to this or that place. Then as the momentum picks up, they have to be open as the opportunities present themselves.

SUMMARY

- » Just jump in. You can think about it only so long. You have to tell stories to be a storyteller.
- » Find stories that you like.
- » Start by telling the stories to yourself—when you are walking or driving in your car.
- » Try telling them to a "safe" audience—to your children at bedtime, to your dog, to a fellow storyteller.
- » Tell "about" the story in normal conversation. That is, summarize it, hit the high points, see if the basic plot is interesting to people. This also helps you get the main images firmly fixed in your mind.
- » Tell the story ten times before deciding whether it works or not.
- » Find a local elementary school that will let you tell one or two stories to three different classes for free. Try the story on different age groups. Make a note of what story appeals to what age group.
- » Volunteer to tell stories for hospitals, churches, day care centers, and nursing homes. Find appropriate stories for each age level.
- » Keep telling. It takes a long time to get good at anything. Enjoy the process. Have fun.

HOW DO I FIND THE RIGHT STORIES?

♦ ♦ ♦ ♦

David Holt has been fascinated for many years with the sinking of the Titanic. Fifteen hundred people died that night in April 1912 on a ship that was deemed "unsinkable." It was a remarkable event and seemed like a natural for storytelling. It had action, excitement, drama, and life and death heroics, but David could never make it work. He tried and tried to fashion a story that would convey the events of that night, but each attempt kept turning into a history lesson.

David needed to find a way to make the story personal, so the listener could visualize that horrible event and become involved in it. He worked on the story for years with no success until at last he found a true account by a survivor—a ten-year-old girl. It was exactly what he had been looking for. As they hear this ten-year-old's point of view, the audience can identify with the narrative and become engrossed. They don't get an entire account of that tragic night, but they get a real story.

Start searching for stories with topics that interest you like David did with the Titanic. It is essential that you find a tale that you like. Your natural curiosity will fuel the search. When you tell it, your enthusiasm will radiate out to the audience. Look for a story that is visually strong so the listener can easily re-create it in his own mind. In a good tale, something has to happen, the more unusual and exciting the better. Keep the plot simple and the action moving.

Another natural place to look for stories is in your ethnic and cultural background. It never fails to amaze us how stories from our own cultural heritage speak to everyone. The folktales of any culture provide a mother lode for the storyteller. Here are tales that have been worked and reworked for generations. They were made for telling. The old folktales, moreover, have a depth and wisdom that adds strength to telling. Many of them have the power to touch an audience at deep levels.

Do not overlook your family stories. Many families have a tradition of telling tales at family gatherings. These stories have been told and retold so often that, sometimes, a good punch line has been established. As a storyteller, your job will be to straighten them up and give the unacquainted listener a sense of who the characters are and what the context is.

Whenever our families get together, the older folks start to tell tales about one another. Luckily, we have had some pretty colorful characters in our clans—like David's Texas pioneer grandmother who had all thirty-two teeth pulled in one sitting with no anesthesia. When Bill's in-laws get together, the "Cousin Otis" stories are always trotted out, told, and retold. There are probably twenty fairly well-polished stories that are told at each of our family gatherings. Every time they are told, we react and laugh as if we had never heard them before. It's a wonderful experience.

These short, mostly true family anecdotes are perfect material for the storyteller. They give the audience a sense of who you are and where you are from. By telling family stories, you encourage others to preserve their family heritage.

There are thousands of stories out there waiting for you. Finding the right ones may seem daunting, but it is really more like an Easter egg hunt for the mind. It may take a long time, but it's always satisfying and never boring.

We are both voracious readers. We're always on the lookout for the next good story. And it takes a lot of reading. We are happy if we find one story we really want to tell in an entire anthology.

Keep notes as you read and listen. After reading several hundred stories, you may have difficulty keeping the various narratives straight. When David first got into storytelling, he decided to read the complete fairy tales of the Brothers Grimm. (There are more than two hundred). It soon became clear that there were too many tales to remember exactly which ones he liked and what they were about. He began to take notes, writing down title, page number, a one- or two-sentence summary, and a rating from one to three for the stories. A "three" meant he should try it out. A "two" meant look at it again. A "one" meant maybe. He made the list of Grimm stories more than twenty years ago and still refers to it today.

After finding a story we like, we make a photocopy of it and file it with similar stories. That way, we have easy access to our collections of stories filed by category: fairy tales, ghost stories, wonder tales, true-life stories, tall tales, and a host of others.

A final note on building a repertoire. You will probably want to "try on" stories that you hear from other tellers. This is only natural and a good way to learn. If you do not plan on being a professional storyteller, you can collect a large group this way. But if you ever see yourself doing this for money, you should start building your own repertoire from the beginning.

Part of the job of storyteller is discovering new material. Sure, the storytellers that got there first had easy pickings, but they got just the obvious, low-hanging fruit. Some of the juiciest, freshest, untouched stories are still waiting to be harvested. Finding your own special peach is only part of the creative challenge, but it's a big part of the joy of storytelling.

Jon Spelman: Finding the right stories for yourself is at least fifty percent of effective telling. It's a long process. How do you find the person that's right for you, or the house that's right for you, or the clothes that are right for you?

You do it by looking around, by experimentation, and by trying on and feeling out lots of different possibilities. Some you reject. Some you say, "I can come back to that later." Some you say, "This feels OK," or "This doesn't look right." And sometimes, when you're lucky and ready, the choice is very clear. I knew the moment I first saw my wife that she was right for me. And you do that with stories, too. The moment that your ears or your eyes fasten on that story or the moment you think of a certain story to create, you know that that's the right story for you. For example, the first time I visited the Vietnam Veterans Memorial, I knew I was going to tell those stories. But usually you have to look around—a lot.

Steve Sanfield: To find a story in text, I probably read two to three hundred stories for every story that I choose to tell. I read stories constantly. A day doesn't go by that I don't read three or four stories from somewhere. Without even the conscious thought that I'm looking for a story, it's just become a habit, a working habit of mine.

The Ibo people of West Africa talk about stories like feathers. They say that there will be a beautiful feather lying on a path and dozens of people will walk by and most people won't see it. A few people will notice the feather, and they'll say, "Oh, what a lovely feather." But eventually, a man or a woman will come along and see that beautiful feather on the path, reach down and pick it up, take it home and make it part of their altar. Now that's how I think you should find a story.

Gay Ducey: I think they find me. The first thing to know is what kind of stories appeal to you and not be misled by what you think is marketable, or what you think is trendy. Find the story that is arresting or that you continue to think about and can't quite forget.

When you start to look for stories, I think the tendency is to look for ones that seem facile, easy to learn, easy to pick up, easy to use. The word "easy" is not a word that should apply to choosing stories—not at all. What I look for is a story that is both suitable for me and one that has something important to say to me. The stories that attract me are usually perverse and not particularly commonplace. But the lessons they teach or the information they share is timeless.

Syd Lieberman: You just keep reading. I have to read a lot before I find something that rings a bell. A lot of times I read a story that I don't like and I'll read it again a few years later and I'll say, "That's a great story. Why didn't I see that before?" But maybe your life is in a different place now, and suddenly the story is talking to you. I can't believe how many stories I have to read before I find one that I think would be good.

Milbre Burch: I almost always find the stories I tell in written collections, usually in the 398.2 section of a public library. In my early days as a storyteller, I especially looked for stories that surprised or haunted, amused or touched me.

As one of the first generation raised on television, I've had a full plate of stories served up to me all my life. I recognize a plot twist when I see one. So I figure if a story takes me by surprise or stays with me, makes me laugh or shed a tear, chances are it will have the same effect on most of my audience. You have to learn to trust your instincts.

Joseph Bruchac: Experience, intuition, paying attention. When I say you have to listen, you also have to listen as a teller to your audience. Sometimes the only way you can answer a question like that is by telling a story.

A friend of mine named John Stokes, who is himself a storyteller in the Southwest and has worked a great deal with young men in teaching them outdoor survival skills and respect for tradition, was called into a high school where there had been just the day before a drive-by shooting and where there was a lot of gang activity. These were tough gang kids, wearing the wraparound sunglasses with the strange haircuts, and that look of defiance that you see an awful lot these days in the eyes of young people.

John got up in front of them and said, "I want to tell you a story. I've studied martial arts for many years and this is a story about that." That got their attention right away. Then he told a story about a man who studied aikido. For many, many years in Japan this man studied—he was an American—until he felt he was really a master. One night he got on a bus. There were a number of Japanese people on the bus and one very, very large Japanese man about the size of a Sumo wrestler. He was drunk and was pushing around the other people on the bus and abusing them verbally.

This young man who had studied aikido was just waiting for that big drunk guy to reach him because he knew exactly what to do. He was ready to be a hero. But before the big drunk man reached him, from the back of the bus, a small elderly Japanese man got up, walked up to that huge drunk, gently put his hand on the man's arm, and said, "My son, what is the trouble with you?" As soon as he did that, the gigantic drunk sat down and began to weep and said, "My wife, she's in the hospital. They say she may not live." It was at that point that the man who had studied aikido realized he was not a master. The old man was the master.

John Stokes told that story to this high school crowd. When he finished, you could have heard a pin drop. Every word he spoke after that, they listened to. That's knowing your audience and knowing your story.

Laura Simms: That's the hardest task of all. For me after twenty-five years as a storyteller, it is still a curious task. I suggest to new storytellers that they begin by choosing one folktale, one true event from their life, and one fairy tale. Begin to outline that story. Just the sequence of events. Learn just three stories for a whole year, just those three. They will know so much about story and storytelling by doing all the research and going through a process of learning.

Then again, sometimes somebody's in the position like I was in the beginning where I had no money, and nobody had ever heard of storytelling. So at that point I got a job where I had to come up with three or four new stories every week. So I poured through books. It took a long time for me to know which stories I really loved or which were the stories that suited me. At the same time, it's like all things in the world, you're not alone. The stories will jump out and come to you, because they need to be told.

There are many collections of world folklore where people can find a big variety of tales and choose something.

How do you know you like a story? First of all, it seems to me that something catches you. Sometimes it's very small. Sometimes it's an image in the story or something you don't understand, something you keep thinking about. Sometimes it's something that is plain irritating. So you go back to it. I always stay with those.

Bill Harley: I think you have to try out a whole bunch of different stories. The key thing is that you should not tell a story you don't like. That sounds obvious, but a lot of times beginning storytellers get put into a situation where they are so eager to do anything that they will tell any kind of story.

I always say in workshops that you are a storyteller the day someone asks you to do a certain kind of story, and you say, "I don't do that." You will be in the middle of a situation that doesn't work and feels awkward and you'll say, "This is just not my story." But you can only do that by trying out different things and getting feedback from the audience so that you know how it feels yourself. You can talk to your friends and people around you. It doesn't have to be just another artist that will tell you what they see. A lot is just trial and error and trusting your instinct.

Doug Lipman: Asking the question is having the answer. Your job is to find the stories that work for you and the audience at the moment. There are three elements to a storytelling event: you, the audience at the moment, and the story, and those three have to work together.

The story needs to be something you can make a connection with and the audience can also make a connection with. Another way to say it is: Can you find a way to connect to this audience through this story? You need to find stories that you love and that draw you to them. You also need to find stories that are a gift for the audience. When you have things that meet both of those, then you have a story that you can tell.

Diane Ferlatte: Just look for the stories that you like. I tend to draw on the culture I'm from—African-American stuff—because I really understand it and I can click with it. I like Southern stuff because my family's from the South and I've heard Southern stories. Other stories just don't click. They're good stories to hear but they're not for me to tell.

To be a storyteller you have to be natural, using your natural way of speaking and your natural way of feeling and being. If you try to trump it up, people are going to know that something's missing. I think a lot of storytellers are getting into that too. So many storytellers are popping up, but they're copying other people, they're using other voices, using other gestures and trumping up stuff, and it's just not them and you can see it.

Michael Parent: I think that moving toward your own passion and curiosity is a good start. For instance, I already knew that I liked stories, and at first I was telling them for kids. So I decided I would do two kinds of stories. I would do stories that were simple and tellable and fun. So I went to folktales. Then I started creating stories around things that I knew about. For instance, I had one story about a kid sister trying to preserve her relationship with her older brother, whom she looked up to. I know about that because I was an older brother, so I made that story up. I was trying to take a feeling and create a story from that feeling— namely, how do you keep that connection with someone you really love and look up to? So I made up stories based on what I knew about.

Margaret Read MacDonald: I've written a lot about this because I feel that you're most apt to find a story that you can tell if you get as close as possible to the words of a good teller. So I've printed up numerous lists of collections that do this. There's a good list in my Twenty Tellable Tales and also in The Storyteller's Start-up Book that list collections that have been taken down by storytellers or folklorists directly from really good tellers.

The point is you've got to find a good teller to begin with, someone who has his or her text refined in a really tellable manner. And then you have to get someone who will take it down exactly as the teller speaks it. If you can find that printed someplace or on a tape you can work from it. You can put that story back into an oral telling very easily because it hasn't been removed from the oral telling.

I probably read two to three hundred stories for every story that I tell.
— Steve Sanfield

The problem with most of our books is that they have been rewritten by authors into a short story format so they've lost that oral feel, that oral flow, and that's why they're so difficult to put back into an oral form. So that's my hint for finding a really tellable story: Get as close as you can to the oral source.

Gayle Ross: If you're tuning yourself correctly, I believe the stories find you. Finding material is the hardest step for beginning storytellers. It's very tempting these days—especially with the resources available—to fill the repertoire based almost entirely on good stories that other people have developed and used effectively and perhaps recorded or published. I think that's a trap. It prevents you from fully developing your own style and your own gift for language. I really believe that the bulk of the world's traditional tales are a gold mine. And for every version of the story there's another that hasn't been told yet and that's yours.

People should be guided in their search for material by what speaks deepest to them, be that a geographical heritage or an ethnic heritage or the love of a particular culture (without getting into all the pitfalls of cross-cultural telling which would take a book in itself). It takes a lot of research, a lot of homework. There are wonderful collections, wonderful bibliographies, mountains of material to go through. I believe that you should just dive in and start looking for what really speaks to you. What moves you the most will be the most effective stories for you to tell.

Len Cabral: It takes a lot of searching to find a good story. Sometimes you'll read a book and the story jumps off the page at you and you go, "Oh, this is great! What a great find!" Other times you will be searching for weeks looking for a story that talks to you. Even when you find a story that just whispers at you, and you work with it for a while but it still doesn't click, it might be a year or two before you find out how to tell that story—before you find the heart of that story and are able to tell it.

Robin Moore: Look at the imagination as if it were a landscape. There is a certain amount of territory there that you can claim as your own and you will know your way around. You can make forays into tales from other cultures and that kind of thing. My own thinking about it is if you don't have a firm grounding in your own culture (for instance, if you are a Christian and you are fascinated by Eastern religions), it would be fine to study Eastern religions, but then you ought to come back and look at the wealth within your own tradition and get a good foundation there. I have felt that way about the Celtic lore, and that's given me a base that I can go out from.

Heather Forest: The right story for a teller to tell is one that fits emotionally, intellectually, and spiritually. There are thousands and thousands of stories in the world. A teller can't carry all the stories. When I choose a story to carry, it must help me in some way or give me pleasure in telling again and again. I am going to tell that

story many times in my life, in many different settings, so it must be a journey that I want to take. Sometimes I find stories that are not right for me to tell. And I know that; it's an instinctive intuitive choosing.

It is important to consider choosing the right story to tell the audience at hand. The age of the listeners, the setting in which the storytelling is taking place, the time of year perhaps, the reason for the coming together are all considerations. Storytelling is a feast for the mind. One must serve appropriate tales in order to best satisfy the needs of the listeners.

Jay O'Callahan: I found a lot of my stories at bedtime or driving, because I would make up stories. So if you have children and you want to try making them up, then you can just wing it. If you do that during the day, you may become aware that you're passing a mailbox—it catches your attention—and maybe that mailbox is going to show up in your story tonight.

Another source for story makers and for those who are parents and grandparents and baby sitters is to let the story come out of a hurt. If a child is hurt, sit down with the child. This has been done for thousands of years. You just say, "It reminds me of the time when this happened ..." and suddenly their attention is taken off their pain and focused on the story you're telling. *Raspberries* came right out of my son's bumping his knee and crying. It's a long story of mine.

The third way is to listen to folktales. I love folktales, and when I hear one that I love, I tell it right away. I grab a friend and I tell it. I ask my wife to sit down, "Let me just tell you this little story ..." Or I get my kids, "Let me tell you this folktale ..." And I keep telling it—three, four, five, six, seven, eight, or nine times. Then I tell it to other people.

The last source has been to read folktales. I prefer to hear them because it's an oral medium and I love the sounds and rhythms and then I know if I like them.

Susan Klein: I think the stories come to you. There is something about putting that energy out into the world. As soon as you really make a conscious statement to yourself, a statement of intent that that's what you are looking for, then that stuff comes to you. And when you know what your intention is, it's amazing how much will be provided for you. Books fall off their shelves and open up to a page. They come in the mail. People call you up and say, "Are you aware of this author and this particular work?" Authors write to me and say, "Will you use my words? Is there a possibility of your doing this?" I'm not saying you just sit back and take a vacation and wait for something to fall out of the sky. You have to do research and make contacts. But the intent really is the underlying part of it and the rest of it is simply walking through the world and picking them up.

Carol Birch: This is one area of storytelling where I know of no shortcut. People seem to think the work of storytelling is learning a story or overcoming fears about performing, but as far as I'm concerned, the real work of storytelling is finding the story to tell.

I'm always looking for stories when I read. The best way to find a story to tell (from printed sources) is to read out loud. This isn't useful if you have nine collections in front of you and you need a story for next week. But if you're involved in this

for the long haul, you'll find more stories to tell by reading aloud as you go along. You feel—and hear—what stories come "trippingly off the tongue" and which stories more easily satisfy your sensibilities.

I once heard a woman tell a version of "Millions of Cats." You know how much repetition is in the story, with the wonderful run: "There were hundreds of cats, thousands of cats, millions and billions and trillions of cats!" The storyteller needs to say it only one time before kids are eager to join in. Well, when the second time to say the line came, this person literally said: "There were hundreds of cats, et cetera."

Et cetera!

It's unbelievable. And yet that is what we all tend to do when we are reading silently. "Oh, there's that run, that rhyme, that name again," and we don't say it. This silence can really cut us off from the joys and the pleasures—and sometimes the arduousness—of a story. When we don't say the words of a story aloud, we lose one of the easiest ways to access the musical quality of a story. When you read aloud, you can more easily find out if this is a story for you.

David Novak: In the area of selecting stories, listening is very important. When you're reading short stories or hearing other people tell stories, you need to listen and see if the story impresses. Does it have any influence on me? Does it appeal to me? If it grabs me, then that's a sign that maybe this is a story I should be working with because I have some connection with it.

SUMMARY

» Start with topics that interest you.

» Look for a story that is filled with vivid images so that the listener can easily re-create it in his own mind.

» A natural place to look for stories is in your own cultural and ethnic background.

» Rummage through your family anecdotes and stories to see if any of them are usable.

» Keep notes on the stories you read. Write a one- or two-sentence summary and rate the stories from one to three.

» Don't be misled by what is trendy or marketable. Stick with those stories that have something to say, that you can't forget.

» Try out many stories. By telling and retelling them, you will find the right ones.

» Never tell a story you don't like.

» Go to the 398.2 section of a library. Look there for stories that surprise, haunt, amuse, or touch you.

» Listen to a lot of different storytellers, either in person or on tape. Notice what stories attract them.

» The right story is one that fits emotionally, intellectually, and physically.

» Read stories aloud.

» Many times the story finds you.

ONCE I FIND A STORY AND LIKE IT,
HOW DO I MAKE IT MY OWN?

◆ ◆ ◆ ◆

Prior to the 1970s, the style of storytelling was primarily literary in nature. The stories came from books that were read or told. But new storytellers started appearing on the scene, sparking a revival in storytelling that kept growing year by year. These new tellers added their own personalities to the stories, which brought them alive. Audiences began to see how the old tales were relevant to their own lives and the storytelling movement burgeoned. Suddenly, storytelling was not just for kids but for everyone.

Making a story your own takes time and work, but the work is creative and fun. This is the work that brings a story to life and infuses it with your personality. In many ways, it is the heart of the modern-day storytelling movement. Take a tale that resonates with you and learn its bare bones, then start to tell it. The more you tell it, the more you will be able to get inside the story.

Gay Ducey does not "monkey" with the story but rather tells it over and over to friendly audiences. To her, it is a process that cannot be hurried. She keeps the story small at the beginning. If you start working up the tale and turn it into a big production number, chances are that you will miss some of the subtleties and deeper meanings.

Milbre Burch once choreographed every detail of her story before she told it to an audience. She then began to realize that a story that has never been heard in performance is unfinished. She needed time to see how the story worked. Then the changes she made became more organic.

Susan Klein does not rehearse but actually lets the narrative work on her. She reads the story over several times, which sets it stewing in her dreams and subconscious. When Susan finally does tell it on stage, she keeps her "inner editor" alert to remember what does and does not work.

Ed Stivender works from a scripted outline, but he lets the audience's response show him what should be kept and discarded. Robin Moore prefers visualizing the images in a story until he has a clear picture of it. Then he simply tells what he sees in his mind.

Steve Sanfield places photocopies of the story in his car and around his home for easy reference. Milbre Burch uses a video recorder to help her critique the work. Diane Wolkstein suggests we practice the words out loud to ourselves. They are like scales to a musician. You play them enough, you learn the notes. Len Cabral sings or moves to a story to find its rhythm. When it is ready, he tries it out before people of various ages to see who enjoys it.

It is important to know what makes the story work. David Novak asks himself what is the most important aspect of the tale, what part has meaning for him. Penninah Schram outlines the plot and considers the point of the story and how her life experiences relate to it. She goes further and asks, "Why do I need to tell this story?"

Good stories are like a pair of new jeans. You have to wear them awhile before they really fit you. It is the repeated telling of stories that breaks them in. At some point, they become a second skin, and you can really be yourself in them. That's when you know they are yours.

David Novak: It's important to use your fascination with a story as a guide to inter-preting it. I don't think of myself as a tradi-tion-bearer, so my objective is not to tell the story in an authentic way or to convey the culture that story came from. I see myself as a revivalist, a story interpreter.

When I'm involved with a story, I'm concerned about the details of the story that are presented to me. I also want to focus on what is the most important aspect of that story, sort out the details to see what gets in my way or what I really want to emphasize. The story becomes your own, if as you work with it, you try to find out for yourself why you like that story.

The audience doesn't need to know that you personally identify with the story. That's the inner work of the artist. That simply gives you a very strong place to stand when you're telling the story. The story will be moving to the audience because it comes from something deep inside you.

Gay Ducey: I think what makes a story your own is going steady with it for a while. It's like anything that is important to you. You can try it on, adapt it, and think about it, but primarily you have to continue to tell it without monkeying with it at first. This is perhaps real purist, but I make an effort to learn the story in my own way. Once I've learned it, I try to tell it and tell it and tell it until it's apparent that the story and I know each other well enough. I don't think there is any way to hurry that process along.

Bill Harley: You tell it and tell it and tell it and tell it and tell it and tell it. Most of the stories I tell now are original, but I still tell traditional tales, especially in school work. When I decide to work on a traditional tale, I look at two or three different versions so that the story itself comes forward rather than the particular idiosyncracies of the teller or the written word. It takes an extraordinary amount of work to get written words off the page.

I read the story over and over again until I know what the bones are—actually know what happens in the story. A lot of times I talk to somebody about the story before I actually tell it; and I usually put those new stories in a safe place within a program. We are better off keeping the story small at the start —taking all the dress off, all the fancy stuff out of it, watching it grow—rather than trying to come out with it full-blown with all the characters fully developed and knowing exactly what they will say. That way you have a better chance to listen to the audience. If you dress the whole thing up to begin with, you will never find out what's at the heart of it.

With my stories, I go back and forth. I usually think about the story for a while. I might talk it through to a friend of mine. I will write it down and then tell it and then go back and rewrite it. I find that writing and telling over and over works well for me, because each process gives you a chance to hone the story.

If you are writing, you may be able to work on a particular phrase which you might not be able to do in performance. This is a crucial part in the story, and you want to make sure that you are saying it just right. Sometimes it takes a long time. Sometimes you learn it in a performance. The audience responds and you say, "Ah, I have to remember that."

Jackie Torrence: To make a story belong to you, you've got to find the bones of it. The bones are what you read in a book, the story that they give you.

In order to add flesh on to it, you have to make it a whole story, a complete story. You add your experience, your wisdom, you see the stories through your eyes. The meat you put on those bones makes the story become yours. You have put your personality in it. I don't mean destroy it, though. The skeleton is there, you just add a little meat to it, a little skin to it.

Ed Stivender: I work from a series of improvisations performed before audiences, working from a script outline. Their responses to various lines and sentences show me where the material must be chiseled away or added to. Once an audience shows me where the hot spots are, the next time I begin to subtly cue my audience until a rhythm is set up that I memorize and do the next time.

A story becomes my own when a bunch of audiences have "owned" it for themselves by responding to me in a telling manner, in which they tell me by their body language and laughter and deep breathing and shocked breathing where the most natural rhythms of the work are.

Margaret Read MacDonald: I don't start a story with a sense that I'm going to make it mine or personalize it or give it my style. I start with a story that I really, really like and think would be fun to play with before an audience.

I read it until I know it well enough to tell it. Then I find an audience and begin telling it. By telling it over and over again to different audiences, it begins shaping itself and rounding itself out and eventually it gets better and better.

Jon Spelman: I belong to the "leave it better than you found it" school of storytelling. The story is not yours until you've "improved" it by telling it your way.

Even if a story ends up back in the form that I first found it, it goes through a process of being made better. James Thurber's "The Night the Bed Fell on Father," for example, is a story that once had a lot of resonance for me about my family and about growing up and how things get complicated in families and become very dramatic when they are actually quite comical. But

Thurber's words seemed very literary and kind of arcane, and at the time I was mostly telling folktales, and I thought, this is just too complex, it's too literary. I'll just get the plot of the story and tell it in my own words. It didn't work. Thurber's story just doesn't work if you only tell the plot. But I had to discover that for myself. I had to go through all that, and I finally returned to James Thurber's words, which are the best words with which to tell that particular story. But I made it my own by going through that process, by really discovering that his way was the best way of telling it.

Every story needs to be a personal story. If it's not, it's not your story. You haven't made it your own. If you are not in "Little Red Riding Hood" someplace, you haven't made it your story. You may not be Little Red Riding Hood, you might be the wolf or Grandma, but there's some important way in which the story needs to be about you. When you discover how the story is connected to you, then you know how to make it your own. As soon as you start to feel yourself in the story, the words in most cases start to change from the original form.

Len Cabral: Well, that's where the work comes in, by telling the story a number of times—telling it to yourself, someone else, a small group. You start to discover more of the story. You tell it as often as you can to see how it works for different age groups. You may tell it one way and it works for grades K through three, but it won't work for four through six or vice versa. Maybe it works for adults and won't work for eighth graders or a younger audience. As you tell the story you begin to see the different ways and approaches of telling it.

Sometimes I sing a story. That helps me to remember it—helps me to get a feel for the story—if I sing or do it in gibberish. I physicalize the story. I move with the story almost like a dance, and I start to feel more comfortable with it. I physicalize that story so that if I get distracted (a bell goes off or a book falls), I can check back where I am physically and that will help me find that thread in the story that I almost dropped.

Penninah Schram: Find a way to talk the story in your own style. I have found four ways to approach a story. They come from the Jewish tradition, originally from Kabbala, of how to learn, how to approach things, utilizing a four-level process. It's an acronym called *PARDES,* which means garden or orchard.

The *P* stands for the Hebrew *p'shat,* which is the literal level of the story. First I learn the story by outlining the sequence of the plot. Once I understand the structure of the story, I memorize the beginning, the middle and the end. I then go to the second level, the *remez,* the lesson or the moral of the story. The focus is: What's the *point* of the story?

I again shape the story to make it my own, because I must relate the point of that story to what I need to take from the story. The third level is *drash* or *drosh,* which comes from the word *midrash,* to interpret the story. This is the part connecting the story to your life and bringing your life to the story. There is an interactive relationship between the storyteller and the story and, of course, the audience.

For instance: What does the story mean to me? What does it have to do with my life? If it is about a king or a queen, well, I don't have a king or queen in my life. But do I? Of course. Very often in Jewish tradition the king will be the symbol for God, and the queen will be the symbol for the feminine aspect of God. Or perhaps there is a story about a young person, a child who wants something so much that he will stop at nothing to get it. So I ask myself what did I ever want so much and how did I get

it, if I did? So there are those questions that the stories ask, because every story asks questions. That problem or that question I first have to relate to me and bring my own life into the story. Then in turn, the cycle, or rather the spiral, continues, and this is how I bring the story back so that I learn from it. That's the third level: connecting questions to the story and taking questions from the story and relating them back to me.

The fourth level is *sod,* which means secret. Somehow, in special stories, there is always a story within a story—that inner core of the story that I need to reveal to understand who I am and why I need to tell that story.

If I work through those four levels, I know how to tell that story. I know how to shape it, how to use the language that feels right to me, how to use my voice, how to use my silence, how to use my images how to use my whole being to tell that story. I also know how to choose the story to tell for that particular time and audience.

Milbre Burch: In the beginning, since I came to storytelling with a dance and mime background, I choreographed every minute of every story I told. I tried to get the story finished before the audience heard it the first time. Now I realize that a story that's never been heard in performance is an unfinished story, and I put it into performance at a much earlier stage. Often, I still use a physical approach to telling, depending on the story, but I've begun to discover the finishing touches in a story through telling it to an audience.

If I spoke the story aloud before writing it, the words usually stay fresh and available to my tongue each time I want to tell it. If it's a story I've written before telling, I must learn it the same way I learn any literary story: piece by piece, image by image. I must also try to be as ruthless in editing one of my written stories for telling as I would be with any other writer's work. Our own words can become so precious to us that if we're not careful, we end up telling the words instead of the story.

I use videotape when I can. I set up the camera and tell the story to the best of my ability. I then turn off the camera and turn on the monitor and critique the story. If I don't have access to video, I try the story out on listeners I trust, and then we talk about what worked and what didn't.

I try to introduce new work in the middle of a show, bracketed with solid, sure material at the beginning and at the end. If you offer a strong beginning and a strong ending, the audience is willing to help you put the finishing touches on a story in the middle.

If the story seems to warrant movement, I sometimes tape-record the piece and then move around the room, blocking out the story. I always try to use gestures, which add meaning to the telling, instead of simply acting out the words. It's a subtle thing, because I'm searching for ways to create some of the story's images with my body without getting in the audience's way. They have their own picture-making to do.

Steve Sanfield: I find a story and then I read it a few times. I also read it aloud so I can hear the cadence and rhythm of the story. I make five or six copies. I try to see the pictures that the story generates. I feel that if I can see it visually, I can articulate it. I can describe those pictures in my mind.

So I carry it around like that and I try to put it together, and I don't go back to the text for a while. I try to stretch my mind and make my mind circle the story. Then at a certain point, I take those copies that I have made, I keep one in the car, one by my bed, one in my study, and one in my woodshed.

At various moments, I pick up a copy. It's usually after having tried to stretch my

mind around the story that I come back and find what I was missing, that one phrase, that one incident, that one idea that escaped me at the beginning. Now it's right there in the text, and everything falls into place like building blocks.

You take the bare bones of a story and flesh it out . . .
add a little meat, add a little skin.
— Jackie Torrence

Susan Klein: I think the very first telling is the best, because you never hit that place of self-transportation again in the same way. That doesn't mean that all other tellings are not good. It just means that first one has a particular kind of clarity that spurs you on to continue to use the story.

I don't choose words or phrases consciously but they do come, and I keep my editor alive when I'm on stage in those early tellings so I can see what things are the phrasings that really stick out like little gems.

I need to have the audience's energy in the room. I can't rehearse. It means nothing to me to rehearse. If I don't have heartbeats and other energy in the room, it's wasted time for me. I have to have them there.

Chuck Larkin: The tall tales I've heard over the years were always told as personal experiences. The conversational style of telling personal experiences should remain the same on stage. The vocal and physical body language on stage should support honesty and show innocent surprise when the audience acts as if they do not believe you.

This kicks in the next traditional technique—interaction between the teller and the listener. If you create an image in the listener's mind and then introduce an incongruent image, this will generate laughter, head-shaking or eye-rolling, and that's the moment to leave the story and interact with the listener. You talk to an individual in the audience and weave in whatever comes to mind but be ready to continue creating humor using quick, witty replies:

"I wouldn't believe it myself if I hadn't been there."

"I was there!"

"I'd walk on my lips before I'd tell a lie."

"Cross wire my heart and hope to fry before I'd tell a lie."

"You know that hurts when you don't believe me."

My mother's favorite was:

"Criss-cross diddle on a horse, hope to die before I'd lie."

After this repartee, return to the story image. How do you move into this type of extemporaneous style? Know the images, know some one-liners, and take a risk. If you are willing to be a fool, God is willing to make you wise.

Next, keep the main story short and expand it with traditional ad-libs. This is difficult if you are dependent upon a memorized script but very easy when you depend on images. You can even shift into a second main story at any place in the tall tale and then return to the first main story as did Scheherazade in *The Arabian Nights*.

Collect one-liners in the humorous, exaggerated tradition of tall tales. These little gems on how poor or small your hometown was or how cold or windy or rainy the weather was can be strung together or used individually. When I find a new line, I tell it to my friends and family at every opportunity until I know the new material is locked into my memory. Later on stage, the new line will automatically enter a story. You can also use the technique of collecting several one- to two-minute stories around the same subject and then patch them together into one story.

Diane Wolkstein: The process changes over the years. I used to lie in bed and tell the story out loud until I liked how every sentence went. When I told it, I wouldn't necessarily use all those words, but at least I had complete assurance that I knew the way I wanted to say everything. I no longer do that as much.

I now think through the idea so I know where the story is going. Because I have practiced enough, I have confidence that I will find the right words when I tell. I think words are like scales with musicians, if you play enough notes, you know the notes.

Robin Moore: First I work with the story in my imagination. The way that story comes out is going to be very individual. Those images are usually quite vivid.

When it comes time to perform the story, instead of repeating words that I've heard or read, I look into my imagination. I see the images the story put there, then I describe to the listeners what I see. The language part of it, for me, is secondary. I, first of all, get a firm foundation by seeing the story clearly in the inner world.

Carol Birch: I'm very interested in being an effective bridge between the audience making a transition from the storytelling event into the time and place of the story.

I am also interested in speaking as myself. For years, I got up before audiences—and though I would have denied it—in a very real way I tried to not be present on the stage. How bizarre! In that desire to not obliterate a story with personal quirks, I often eradicated my own personality. It must have seemed terribly artificial sometimes. Although I spoke against merely being a voice intoning the words of the story, I can see now that without my personality behind my voice that is what I was actually doing.

Now I take responsibility for being the person telling you the story that day. I tell the story on a given day based on my mind set, my quirky feelings *towards the audience* and my feelings *toward the narrator* who originally told or wrote the story. Storytellers have to give up trying to *be* or replicate the tale's *original* narrator. Instead we have to take responsibility for who we are and how we bring the story alive *this* day with this *audience*.

David Holt: The mere act of selecting a particular story makes it personal. It touches something in you. At first, I don't usually analyze a story very much. I just know I like it. I try to get it ready to tell quickly so I can see if it works for me in front of an audience. I have many stories that I love but just can't make them work in performance.

If a story seems like it may work, I ask myself, "What are the interesting parts of this tale? Why is it appealing? Is it the mystery? Is it the characters? Is it the action?" I expand on these parts and show who I am by what I choose to emphasize. I try to find the heart of the tale and make it beat a little harder.

HOW DO I SHAPE STORIES FROM PRINTED TEXTS?

◆ ◆ ◆ ◆

The Cherokee Indians called pages from a book "talking leaves." It is a wonderful image for storytellers to remember since it is our job to get those pages talking. We must bring the printed page to life. By using natural oral language, strong kicking images, and our own personalities, we can vividly re-create a story in the listener's imagination.

While printed literary tales offer an unlimited resource for the storyteller, few of these can be told exactly as they appear on the page. Take the stories of the Brothers Grimm, for example. It would be nearly impossible to engage a modern-day audience with the stilted language used in the literary versions of the stories. But, it is easy to imagine that, when the Grimm brothers collected the tales, the original storytellers were full of animated gestures, emotion, and compelling language.

What works for the ear does not necessarily work for the eye, or vice versa. As storytellers, we must "translate" the written word into the spoken word. Every storyteller has his or her own technique for breathing life into book prose.

David Novak likes to work from a scaled-down, bare bones version of the story. This allows him to use his imagination to flesh out the tale. Doug Lipman urges us to tell the story in our own words and to notice how phrases begin to be repeated with each telling as we create our own oral version.

Trying to memorize a story can be a deadly trap, as Jon Spelman reminds us, for when we memorize, we end up concentrating on the words, not the images. Jon reads a story many times and then starts telling it naturally by seeing the story's images and then simply describing them to listeners. Both Jon Spelman and Diane Wolkstein tell and retell, write and rewrite the story until it takes the shape they desire.

To Pleasant DeSpain and Beth Horner, it is essential to find all the different variants of a tale before working up a personal version. Beth emphasizes the importance of understanding the cultural context and meaning of every story before presenting it to an audience.

David Novak: There's a distinction between the two types of printed texts. One is the recording or adaptation of folkloric material—material that has come out of the oral tradition that is now in printed text, for example, *Grimm's Fairy Tales*. The other is the story that is created by an author as a piece of printed literature.

You have more license with the printed text of a story that comes from the folk tradition. It's a story that has been interpreted by somebody else and printed. So you want to synopsize that story as much as possible, then try to retell the story using your own words. It could be that the person who wrote out the folktale used very nice language and interesting wording. If you use their wording, you have to honor the fact that it is someone else's work. It is appropriate to seek permission or at least acknowledge the author of the work.

I like the bare-bones synopsis of a story. I find it gives me more room to work with it. For example, when I work with a Greek myth, I don't look for a full-blown literary retelling of that story. I look for a nice concise synopsis. Then I can put in my own lyrical details.

The way I would approach a literary story would be as an actor approaching text. That doesn't mean that I wouldn't take a pen to it and make some cuts, but my editing makes the story sound better spoken. It is also important for a public performance of a story that clearances are received, permissions granted, and royalties, if any, are paid.

Laura Simms: Let's say it is a Pawnee story and I've read it in a book. So I have read it out loud and then I make an outline of that story and the story's events on half a page. One-half is for my outline, and the other half I leave empty.

I have a lot of questions about the story: Who were the Pawnee? Where did they live? What was their environment like? Was this story told in a particular situation?

Then I want to know about Morning Star, Horse, Medicine Bundle, and Three Brothers. I make a list of all the things that are in the story. How did they look at these things?

I will never be a Pawnee storyteller. I will not know the context of cultural mythology. But I can find out some things about it. I look in a folklore dictionary. I try to get a feeling for what it means.

The next thing I would do is figure out the "what," "who," "where" that occurs in the beginning of a story. The beginning of the story almost always lets you know, what change occurs to lead into the rest of the story. So once I can find the beginning—who's *not* in the story, where it is taking place— something occurs to start the journey of the story.

Then I look for the middle, which is the actual journey. Then I try to ascertain what the end of the story is and how the end relates to the beginning. Suddenly, the story starts to have a crystalline structure. It starts to have an inner logic.

Mapping the story is really important. I ask people to walk through it and touch and smell it. What are the noises? What's the time of day? So when you are telling the story, you are in it. But you get a lot of pertinent information, because a story is a code and a hieroglyphic. You start to tell this hieroglyphic and the sound of your voice and presence make it a full-blown Cecil B. DeMille visualization in somebody else's mind. It's magic. It's how everything is created. It is mirroring creation. That's what the joy is.

Doug Lipman: People tell stories about what happened to them. Maybe they tell a story about how they went to the store. When they do that, they imagine what happened with all their senses—sight being one of them, but sound, touch, smell, and taste being the others. Then, having re-imaged the events, they apply oral language to communicate what they are imaging to the person next to them. And that's what you have to do with a story whether it's initially oral or written.

If you tell a story from true life over and over again, you end up telling it more or less the same way. You may even find yourself using the same words. You use those words, not because they're the words you started with, but because they have become the most efficient path to describe what you're imagining. The words are in the imagination. When you start to tell a written story, there's a real temptation to repeat exactly what you have read. That doesn't work.

You need to get it off the page and totally imagine what the story is, and then forget those words ever existed. Deal with it as a story that happened to you or that you imagined, then make the oral language work from there. If you tell it often enough, you'll phrase parts of it over and over the same way. Then you can compare your version with what was on the page. You should always be spurred by your imaginings and let the words follow that.

Gwenda LedBetter: "Once there was a peasant and he was rich. More animals than he could count and more land than he could see. But he had no children."

Incredible! You've got place, character, timeframe, and conflict in just a few lines. What follows increases the suspense until the climax and ending feel right, and there's just enough description to take you into the story. I love its spareness and it has saved my life in trying to peel off too much prose in a literary tale. I try to stay true to the author's intention, using phrases that I have a strong connection with in experience and memory.

Jon Spelman: Don't honor the text too much. For a beginner to tell a story from a printed text, the way it's written, is the most difficult way to start. Because on top of everything else you have to remember the words and very often remembering the words becomes your chief focus and then you're not telling the story. Stories ultimately do not really consist of words; they consist of images that the teller translates into words, which the listener hears and then translates back into images.

My basic advice to beginning tellers is to not use the written literary version of a story. Read that written version many times and get a sense of the story's plot and how it flows. If you really like the way the story's written, try for a flavor of the dialogue, the language, or the rhythm of the story. Then tell it in your own way, in your own words, until you're really confident of the story. You may be able to go back to the written source and increasingly add in some of the specific ways it's written.

Currently, however, in my own work, I'm using a process of carefully writing out and rewriting stories several times and memorizing the text.

I scan a typed or printed text into my computer and then start playing with it. I cut and add just based on my hunches about the story as oral text. Computers also make it easy to keep track of each of the edits of a story, so you can go back and catch things you might have cut or changed too soon.

Milbre Burch: Unless I'm working with the sparse text of a picture book, I do a lot of editing. It's clear that the written word and the spoken word are two different creatures with different needs. Of course, I try to capture a sense of the writer's language, which is part of what attracts me to a literary story to begin with. But I do not use every word nor, sometimes, every scene.

Some years ago, for instance, I worked up "Dragonfield," a novella by Jane Yolen. If I read it aloud from start to finish, it's a sixty-minute story. The version I tell is twenty-five minutes. With Jane's encouragement I have cut out every subplot, every minor character and have told only the heart of the story. The written story is its own experience, and the listener is encouraged to follow up hearing the condensed tale with reading the expanded form.

Diane Wolkstein: By writing and by telling. I would write something that I thought was a little better than the academic version I was given. When I tried to tell it, though, it still sounded very stilted. I changed it again and then came back to the writing, because it sometimes was still too loose. I would record what I told, play it back, and then rewrite it. That's the work that I did with *Innana*. I would say it took a good thirty tellings, at least, maybe more, to come to the place it is now. And even the way it is printed now is not how I tell it. I have changed it since then. It still keeps changing. I keep listening for the underlying rhythm and the words to match.

Pleasant DeSpain: I do whatever research is necessary to find all the variants. It's so fascinating to see where a story has traveled and what has happened to it. It is most important, however, to see what has survived in that story from culture to culture, because *that* is the most important aspect in a story to remain true to. The integrity of the story exists in what has survived in the adaptations from culture to culture, from time to time. I stay with those parts of the story, and then I say, "OK, now, it's the 1990s. How do I tell this story? Who is listening today?"

Bobby Norfolk: I generally shape stories to make them my own by using the proverbial technique of "artistic license." The adage that stories don't have to be told the exact same way twice is a recurring theme in my research and development of a story. From the standpoint of a printed text, I use the powers of imagination. I see through the mind's eye the story being told in a slightly different manner that reflects my personality and style. Colloquial terms are modified, and certain words are substituted if they are archaic and/or questionable.

SUMMARY

> » Find the story you like and search out as many variations of the tale as you can find. Compare the different versions to see what are the essential characteristics that make up the basic narrative.
> » Choose the version that is most compelling.
> » Read the story many times to get the images in your mind.
> » Outline the important parts of the tale.
> » Decide what aspects of the story are most interesting to you. What do you want to emphasize and expand? What can be deleted?
> » Start telling the story to yourself and others in your own words to get a feel for what words best describe the action and the characters. Don't try to memorize the words. Visualize the images of the story and tell what you see.
> » Remember and reuse phrases that work particularly well and that tell the tale concisely.
> » Rewrite and edit your new version.
> » Research and understand the cultural context and nuance of the tale.
> » Decide if you need to give credit to a particular storyteller or author. Then make sure that is always part of your introduction to the story.

FOR A LITERARY TALE

If you wish to use a copyrighted original story, you must first get permission from whoever owns the copyright. It is always wisest to contact the publisher first.

If you have permission to tell a literary story that is under copyright, you must always let the author know how you plan to alter the story, whether by cutting it or putting parts of it in a more spoken language. Exact memorization is required.

If you are telling a literary story that is not in the copyright domain, you should respect the author's intent and language. Memorization may be in order.

For more information on copyright, see the last chapter in this book.

HOW DO I CREATE STORIES FROM TRUE-LIFE EVENTS?

♦ ♦ ♦ ♦

Each of our lives is filled with stories—stories about the day we got our first kiss, the time our car broke down, how we met our spouse, the crazy things we did in high school. Our conversations and gossip sizzle with true-life stories. Although few of us ever write the stories down, our family histories are kept alive by the telling and retelling of these stories.

True stories don't have to be dramatized or acted out. Most of them are best told in a simple, straightforward manner. The key is having a good story to tell. The most difficult aspect of true-life stories is deciding on the incident in life that will make the stories intriguing to others. Since you lived your stories, it is sometimes hard to decide if they will appeal to someone else. A lot of us tend to overlook the very things about ourselves that other people find most interesting. We take them for granted. If we look long enough, however, each of us can find interesting, beautiful, touching, funny, and very human stories from our own lives.

For anyone (teacher, business executive, performer, preacher) who appears before an audience, it is essential that you get the crowd on your side. You have to give people a reason to care about you. There is no better way to let them know who you are and why they should be interested in you than by telling engaging stories about yourself. The stories do not have to be full-blown productions, just interesting anecdotes that the audience can identify with, that help to create a common ground between you.

The most interesting parts of history are the unusual and intriguing stories that happened. These stories give us insight into who the people were and why they did what they did. True anecdotes can be used to set up and introduce longer stories. They give the audience a reason to care about you.

Finding our own stories can be both joyous and painful but always rewarding. It takes time and attention, but you have the rest of your life to work on it.

Penninah Schram: I start with a lifeline. I draw a line across a page. On the left side I put the date of my birth, and on the right side I put today's date. Without giving it much thought or editing, I put on that line—in some kind of chronological order—memories or moments that come to me. It could be my first day at school, the birth of both of my children, the death of my first husband, my first remembered memory of the trauma of the hurricane of 1938, a time when I was turned down for a job, a letter I received, a sad moment, a happy moment, whatever comes flooding to my mind. Moments.

After I've gotten ten or twenty of these lines down with identifying tags, I look at them to see if there is some kind of pattern—several of those moments or memories that connect in some way—journeys I've made to another country. Maybe the different trips I've taken to Israel. Some exhilarating moment when I was in a certain place. And all of these begin to trigger other memories.

Then I write down a whole list of emotions on another page and think of what was the dominant emotion of that moment. By retelling that moment, focusing on how I felt and how empathically I want you to respond to the way I felt, I can then begin to fill in the outline: where I was, who was there, why I was there, what was happening. But I always focus on the point of the story—why I'm telling it—not just the sequence.

There are a number of other triggers. One is places. Memories of places bring with them memories of events. To retrieve stories that happened in a particular location, move back through the place and time when a particular holiday happened.

Go back to a place in your home. Very often by re-creating your first room, your bedroom, or a particular room with a particular object—like the dining room table and what happened around that table—you will be able to create stories from your own life.

You can also focus on people—make characters come to life. Choose people and describe them. Bring them alive through mannerisms, favorite phrases, certain gestures. Recall favorite jokes or quotes or sayings that they had. All of those people in your life give you the triggers for personal stories.

Look at objects you possess or that have been the legacies given to you by somebody. A recipe. A particular food. A photograph. If you describe those objects or how they were used, they will trigger stories from your memory.

Think about the experiences that we all go through. The funniest thing that happened to you. The most poignant moment. The best gift that you gave or received. A special visit. They trigger not only the high points, but those tinier moments that are so important in shaping our lives and our relationships. So any one moment or a combination of them can help you create your stories, or at least trigger ideas. Then you start to shape them—adding the who,

what, where, when and why—creating the beginning, the middle and the end.

Michael Parent: You have to find the "hook" or the problem of the story. If you want to make a story that has some shape, the key is to find the elements that hold stories together. If you already have the "someone" and the "someplace," you need to have the problem, the conflict—the hook—something that needs to be solved or changed.

Connie Regan-Blake: A lot of people think they have to be good to begin with at creating a true-life story, but it's like anything else. It takes work. If that's something you want to do, you need to work at it and play with it some. In our workshop, Barbara Freeman and I do a thing called "Walk through Memory." It's a way of looking inward. People are often amazed at how much they can remember. A lot of people start out by saying, "I can't tell real-life experiences because I don't remember anything; plus, it was all pretty boring." But once you get them looking inside, it's as if they are literally walking around in that scene and remembering all the details.

I encourage people to be aware of their senses when they're looking at their memories, not only the images but the smell and touch and sound of things. All those things help bring back memories. I also encourage them not to necessarily start with a complete story. Just use something that happened as an introduction or a sidebar to a story. That helps in getting comfortable with true-life stories and seeing what works and what doesn't work.

Bill Harley: I bring in different elements from different parts of my life. I will change things, because a story that's told is very different from a story that's written. The structure has got to be strong if it's going to work. You've got to have that kind of blow-off at the end that gives a summing up. The plot has to be well-formed. You have to introduce strong characters and idiosyncracies at the beginning and then return to those images at the end. A lot of times with personal stories, they just run on and on and there is no sense of that "coming back." If a story is about your grandmother's gloves, it starts with the image of the grandmother's gloves, and somehow you have got to bring that image back at the end—even if you have to twist things a little bit from the way they really happened. What you are trying to do is touch people. That's the most important thing. For me, emotional honesty is more important than historical accuracy.

Beth Horner: I have attempted to sit down and write out a personal story or a true-life story and it has never worked. The best way I know to work up a personal story is just to talk with friends, or family, or other storytellers, and start out by telling an anecdote and see what rises to the top, what the high points become. Just doing that over and over and over and over and over—sometimes it takes several years. After doing that, I might try it in performance, in a non-threatening performance and see if the audience is reacting to the same things that my friends or family did. Then I take all of that and I start writing. For me, it's very difficult to begin writing a personal story. I have to tell it first.

Jim May: It's really related to images and memory. When I'm beginning a story, I keep it conversational. I say, "Here's what happened. I'm going to tell you something funny that happened in my family." I make it as short as possible, and it's just like a little nugget you give to the audience. Then you see what happens.

If you're looking for a plot structure for family stories, I often tell people in my workshops to look at heroic folktales. You can overlay that plot structure on your own life. Perhaps there were times when you were wrestling with demons. Times when you accepted the heroic call and crossed the heroic threshold where you knew life would never be the same. Times when you were the little girl going out in the forest, the Little Red Riding Hood. Times when you could have stayed in the comfortable castle but decided you would give up everything and go live among the poor people. All those moments in heroic stories—when did it happen to you? When did you make a decision and know that your life would never be the same as a result? When did you have a mentor? When did you get the gold in your life? Where's the magic in your life? I use that as a backdrop to identify places where people can find their own stories.

Pleasant DeSpain: When I want to tell a story from my life or a story that is about someone else, I wait until I'm actually ready to share it. If it's a dramatic story that contains human pain, then it's vital that I wait until I am healed so that I can share the story as a teller rather than as a sufferer.

Judith Black: Your life, unless you've modeled your every look, move, and feeling after a film character, is original—all yours. When you want to brew fresh tales, begin with what you know. The result is sure to be honest, compelling, and grounded in human experience. Begin with a person, an experience, or memory that has stayed with you. Try to recall it in all the detail you can. Close your eyes and relive it. Make a little cartoon board of it with pictures representing each episode or scene. Retell it to friends and family.

The difference between a reminiscence and a story is that you understand why the experience or person has touched you and allow this understanding to shape the memory. For instance, as a child I would ask my mother to tell the same story *ad nauseam.*

"Mommy, tell me what happened when grandma found the prune pits on Yom Kippur (a twenty-four hour fast for people of the Jewish faith)?"

"Oh, she found them behind the couch and I don't know how, but she knew they were mine. I had snuck them on Yom Kippur! She was holding them in her hand when I heard her call my name, 'Helen Edith Gruskin!' She only used all three of my names when I was in big trouble."

This was a minute piece of family trivia until I thought about why it was important to me and integrated that reason into the telling.

My mother was perfection. You could eat off her floors. My room was a constant mess. Her hair was strand perfect. Mine flew away to the Bahamas. She kept the family books. I still flunked adding in high school. But there was this one story. So my mom made mistakes too!

The anecdote without the frame would not have accomplished the goal. It required a little thinking. Why did I want my mother to repeat this story so frequently? By translating those thoughts into a frame, I was able to make a story that spoke to the experiences of others. We all have stories to tell. Words and images emerge from the personal, but with a little work we can often discover a universal base of understanding that they ride upon.

Len Cabral: I am trying to find more personal stories, thinking back on growing up in high school and the names of different teachers. I do little exercises so that I can remember each teacher that I had from grade one to grade twelve. Then I try to remember something about each teacher, and what I could say about them and to them if I saw them today.

It's a dancing lesson from above when you bump into someone who might have a story for you that is about you and something you had forgotten all about. It marked them so much that it stayed with them. They can recall it like it was yesterday.

Kathryn Windham: The personal stories I tell are already put together for me. I mean they really happened. They happened to members of my family, to people that I know, and so they are ready.

Ghost stories I research very thoroughly. I was a newspaper reporter for more than forty years. So when somebody says to me, "Do you know the story about that ghost at, say, Bald Mountain?" and they give me a little brief sketch of it, if it interests me, I go to that site and then I talk to people who may know something about that story.

I go to the library and look at all the old newspaper clippings about that story. I find out the names of the people who were involved in it. I find out all I can about their lives, who they were, where they came from, and why they were involved in this story. You can go to the neighborhoods where they lived. Newspapers can be very helpful and so can libraries, because around Halloween every year editors send new reporters out to write ghost stories. Through the years, they are very likely to have written something about this episode, and it will be bare facts mainly and not be too interesting, but they will have names in there that you can contact.

I've visited cemeteries to be sure these people lived at the time they are supposed to have lived, checking the dates on tombstones. I read death records and old diaries, and if you just have the name and approximately when they were living, and where they were living, you find people who will say, "Yes, my grandmother used to tell me about that." I go to their houses. I think you do better when you are talking face to face with people. They will be a little apprehensive over the telephone, to tell a stranger about this unusual thing that happened in their family.

There are too many people who will think you are crazy. But if you go to a house (and the very fact that I admit there is something strange in my house in Selma) … well, then they feel a little bit easier about telling me about something strange that has happened to them or their family.

[Do you take notes or record it?]

No. I think if it's not interesting enough for me to remember, it's not going to be interesting enough to tell. Now I may go back again and say that I want to verify these dates and the spelling, but I never interrupt the original telling of a story to ask any question like that.

[And when you get this information, I assume you write it down and see if you have a story.]

The story evolves in my mind as I drive back to wherever I'm going, and by telling the story to myself, I become aware of any gaps of information that I need. Then I pay another visit and we fill in those gaps.

[How important is it the stories be factual? Or if you need to build a bridge because the story doesn't quite work, how often do you do that?]

I try to make them as factual as possible. You can do that. Facts usually don't get in the way of a good story. I think it's rather unusual that my first book of ghost stories, *Thirteen Alabama Ghosts and Jeffrey*, is used in many Alabama schools as a supplement for teaching Alabama history. Because the events in it are absolutely factual and historic events. It makes the students more interested in that aspect of history, the fact that there is a little ghost tale connected with it.

[I assume that you then tell it before you write it?]

There is no rule at all about that. If I'm on a deadline, and somebody is waiting to get another chapter for a book, I write it first. If I have a speaking engagement somewhere and need a new story, I tell it first.

SUMMARY

» You can find true-life stories all around you— from your own life, your family, current events, and history.

» In any good story, *something* has to happen. A laundry list of events is not interesting. A story moves from a beginning to a middle to a climax to an end.

» Look for strong images—something that captures the imagination.

» Search your own life for stories—memories of special places and people, heroes, tragedies, coincendences, family secrets, successes, failures, accidents, travels, food, et cetera.

» Many families have stories that have been told for generations. These are often little gems, already worked up and prepared by your ancestors and ready for telling.

» Make a timeline of your life. List all the turning points. Which of these would be most interesting to people?

» The audience is not your therapist. Be sure you have already worked through your emotional issues with each story.

HOW DO I CREATE ORIGINAL STORIES?

♦ ♦ ♦

There is a great joy in bringing to life an old folktale and making it relevant to a modern audience. But there comes a time for many storytellers when they want to create something new, tell a story that has never been told before, a story that is their very own.

How do we begin?

Usually a story begins with just a germ, a seed. It is rare when stories leap full-blown into our brains. Perhaps it is something we read in the newspaper, something we overheard on a plane, a smell that brings back a long-forgotten memory.

Bill Mooney's story of Morris Frank, the founder of The Seeing Dog (a school that trains guide dogs for blind people) began by reading the notice on post office doors, "No Dogs Allowed, Except Seeing Eye Dogs, and being curious, he telephoned the school and discovered the story. Another story was prompted by hearing about Navajo code-talkers during World War II, still another from reading about Smokejumpers being caught in a wildfire.

David Holt's "Hogaphone" is an original story based on a real-life Uncle Ike who was an inventive mountaineer. David collected the anecdote about Ike making a telephone from a groundhog hide, but he could find no more information. David created a complete story using the original anecdote as the inspiration for the tale.

Jay O'Callahan looks for a striking image to build his original story upon. Sometimes his imagination is triggered by something amusing like a word, a rhythm, or a character. Sometimes it is a specific emotion like fear or anger. It might sometimes come out of a hurt, something that is still raw in his life.

Jackie Torrence's original stories about her childhood were brought about by the grief she felt at losing close family members. For Jackie, the smells she associates with growing up evoke vivid memories—sometimes something as simple as bathroom disinfectant or cedar branches being heated over a stove.

For Donald Davis, as with all of the storytellers we interviewed, it ultimately comes down to having a memorable character in your story. Donald makes sure the people and the places of the story are clearly set up. He spends a lot of time building a normal world in his listener's imagination and then turns it upside down.

Pleasant DeSpain does not hesitate to use a school audience to help him finish a story he is working on. He receives literally hundreds of plot possibilities from their suggestions.

Bobby Norfolk suggests always starting with the five senses. And David Novak tells how he came up with the idea for his signature story, "Itsy Bitsy Spider."

There is no one right way to create original stories. But see if your imagination isn't jump-started by reading the following ideas.

Jay O'Callahan: When I'm creating a story, I'm always on the alert for an image. I'm looking around all the time without thinking about it.

In the story, "Petrukian," wild twisted trees are very important. There was "that wild twisted tree" at the edge of the marsh and I loved that tree. I think because I preserved it and liked it, the tree crept into my story.

Observing things that strike you—perhaps trying to bring things like that into the story—is a good way to start. Another way to start is to find something that amuses you: a word, a rhythm, a character. If you're drawn to a character, it can be a real one. It can be some funny old uncle. Indulge your imagination a bit with a character and let the story grow out of the character.

Be aware of those things that still are raw in your life. Maybe you find yourself very upset if someone slams the door. Maybe it brings up a mood. Well, the mood that's unpleasant in your life may also be an invitation to a story.

Sometimes the weak parts inside us are really stories. If you are close to an emotion and you create a story around that emotion, the listener will realize that, deep down you know what you're talking about. You're not inventing it. You're feeling it at that very moment. Many a story starts just with an emotion—fear, laughter.

Sometimes a story starts with an image—a man with a hat. He pulls it down, so there are questions: Why doesn't he take it off? What's he hiding from?

What I really want in my story is for you to meet people. I love for people to be excited and interested in adventure, but I want something beyond that. I want them to meet the people and to be moved. So for me, I think my advice would be to find something specific—an object, an emotion, a character, a single moment that is moving.

[Once you do that, do you start telling it as a story? Do you start talking out loud? Do you end up writing first?]

Some of my stories begin with writing, because it's like interviewing myself. What I do is sit down in a little barn and I'll say to myself, what was my Latin teacher, Miss Manther, like? I start writing down a lot of phrases, trying to bring back the Latin teacher and her love of life. Images begin to pop in: Miss Manther loved Latin so much I was sure her cereal box was written in Latin. I could see her sitting there reading it, and I could almost hear her parrot conjugating in Latin. So that interview process gets me started and that brings up the emotions and I pace around and shape some of it out loud. Then I call a friend and tell the story out loud.

Jackie Torrence: I used to use stories as jokes. They were conversation sort of things that, when I was with somebody and really didn't know what to talk about with them, I'd just tell them about my childhood and all these crazy things that I did with my grandparents.

Jim May said to me one day, driving into Chicago, "Those are funny stories." Sometimes when I'd tell them he'd have to stop and laugh so he wouldn't run off the road. He said, "Why don't you tell those stories?"

I said, "No, nobody wants to hear about a back-in-the-country child."

Then in 1988, my mother, my father, and my stepfather died within three months of one another. I became depressed. I didn't know what to do.

I found a psychiatrist. One day he gave me a legal pad and said, "I want you to go home and write down all that you can remember about your life growing up, as far back as you can get into your childhood."

Seven legal pads later, I came into his office for my appointment. He had my pads and was reading them. He looked up and said, "I think this has healed you." Now I'm not saying this would work for anyone else, but it sure seemed to work for me.

How did I remember all the things that I do? Like being four-years-old? I was in the kitchen one day making bread. I had a loaf of bread in the oven and I was standing there kneading some more dough and the odor of that bread came across my mind along with …

I had also been in the bathroom using disinfectant and it smelled like pine. And the odor of that pine and the odor of that bread clicked my memory. My grandmother used cedar to deodorize the house.

In the wintertime, when the house would get stuffy, she would go out and pull off a branch of a cedar tree and bring it back. She'd stand in front of the stove and rub the branch across the fire. Then, she'd turn it over and rub it in some more. The odor of that cedar would penetrate the house. You could smell the cedar and the bread baking in the oven and with that it triggered a memory of a story that I had heard from my pa.

Sometimes when I'm shopping, I'll come across a fabric. I'll feel it and that will trigger the memory of something that happened.

Donald Davis: I start talking about a story that I am thinking about telling, because that's not very scary, just to talk about the story. Rather than say, "I am going to tell you the story," say, "I'm going to talk about the story." I find a friend to talk to about the story. I'll do that again and again, and I'll start to notice what works—what a person does or doesn't react to.

I leave out those sections that get no response and the things they react to get bigger and bigger. Basically I orally work the story to where it's ready to be put in performance. Writing comes much later for me. I write eventually just to document the story after it already exits as an oral entity.

Telling is a different medium from the written word. It's not the written word said out loud. There's a different preparation process; there's a whole different creative process. It reverses the theater process. In my stories, the script comes last, not first. It's a very backwards kind of process.

[You base a lot of your stories on things that have actually happened, correct?]

Yes.

[What would you suggest to someone who is creating an original story and had the basis of a pretty funny story, how could they make it funny all the way through?]

Well, you can't make it funny. If I try to make it funny, it sounds like I tried to make it funny. It doesn't work. The funny things in stories are not punch lines. They are descriptive places. And when people laugh, they are saying, "Ah, I see that. Ah, I've been there." I work on description, and then I try to notice what people laugh at. A lot of times I won't know it's funny. Then when they laugh at it, I say, "Ah, that's something to keep."

I try to identify humor when a story is in its early stages, and let those things grow and build.

A lot of people tend to start a story too late. They start it in the middle of the crisis event, instead of setting up the whole place and the people and what is normal before the world all falls apart. If you start the story too late, people are listening to it, saying, "Well, so what? Well, so?" I try to build a normal world and then turn it over. Often I see people not taking that step back.

[I understand what you are saying, but on the other hand, I see a lot of weakness in people telling you how to build a clock when you just ask them to tell you the time.]

Well, that's one of the differences between the written and oral mediums. In writing, a reader who gets lost can look back, and a reader who catches on fast can skim ahead. But in the oral medium, a listener can't do either of those. If I am as verbose a teller as I am a writer, I bore everybody to death. I've violated their imagination, their integrity. So I have to watch those people as I lay out little pieces of the story. As long as their faces are going, "Huh? Huh? Huh?" I keep laying out more. As soon as their faces go, "Ah ha!"

that piece is finished and it's on to the next. That is something that won't work from a script. It's got to be negotiated with a living audience.

There is a norm that settles in a story after a while. In other words, you can predict how the audience is going to behave. But until that story's been told, say two hundred times, I'm still finding those places. So it's a long process for me.

[Are there any tips that you could give someone who has a story that aims toward humor, something about how to find the humorous points in it?]

I don't know that. I find I just can't make that work. Again, I'll tell a story and I'll think there's absolutely nothing funny there. But somewhere along the way, somebody will laugh. That's the crack! When that happens, I say, "Ah, I see what its possibilities are." It's not a possibility I've created. It's a possibility I've been able to identify by seeing people's reaction to it.

What I notice more than anything is that we're so geared toward television punch line stuff that we think punch line equals funny. But that's not it in story. In story, laughter is the way the listener identifies with the teller. It's the way the listener says to the teller, "You've got me, I know her, I've been there, that's happened to me." They're all matters of description.

When I tell you I had a teacher who was especially built by the school board so she'd never blow away in a hard wind, that's not a punch line, that's a description. That's a picture. You immediately see the teacher, whom you would describe the same way. It makes you think, why didn't I describe her that way?

Story is a visual entity. When a story works, we see it happening inside our head while we're telling it. So I never ask, how do I tell the story to people? But rather how do I show them the story? How do I show them the way through the story including not just vision, but sound and

smell and touch and feeling? The moment I deal with thinking, concepts, prescribed feelings, I've lost it.

Michael Parent: I think the process is similar to creating stories from true-life events, except that you have more leeway. If you're using your imagination, you have more room for shaping and manipulating events. The starter-image or starter-character for an original story can come from something that actually happened that you fictionalize. It can come from something that is totally imagined. You may take some real people as your characters and shape a fictional event around them. It still boils down to someone, someplace, having a problem, making a number of good tries, and eventually changing the situation.

Susan Klein: Some tellers take stuff that has all the pieces for a gorgeous story, but it isn't honed yet. It may be ready in six months, but you wish you hadn't heard it yet. There was a phrase that I thought was a magnificiant way of describing it. I was walking out of a tent a large storytelling festival, and I had just heard something that I consider trash-telling. I was ticked off because I had spent my time and energy hoping we were going to get something out of a story. A woman nearby said, "You know, that might have been a story that teller needed to tell, but it certainly wasn't a story I needed to hear." That's *couch syndrome.* You should be horizontal, not vertical, and you should be paying someone $75 to listen to it.

Pleasant DeSpain: I work them out over several months in schools with children. In the middle of my programs, I say "Stop! You are such good listeners and we are having such a great time, let's all work on a story together." I'm in the middle of one right now, but I've created the structure of it, the bare bones. It's called "The Laughing

Hat," and I bring the hat. I show it to the kids and they laugh.

We work out the story together through quick, active participation. But I get to a part of the story where there are many possibilities—I'm not going to give it away—but there are many possibilities of what can happen. Essentially, how are we going to get the hat off this kid's head without hurting him? I let the kids give me all the ideas and, of course, we use one of them and go on. By now, I've heard more than a hundred possibilities.

Now that I am writing the story down, I have so much to draw from. So I always start either with a character or an object, and I go out and work with it. There is so much fun once we all realize we are creating this together that we really can't go wrong. I've gotten a lot of bad answers, but so what? It's a lot of fun. That is one way that I create original stories.

I work a lot with characters when I teach kids and adults how to write stories. I show the difference between a plot-driven story—a folktale—and a character-driven story, which comes more from the imagination.

Bobby Norfolk: Original material is usually created by stream-of-consciousness and embellishment. Stream-of-consciousness emanates in that part of the mind that houses memory. Memory is triggered by the five basic senses. For example, when you were young and Grandma always baked apple pie from scratch on a Sunday when you and the family got together for dinner, the combined aromas of cooked apples, cinnamon, nutmeg, butter, sugar, and vanilla wafting through the air of the house entered your olfactory nerves and lodged in that part of memory that governs *smell.*

Decades later, you are invited to a friend's house for dinner, and unknown to you, apple pie is the dessert. Upon entering their home, the same aromas wafting from the kitchen enter your nostrils. Immediately you are psychically transported back to Grandma's house, reliving the events of Sunday dinner. Your host may have to grab your attention back by calling your name, or you may make an immediate comment about your Grandma's pie smelling similar to theirs. The emotions of our heart are the fuel and fodder for original stories. Whatever goes to your emotional core and triggers events is excellent material for personal stories.

David Novak: It is very important when working with original material to have a sense of play, to be constantly toying with an idea. When I put together "Itsy Bitsy Spider," I was asked to do a series of workshops at a local school. In the kindergarten classroom, the teacher wanted me to work with story structure. That was my instruction—teach about beginning, middle, and end. So I thought, well, what is a story that these kids know that I can examine with them and explore the concept that a story has a beginning, middle, and end?

"Itsy Bitsy Spider" presented itself because, really, it is nothing but structure. I used dramatic activities with the kids during which we played out each part of the story. We asked creative questions about each part of the story. Then the latent power of the story took over. It had many possibilities, but it had what any good story needs—good structure. My telling of the story was born from those first explorations. New stories always come from somewhere. They don't just come out of a completely blank void. They come from old stories. If I'm going to make myself a meal, I'll refer to my recipe books, then kind of improvise while I work with the recipe. It's the same way with a new story.

SUMMARY

» The process is the same for working up any type of story from folktale to true-life to original. Keep in mind that true-life stories are sometimes more difficult since their form can be rather nebulous; however, working through these steps will help you flesh them out.

» Decide what is interesting about your story—what part of the tale seems to capture people's imaginations.

» Always remember that in any story *something* has to happen.

» Outline the important facts. If you mention, for example, a gun hanging on a wall, that gun had better go off before the story ends.

» Know the story's climax. If you know what the climax is, then you know what you are building toward.

» Know the facts needed to build toward the story's climax.

» Decide what facts can be omitted. Generally, the best stories cut to the chase and get right to the action.

» Do story bridges need to be added? If it is a true story, you will want to stick to the facts. Sometimes, however, the truth needs to be simplified, amplified, or bent slightly to make the story pay off. If you tell every detail, the narrative will get boring. Bridges are built between the various parts of the story to make it unfold logically.

» Make sure the story has a strong definite ending. Even though our lives are one long chain of events, we must have a conclusion in a story-for-telling. The audience must clearly know the story is over. Try several different endings. An audience can sometimes help you choose the best ending. Never end with "It was so funny!" or "You should have been there …"

» Create the beginning last. Now that you see where the story is going and how it will end, you can go back and create the beginning. If you set up the ending of the story by foreshadowing it at the start, you will often get the greatest response.

WHAT MAKES A STORY STRONG?
WHAT MAKES A STORY WEAK?
◆ ◆ ◆ ◆

The tellers all agree that each story needs characters that are strong and ring true. The characters may be trapped in outlandish plots, but if they are real, listeners will empathize and become involved. Gayle Ross thinks that, for her, "A really good story resonates with some basic universal aspects of being human." John Spelman adds to that. "The strongest mark of a good story well-told is its sincerity. A story becomes wimpy if it is insincere, unauthentic, untrue to the person who is telling it."

But what happens if we have a real protagonist and nothing interesting happens in the story? Susan Klein reminds us that, just as in theater, a story needs conflict and resolution. "The protagonist … needs some kind of action that signifies growth and redemption." Susan says if the story doesn't have that, it's just another cute piece. "Strong stories make you think about them afterwards."

Heather Forest also feels that a good story is one that touches people deeply, moving them beyond the moment they are in, allowing them to transcend themselves.

Storytellers often talk about the basic outline of a story—its skeleton or "bones." If the skeletal structure is strong and fits snugly, chances are you have a good story. Sometimes you find all the pieces but no backbone. David Novak believes that a good story has substance to it, real dramatic weight. Deep truths run through it. "There has to be a living idea in the story," he says.

Sometimes a good story is told badly. Bill Harley states that many times the weak story is simply the weak performance. Margaret Read MacDonald echoes that with, "I don't think there are any weak stories … just weak storytellers."

Laura Simms: If storytellers don't do their homework, if they don't know how to distinguish between themselves and the story, then even a great story can become wimpy.

I was once at a festival in England and I heard the Tinkers telling stories. The Tinkers are Gypsies. We were all performing in the Royal Festival Hall in London and this twelve-year-old boy got up and told a Jack tale. Now I personally do not like Jack tales. They're not my style. There are wonderful storytellers who tell them and it's their style, but I can never really get interested in them. We had been all over England, and we were wiped out. We liked each other, so we were staying up all night long. I was very tired. It was one of those if-I-hear-another-story-I'll-vomit kind of festivals, but we were having too much fun. Then suddenly I was sitting up straight, alert like a lion, because this boy's telling was so vivid. I was thoroughly engaged. Suddenly that story was different from any version I had ever heard and I was completely refreshed by the telling of it.

A wimpy story is one that points toward something very obvious, that doesn't have resonance inside, that doesn't provide an experience. You might tell very different stories than I would tell because our personalities and experiences are different, but they could be very good stories, because of our relationship to the story and our care about it.

Bill Harley: A lot of times the weak story is the weak performance, or the teller doesn't know why he or she is telling the story. I once saw a performer who said, "I don't know why I have to tell this story, but I do." It was a mess. There were little extra parts and you didn't know what they were and they were disturbing. There was a lot of violence in the story that didn't make any sense. Hearing it, I said, "These things are disturbing to me because she doesn't know where she's going with them. She doesn't know what the functions of them are. She just knows that they are somehow interesting to her and that's a sign of somebody who hasn't done her work on the story. She doesn't know what the story is about."

David Novak: A good story really has to have some substance to it. It has to have some real dramatic weight. It doesn't matter whether the audience for your story is four years old or fifty. I often hear stories told that were designed for a young listener that are almost insulting. They assume that the young listener is not discriminating, so the teller simply tapes together a bunch of details that are superfluous with a story line that doesn't track and has no point to it. That is a wimpy story.

I think a really good story has to come from a strong center in the person who creates it, whether that person is a writer or a storyteller. For example, I started the "Itsy Bitsy Spider" story as a lark. For me, it was something of a lampoon of an epic tale, a Homeric retelling of a Mother Goose story. It still is in many ways.

But a short time after I started telling it, a friend of mine ended up in the intensive care unit of the hospital. I went to visit him. An adult male, my age, a peer of mine, a longtime friend. He was under medication. It was an extremely depressing setting. Here we were, two guys, not knowing what to say to each other. He turned to me, lying in his bed, and said, "Tell me that story about Itsy Bitsy Spider." So I sat in the intimacy of this hospital room with my friend in trouble and under sedation. I told him this story, which I had been treating as a burlesque. And suddenly, *Bang!* it hit me in the face, that this was much more than simply a burlesque of a children's nursery tale. The story taught me a lesson about its own latent power.

If the story is a good story, it is good because it has some deep truths running through it. I am reluctant to say that a good story has to teach a lesson. Many bad stories make an effort to teach a lesson, in a very pedantic, didactic way. But there has to be a living idea in the story.

Heather Forest: A good story is one that touches people deeply in some way. It moves them beyond the moment they're in. It allows them to transcend themselves. They forget they're sitting in the chair. They forget they're looking at a storyteller. The "what's good" is the story and not the teller. If someone walks away and says, "That was a great storyteller," but they can't remember what the story was about, then somehow there's been an imbalance between the technical prowess of the teller and the power of the plot. I'm attracted to the ancient stories that have been tongued by tellers over time. Centuries of telling have honed these tales so that there's nothing extra in the plot; the tale makes sense, it's satisfying, it scratches deep emotional itches. After hearing a plot such as this, the listener feels like he has sighed deeply or wept soundly or shuddered severely. There's something about the story that has gone to his core.

Donald Davis: To me, a wimpy story is a story that is thoughtful but doesn't land concretely enough in any particular place for me to be able to really see it.

"Once upon a time …" When was that? Where was that? In a pre-television era, people could take, "Once upon a time," and go anywhere with it. But for people who have grown up on television and illustrated children's books, "Once upon a time" is meaningless. People sit there and say, "When?" "Where?" So, the more specifically and visually concrete a story is, the more it really works well. The more it loses that concreteness and becomes an exercise in thoughtfulness, the more wimpy it gets. I think a lot of people (especially inexperienced listeners) will often find that traditional stories leave them unhooked. Traditional stories are not very clearly established in time and place, because the original listeners knew the times and places and didn't have to have them described.

When I tell my Jack tales, I clearly describe the setting in which I heard them. I describe the people who told them to me. I try to get them to be as concretely experienced by people as they can be. So I don't start right in with, "One time Jack did so-and-so …" I take them to my Grandmother's house and describe where we are and what the world is like. Then I have my Grandmother tell the story. Maybe somebody else can pull it off another way, but that way works better for me.

Ed Stivender: The only good story is a live story, told responsively, respectfully of the widows and orphans in the house, and responsibly to the etiquette of the tribes and wigwams where you work.

Wimpy was a friend of Popeye's, and what makes a story wimpy is the demand a storyteller makes on one's audience to gladly pay them back Tuesday for the attention they are paying today by delivering an unfair return at the moment, by not following the three R's outlined above. By insulting, boring, kidnapping, or embarrassing them with a moral that outweighs the plot, for instance.

Michael Parent: The difference between a good story and a wimpy story for me is the wimpy story gives too easy a solution. Now you wouldn't want to resolve this story with a lazy solution, or a "fairy godmother" solution.

Here is an example: Sarah Lee Hoskinen was ten-years-old in 1952. She wanted to be on the Little League baseball team, and the league would not allow her to do so. For instance, all of a sudden someone comes along and hears about this kid's problem, that she wants to be on the Little League team and is not allowed to be. The fairy godmother solution would be that some rich guy says, "Oh, well, I like this kid and if you'll let her play, I'll give $50,000 to the Little League." And then she's allowed to play. To me that's a wimpy story because the character doesn't learn anything; she doesn't struggle.

I think it's OK for the character to get help in a good story, but usually the best help is the kind that moves the character along so they can solve their own problem. For instance, if this kid who wants to play in the Little League just hangs in there and tries a number of different ways to get them to let her play, even if she doesn't get to play on the Little League team, if she somehow makes a statement and at the end of the story she (or maybe someone else in the story) has learned something, then, to my way of thinking, it's a good story.

Now as long as the problem is a possible human one for the main character, then it's a good problem. Even if the problem is that the person has curly hair and wants straight hair. As long as the problem is really a problem for the character, we will relate to it.

Connie Regan-Blake: A good story has a sense of truth. Not that it has to be a true story, but it has that sense of truth. I think the stories that have been around for generations and generations are the ones that have some sense of truth about them.

Pleasant DeSpain: What makes a story good is the action—believable action—that moves rapidly from beginning to middle to end.

The other thing that makes a story good is that the question, "And then what happened…?" is always being answered, so that we can move swiftly to a satisfying conclusion, and the audience feels involved and is allowed to participate. When I let my audience be a part of the story's unfolding, it works every time.

What makes a story wimpy is all the unnecessary descriptive aspects that do not allow the listener to participate. If the story does too much or if it's acted out too much, I am not nearly as involved. I want to participate, and I think, most of my listeners want to participate. It is a "control" versus "allow" issue. A good story "allows."

Gayle Ross: A really good story resonates with some basic universal aspects of being human, be those humorous, moving, or grief-stricken. Regardless of which string is plucked, good stories are going to set up a resonance within the people who hear them, because they touch on some aspect of our existence as human beings that transcends geographic and cultural borders. Even stories that are very heavily rooted in one particular tradition or place—the geography, the people, the nature of pioneer experience in the hill country—the deepest essence of the story transcends all of that and speaks to a universal experience.

Margaret Read MacDonald: I don't think there are any weak stories. There are simply weak storytellers. Any story, absolutely any story can be marvelous in the hands of a skillful storyteller who is right for that story. It's probably more a matter of a match between story and storyteller. If it's a bad match and the teller begins trying to tell a story that isn't right for him, the story comes out very poorly. But if the teller has a story that he loves and really wants to tell and which can fit his style, the simplest little story can become marvelous. So I don't think there are any weak stories. It's simply a matter of finding the right story for the right teller.

Jon Spelman: To me, the strongest mark of a good story well-told is its sincerity. I think there's something about a wimpy story that is insincere; it's unauthentic. It's not true to the person who's telling it.

Gay Ducey: A story is wimpy when it seems to work out too easily or is too predictable unless it is for the very youngest kids, where predictability is sometimes a good way to learn and to anticipate with joy what is going to come next. I look for stories that are less predictable and have characters that seem interesting enough to spend some time with. I think there are a lot of stories that we pick as a community because we think they'll play. We think they'll market as opposed to stories that slightly disturb us or that cause us to think about them again and again and again.

Kathryn Windham: You need strong characters to be involved in the story. It's people who are important in all of my stories. When you find interesting people, you are going to find interesting stories. I think, if you open your senses and maybe even your heart to people, you will find an unending source of unwimpy stories, good strong stories.

Jackie Torrence: First rule: Never tell a story you don't like. How do you find a story that you like? You read, over and over again. You concentrate on what it is. You look at the pictures in the story, and what the story is saying. When you know exactly that the story hits, that there are things in the story that people will just die to hear, that people will laugh at, they'll get excited about. Things that might even cause somebody to question something they have somewhere deep in their mind. Does it solve problems? Is it a universal truth? Does it love; does it hate? Does it show all of these things? Is it exciting? Are there adventures? Is it scary? I mean real scary, not some soppy kind of scary. I love the poem *Little Orphan Annie.* "Little Orphan Annie came to our house the other night …" But that's not scary. Kids nowadays are not scared of things like that. In my day when I was little, you tell me that poem and I'd get under the nearest bed. Nowadays, you have to bring out Freddy and all of that to frighten these kids.

Think about who you're telling the stories to when you're choosing a story. If you've got a senior citizens' group to talk to, don't find something like *Little Red Riding Hood.* Remember that these people have lived seventy, eighty, ninety years. They are wise, they have had experiences in life. They might enjoy love stories. They might enjoy stories about a terrible villain who killed his wife. Something like that. Find something that will hit that particular audience, where they are.

Susan Klein: Just like theater, a story needs to have conflict and resolution. The protagonist, whether it's a he or a she or an animal or a machine or whatever, needs to have some kind of action in the story that signifies personal growth, and the story needs to have redemption. If it doesn't have those aspects, then it can be considered as "what a cute piece"—or "wasn't that dear"—but it doesn't have the kind of thing that leaves you pondering, which is what good stories should do. It should make you think about it afterwards.

Syd Lieberman: I think it's a matter of personal taste more than anything. I like a story that moves me, makes me laugh, makes me think, something that rings true. It doesn't have to be profound. I like to recognize something of life in it that seems real to me. However, there are some tellers who think that just because it's life it's powerful, then they get up and do personal stories without really thinking about how to put them together. You can't just get up and talk. The story has to be crafted.

I dislike a story if I know where it's going by the third sentence. A lot of folktales are like that. I know basically what's coming, and I know it's going to happen three times. I like surprise endings, endings that make me laugh.

I used to worry about changes of mood and stuff—telling something really serious and then wondering how to get out of it. A friend who watches a lot of television told me, "Just change the channel."

HOW DO I MEMORIZE
AND REHEARSE A STORY?
◆ ◆ ◆ ◆

For many storytellers, working up a story to tell is the least enjoyable aspect of the storyteller's art. But there are shortcuts, tricks, and proven ways to make this process seem less painful—maybe even enjoyable.

We want the telling of any story to be full of life and vigor. The storyteller's job is to help the listener re-create in his or her own mind the images of the tale. This works best when the teller is re-creating the story for himself with each telling. Memorizing a narrative word for word generally gets in the way of this process. As Jim May relates, it is best to get to know the entire "landscape" of a story rather than just memorize a certain path through it. If you get off the memorized path, you will get lost. But "if you know the whole story, if you know its emotional content, and general direction, you can always find your way back if you get off the path," May notes.

If you can see the story's images strongly in your mind, you will usually be able to communicate those images to others. The first step is to remember how the story goes. If the tale is from a printed source, reading it over several times helps set the plot and language in your mind. Some prefer to read aloud; others learn in concentrated silence. Connie Regan-Blake sometimes reads a story fifty times or more over several weeks. Without thinking about it, the story is planted in her memory.

Another simple and effective memory technique is to read the story right before you go to sleep and as soon as you wake up. This is one of the fastest ways to learn a narrative. It invites the unconscious mind to play with the images. We find it quite effective to just think through the story as we are dozing off. It's a relaxing way to go to sleep and allows effortless practice.

Many tellers read the story into a tape recorder. They listen to the story over and over as they take walks or ride in their cars. While listening to the story, you can re-examine it for appropriate language and strong and vivid images. You can then rerecord the story with the revisions, which gives added practice. When we were working on the audio cassette *Why the Dog Chases the Cat*, we talked the story through several times, then wrote a first draft. After it was written, we read it into a tape recorder. We kept rewriting and rerecording it until we were satisfied with the final telling of the tale. That final draft was then told to various audiences to test what worked and what didn't. We finally came up with an effective version that we were happy with only after making many revisions and testing them. By the time we recorded it, we had told the story so many times we knew it perfectly.

Michael Parent finds one of the quickest ways to learn a story is to record a paragraph of written text and then leave enough space on the tape so that he can repeat what was said. He does this intermittent recording technique for the entire tale, breaking it down into bite-sized chunks.

Outlining a story can also help you learn and remember the structure and main plot points. This outline can be saved and used again to quickly refresh your memory if the story hasn't stayed in your repertoire. Some tellers prefer a storyboard, using simple drawings of the main scenes to jolt their memories.

Some of the tellers interviewed find it most effective to rewrite the story in their own words. They work and rework the written draft and learn from that version. Conversely, writing is an impediment to memorizing for others. These tellers like to tell the story "on their feet" orally.

Getting the story "in your bones" through movement and song is another way to literally "get the feel" of the material. Len Cabral puts movement to the story after the first reading. He sings the words instead of speaking them. Only after exploring various expressions of the tale does he go back to simply telling it. Milbre Burch was trained as a mime and visualizes the action in her imagination. This in turn often translates into gesture.

Memorizing the beginning and ending of a story, as well as any essential language, repeated phrases, or songs should be the next step after you get it in your bones. You need to know the first few lines of the beginning so that you can confidently launch into a tale when nervousness strikes. You need to know of the ending so that you can direct your tale to that point and leave the audience satisfied.

Many tellers take time to think about the "landscape" of the story—fleshing out, in their minds, the story's setting and characters. Milbre Burch says, "In my mind, I try to fill in as many details of the story as I can. For instance, if I say 'the boy,' I need to know how old he is in my mind and picture him that way. Otherwise, my ambiguity about his age 'leaks' to the audience."

You can think about and rehearse a story privately forever, but until you actually tell it to someone, the story will not be a part of you. It is an amazing thing, but until you take a chance and communicate the story to someone, it will never be fully realized. All the tellers agree that a story must be worked in front of an audience to really understand it and for it to come alive. In fact, Doug Lipman goes so far as to say that it is not a good idea to tell a story without someone there. But in the beginning, when the story is raw and new you must, as Bill Harley says, "find a place where you can feel safe and let the story grow." For many of us that "safe place" is with our children or family and friends. David used to try out his stories on his two-year-old son, Zeb. "I knew if I could hold his attention with rhythm, action, and movement, I had something."

A number of storytellers get together in pairs or small groups to work out stories in the early stages. Jay O'Callahan has a group of friends who are not storytellers who will listen to a new work and discuss it with him.

Children from four- to ten-years-old are always a forgiving and appreciative audience. Many tellers will have an ongoing relationship with a neighborhood elementary school. When they have several new stories ready, they will set up a fifteen- to thirty-minute session in two or three classrooms. This gives them a chance to try the same stories several times in a row to new audiences. Telling to different grade levels lets tellers see how the material works for various ages. Of course, this is done gratis.

Don't expect the first performance of a story to go well, no matter how much experience you have had. "I call it rehearsing the first ten times I tell it live," says Pleasant DeSpain. Jay O'Callahan notes, "One of the absolute sure steps is failure." Jump in and tell the story. Knowing that it will not be perfect, realizing that it will grow with each new telling. It's all part of the process.

When you do begin telling your new story in performance, place it between two pieces of strong material. That way, the audience will be satisfied no matter how you do. Donald Davis asks the audience if they would like to hear a story or even part of a story he is working up. Most people like to be let in at the creation of something new. No need to apologize. Just jump in and do it.

Jon Spelman: In film writing there's the useful concept of storyboards—a little picture of what's happening in each scene. When plotting out a story or working in detail on a story, you may not actually draw out the pictures, but you see them. What you're doing is moving from one picture to another and talking about them and going over and over them. The more you find the words you want to use to talk about the pictures, the clearer the pictures become. The clearer the pictures become, the easier it is to find the words. So you don't memorize the words as much as you memorize the pictures of the story. It might feel to you like it's always the same text, always the same words, but if you recorded multiple tellings of the story there would be a lot of different words conveying the same pictures. Even in that process, however, it is sometimes important to memorize some specific words or series of words: how the story begins, or maybe a clear description of a character who has to be very economically described. The story's climax has to be vivid and economical, and therefore you want to find the best words for that and usually for the story's ending.

Sometimes I have a story on tape that I have tried to record in the flattest and most uninteresting way. I just try to hear the words as a process of learning the story. It's also on tape because I want to make those words portable, so I can walk along and listen, or run along, or drive my car and just listen to those words over and over and over again.

I can do it for longer than I think I can, and then when I get to the point of "Oh, no, now I've got to start facing the fact of learning all these words," I realize that learning has been going on the whole time and I actually know more of the story than I thought. But almost inevitably there are some places where it's like the multiplication tables. You simply have to sit down and do it over and over and over again.

Margaret Read MacDonald: I take a story and read it through a few times until I have the plot, a lot of key phrases, and the flow of it straight in my mind. Then I usually go into a private room or someplace where I can be alone for about an hour and talk out loud. Go over and over it out loud. And then I begin working with an audience. I let them help me work the story. I don't attempt to perfect the story before I go to the audience, because the audience is half of what's happening. To me they're the most important part of building the story. Of course, you have to be fair with them and give them some of your best stuff that's really pretty polished along with some of the stuff that you're just trying to work on.

I was trained in the public library school of storytelling where you were supposed to rehearse the story and tell it letter-perfect before you ever shared it with an audience. I think that training, while it's very fine in theory, has kept many, many people from ever telling a story or more than a couple of stories. So a lot of what I've done with my writing and my lecturing in workshops has been to try to get people to break through that block—the feeling that they have to be perfect before they start. They can jump in with both feet and start telling. That's the only way you're going to get them going. Of course, once they do it they get so excited about it they don't stop.

Bill Harley: The story doesn't really happen until there is an audience. For me, the story has to grow in performance. You need to find a place where you can feel safe to let the story grow. Don't do new stories in front of the most important audience you ever work for. Do them in the classroom or for friends. I run over the pictures (the plot) in my mind, so I know what happens. Then I go out there, see the images, and tell people what I am thinking. They are all comfortable, and I try out this little eight-minute story and see what it's all about.

Beth Horner: I always have to get the story on tape. I listen to the tape over and over again. Sometimes when I try to write something out and it won't come, I speak it and it comes out perfectly. So I listen to myself over and over and over again.

A folktale is easier. I just chart out or write out the main plot—outline it—memorize any song or repeated point, then put in anything that ties it to a particular culture. That's how I learn it.

Ed Stivender: Read or view or review audibly the story fifty times. Outline it in longhand. Outline the outline. Print buzz words on shirt cardboard in magic marker. Hire a child in the front row to keep up with you, holding them or laying them out below your audience's sightline. Do it again. And again. And again. Get to Carnegie Hall or taxi there.

Jim May: For a lot of storytellers, memorization is a trap and they need to be careful. Let's say you go on a journey, and it's the difference between memorizing only the path or learning the whole landscape. If you memorize the path rather than learn the landscape, you're going to be lost if you get off that path even a little bit. But if you know the whole story, if you learn it well, know its emotional content, its general direction, its landscape, then if you get off the path, you can always find your way back. If you cut behind that mountain over there, you will know that you're going to come back on the path again. If you have a glitch and go off, you can sometimes construct an extra little part of that story. You can construct some narrative stuff the audience may not even know about. You may discover something extra.

Doug Lipman: I've come to what is a radical position on this, which is, basically, it's not a good idea to tell a story without somebody being there. Oral communication is much too complicated to teach anybody. It is many simultaneous layers of facial expression—eye contact, tone—all those things. And when practiced without somebody there to give the feedback that you're used to in oral communication, you practice bad communication. There are times when you need to imagine the story through in your mind to experience the story. It's actually irrelevant whether you're speaking aloud or not. It depends on what works for you.

Most of my time with the story actually needs to be spent communicating it to people. Now I can't do that the first time at the level that would enable me to be at the National Storytelling Festival, so that means I have to take charge of getting people who can listen when the story's raw. In fact, I make a whole hierarchy of practice performance audiences, so that with each level of a particular story, I can tell it at the appropriate level and practice it.

Donald Davis: Well, to me, a story is a relationship between a teller and a listener. The word "communication" comes from a Latin word which refers to things that are two-sided, like "communicable," you don't catch that by yourself. If a story is a communication event, you can't practice it unless there's somebody there. It's like a line, a wire between the teller and the listener. Both people hold each end of it and the story walks on that wire between them.

It doesn't work that way in the theater. You have a script. You practice it and present it, but you negotiate the story. You constantly say (not with words, but in essence), "You got it? Are you with me?" and negotiate the story from there.

I put a story together as a series of pictures. I walk people past those pictures and show them each picture until they say to me, "I got it."

Every group's trip past those pictures is a different trip. If they're kindergartners, if they're Japanese tourists, if they're from the retirement home, if they're mixed-age families. As far as the words go, those words are going to be different every time. They're different because I'm taking them up, I'm showing them this picture and working with them until they say to me, "Ah, we've got it." That's very different from a theater event in which whether the audience gets it or not is their problem, not Shakespeare's.

So rehearsal for me is what you do with your kids in the car or what you do with your friends when you're talking about the story. It's finally what I do when I think and talk to myself but that's way down the road somewhere. Typically in a festival weekend where I'm doing four hours of stories, by the time I've told stories one hour, told stories a second hour, I'm in the third hour, and I say, "Do you want to hear a story that I'm just kind of working on?" Then I'll share with people a new story that may not be finished, and I may not even finish it then. I may say, "OK, that's the story I'm working on now. Thanks for listening to part of it." Because then I'm coming back for a fourth hour with finished, solid stories later in the day.

People delight in being let in on that process. They'll come back later and say, "Remember that story you told us? Do we get to hear it now that it's all finished?" It can be fun to do, to let people in on a story that's in the works. I don't say, "I'll tell you a story." I say, "I'll tell you *about* a story." Because if I say, "I'll tell you about it ..." I can stop at any point along the way and say, "OK, you may hear that when it's all finished later on." But what I'm doing is checking out some pieces of it and seeing how they work.

Robin Moore: I spend a lot of time in the car, so when I'm working on a story I will usually tell the story out loud to myself so I can experiment with the sonic qualities of the stories. I don't ever pretend to myself that it is the same as telling it in front of a live audience. What I am doing is just playing with words and sounds at that point. I'm seeing the different possibilities that the story has aurally. By the time I get to the words, I've already done all the inner work and I see the story clearly in the imagination. So that is really great preparation, but the best thing is just being on your feet in front of people and telling them.

Milbre Burch: I don't memorize, I try to *learn* the story. This means I spend time seeing the action in my imagination and often that translates into gesture. For me, having "imaged" the story and translated it through my body helps me in the inevitable moments of lost concentration when the words suddenly drop away.

In my mind, I try to fill in as many details of the story as I can, including details I don't necessarily "speak" to the audience. For instance, if I say "the boy," I need to know how old he is in my mind and picture him that way. Otherwise my ambiguity about his age "leaks" to the audience. And then in the listeners' minds he may shrink or grow throughout the story depending on the action. How much simpler to commit myself to his age and see him that way in my mind; that clear picture is then conveyed non-verbally to the audience.

My first mime teacher, Meli Kaye, was a protege of the great modern dancer Doris Humphrey. Humphrey's movement style was based on gesture and natural breath: one movement led to its complement, like breathing in and out. Humphrey once made a statement to her students that applies to my work as a storyteller: "Don't just do something, stand there."

Jay O'Callahan: This is the exciting part of learning and creating. They go together for me. Whole new scenes and possibilities appear; I write them down; I tell them. I rush into my study and write down this possibility of the scene. Then the next day, I write out and pace out and talk out the story. As it's taking shape, I tell it to one trusted friend. Afterwards, the two of us talk it over. Then I get a group of three or four people together and tell the story again.

I find in the growth process of the story there's a different energy with four people. It pulls out different things. It's very mysterious. If you're telling the story to one person, there isn't quite the energy to pull out certain things. In this process of creating, making, learning the story, I find one of the absolute sure steps is failure. Tell the story and a scene won't work at all, or some person will be confused about the character. I don't like this part of the process, because I usually feel terrible if I sense they're really lost in the story or if they ask a question that makes it clear they don't know what the whole scene is about. But that's part of the learning process. I feel badly and I say, "What can I do about that? How can I speed that up? Shall I cut that out?" Failed tellings are programmed into the process of learning the story. All during this process, I'm thinking about what the image is so that when I lose what's important to the story, or what draws me to the story, or what I love about the story, returning to these questions keeps me on track.

Pleasant DeSpain: I don't memorize stories verbatim, never have, never will. I memorize the bare-bones structure. Then I rehearse from thirty minutes to an hour a day. I learned this on my TV show. I rehearse in a closed room, no interruptions allowed. I always rehearse standing up which means I am moving. I'm on my feet, because my body has to learn the story as well as my mind. Once I can tell it bare-

boned, then comes the joy of fleshing it out, then the enlivening. I hear its rhythms. I allow the story to breathe from its early conception right on through to the finish. I know when I am ready to tell a story, because at the end of the rehearsal I am so calm, and it comes effortlessly. Of course, I'll learn more. I call the first ten times I tell the story live my final rehearsals.

Steve Sanfield: Here's how I learn a story. I walk around telling the story aloud over and over and over again. I don't think the story and mumble it to myself. Because when you think you use one part of your mind and when you speak you use another. So if you're going to learn a story to tell it, you have to tell it again and again and again and again. I used to embarrass my son when he was younger. He said, "You know, Dad, you've got to stop talking to yourself."

I practice a lot. I practice when I'm doing dishes. I practice a lot when I'm walking or sitting in the woods. I keep doing that until I can go from the beginning to the end, and I know that I've learned the story in two ways.

If you look at my house, you'll see that paths go off in all directions. I just start to walk and tell the story, and if I end up somewhere without really knowing how I got there, then I'm sure I know the tale. Sometimes I climb out on a rock in the Yuba River, look upstream, and watch the river coming at me. If I can tell the story from beginning to end without being distracted by the sound of the water, by the play of light on the ripples, then I know I can tell it to any group at all. I won't be distracted.

David Novak: I do a lot of daydreaming. I can do that easily on the freeways here in California. So I do the story in my head a lot. But for me to practice a story, I need someone to listen. So often I do my practicing of a story in performance. I think that, unlike acting, where I can go and do a rehearsal, the performance is in many ways the rehearsal. I meditate a lot about my stories. I have a very specific point about memorization, however, that works well for me. If you need to memorize a text— let's say you're doing a literary tale and you want to do it verbatim—most people when they try to memorize, start at the beginning. They know the first part extremely well. But the stuff they learn later, they're a little less solid on. They start going up in their lines. Whereas when I'm speaking, I'm moving forward to the point I'm trying to make. My ideas are coming to me and I'm really strong on the point I'm trying to make. Takes me a while to get there, but I know where I'm going. When I memorize a speech, I start at the end of the speech, because that's where I'm going. Learn the last line, and then reconstruct the speech one line at a time (i.e., the line before that and put the two lines together, and then the line before that). When I perform the speech, I'm getting stronger and I accelerate towards the end of it.

SUMMARY

There is no one way to learn a story, but here are some suggestions:

» Read the story over ten times. Read it before going to bed and when you wake up. Walk through the story in your mind as you fall asleep.
» Make a tape of the story to listen to in the car or while doing other activities.
» Make an outline of the story. Keep this in a notebook for later reference.
» Try telling the story in your own words. After several tellings, make a recording of it and critique it. Revise the recording until you have the one you like.
» Try opening up the story with movement.
» Visualize the "landscape" of the story. Draw characters, scenes, and action of the story very clearly in your mind. Understand who the characters are. Give them personalities. Think about what the story means to you.
» Create a set beginning and ending and memorize these.
» Memorize any essential language, poetry.
» Decide how you are going to introduce the tale, giving credit where it is due.
» Tell the story or tell about the story to someone.
» Practice the story ten more times in front of small friendly audiences.
» Sandwich the new story between two strong pieces of material and tell it in performance.

WHAT PERFORMANCE TECHNIQUES DO I NEED TO KNOW?

♦ ♦ ♦ ♦

There's an old adage that states, "You only get one chance to make a good first impression." How you look and sound are vitally important to the success of your stories. Equally important is the setup of the performing space. Can you be seen? Can you be heard? Is it too hot in the room? Too cold? Are the people scattered about in small clusters or all bunched together so that you can "work" them as an audience? Are you close to them or far away? Are you telling indoors or outdoors? If outdoors, are you sandwiched between a clown making balloon animals and a polka band?

While storytelling is more relaxed and informal than most types of performing, you don't want anything to get in the way of your being able to tell stories to the best of your ability. Good performance techniques enable you to seemingly spin out your stories with little or no effort.

Milbre Burch thinks good performance technique begins with how you feel about yourself and your craft. She says you should feel secure enough to walk into a performance space and own it completely. Steve Sanfield notes your job will be easier if you trust who you are. Before you begin to tell stories, Jay O'Callahan feels you need to let the audience know "I really want to be here, and I'm so glad you've come." Margaret Read MacDonald discusses the importance of being centered, and what that means.

Doug Lipman explains why your first story should be one you've told a thousand times. He says not only will it make you feel more comfortable, but you can judge the audience by their response to it. Jim May and Jon Spelmann offer advice on controlling the environment and taking charge of the setup. Following that line of thought, Len Cabral counsels us to be sensitive to the physical needs and wants of the audience, keeping in mind the time of day, how long they've been sitting, what they've been sitting on, the temperature, and the listeners' ages.

Bill Harley explains how the pacing and dynamics of your storytelling set can make a big difference. Both Donald Davis and Heather Forest emphasize the two most basic performance techniques: being seen and being heard.

The chapter ends with reminders about vocal technique and ways to take charge of your storytelling event.

Milbre Burch: When it's the storyteller's turn to tell, she or he needs to be willing and able to enter the performance space, claim it completely, breathe, acknowledge the audience, start the story, stay connected with the audience, finish the story, acknowledge the applause, and leave the space—preferably without having an out-of-body experience anywhere along the way. As the sweepstakes ticket says: "You have to be present to win."

Jay O'Callahan: I want to be present when I go out on stage. I want my attention on the characters. I sometimes make a conscious decision to say in my mind, "You're good at this," and "Welcome, welcome to all you people who have shown up." The audience needs to sense that I really want to be there, and I'm glad they've come. It's important to not just do the work but to have that sense of welcome.

In terms of performance, I want my body to be limber. I want to be rested. I want my voice to be relaxed. That means I do a lot of my performance technique off-stage an hour or so before I go on. I do a lot of warmup and voice exercises. My stories are often long dramatic ones so I need this. Then I'll actually do several of the scenes to calm me down, right there on the stage before people come. I'll be doing a few of the scenes that really draw me into the stories, scenes I love the best, and maybe some of the hardest ones. This is all to draw me into that story as intensely as possible. Again, this is pre-stage. I will try to be very relaxed before I go on. I hope there's no tension in my face or my back. Those ordinary pre-story jitters are fine. I pay a lot of attention to the breath, the voice, the body, the characters, and the audience.

In terms of techniques, I try to be aware, even with a short folktale, what the important moments are in the story. Maybe there are three moments, maybe there are forty-two moments. If there are several moments in the story, I want those moments to live and they can't live often unless I'm really aware of them.

I don't rush through it; I don't back away from it. I don't overdo it. I try to give it all the concentration that it deserves. I do that because it's very easy to race over them, and if you race over them, then you don't have those peaks.

Donald Davis: Well, the point is to get the story to the people in the audience. And so the three important things to me are: Can they really *hear* me? And can they really *see* me? And what can I do to enable them to really hear me and really see me? You know, I hear people say, "Well, I just don't like to work with microphones." Too bad! If that's what it takes for people to really hear you, that's your job.

I prefer hand-held mikes because I have real control over what I'm doing with the mike. A mike that's clipped on, I have no control over the relationship between that mike and my mouth. I'm limited sound-wise, so I like to have something I can work with.

I like to work up close to an audience. If they can't hear me or see me, I've lost the point of being there. I ask myself over and over again, Am I doing all I can so that they can hear well and see well?

As for the performance itself, I avoid using any kind of scriptedness. I want to be real sure that I don't fall into word patterns that are comfortable and come out like they're from a vending machine. I avoid that by not telling the same story too often. I want to be reaching for a story while I tell it. I want to be trying to remember it while I tell it. If I told a story, say, yesterday, I don't want to tell it today, not even to a different group. So one of the things about telling stories is that it takes a lot of stories.

I want to be sure that I see the story in picture blocks, not in words. Once in a while, one of the ways I use to keep a story fresh is to take a forty-minute story and tell it in twenty minutes. I must pull out of it the pieces that are essential and junk the rest. I fight ever letting the stories become rote. I always try to say, OK, don't let it ever become 'these words equal this story.' Instead, these *pictures* make the story and every audience is going to pass by them in a different way.

Jon Spelman: The best way you can be a better performer is to really invest in the story. If you really find yourself in the story, really know why you're telling the story, really think about the images in the story, then a lot of your performance problems are going to be solved or at least greatly lessened. And, as they say, check your fly and your zippers and your buttons before you start. I'm surprised by how many people don't do those little checks.

For informal storytelling, do as much as you can to control your environment. Should I sit or stand? Where am I going to be in relationship to the audience? What's going to be visible behind me as I'm telling? Will people be moving behind me? Are there windows behind me? Are there mirrors behind me? Will bells be rung while I'm telling? Are there announcements that might come over a speaker? Am I right by the garbage dump? There're a whole lot of things that you can start to think about environmentally, that you might have some control over so that you can set up the room or move from where you are or ask to have the truck not pick up the garbage until you're gone.

Steve Sanfield: The very thing that makes a person an individual is what's going to make him an outstanding storyteller. Everybody will tell a story in a different way; no two people will ever tell it the same way. My suggestion to any would-be storyteller is trust yourself and trust who you are. I think that storytelling is an art, but I think it is a folk art. I think one of the great things about folk art is that the self is not there, the self is out of the way, and it's the song that matters. It's not the name of the woman at the bottom of the quilt. It's the quilt that matters. The same thing is true of storytelling. It's the story that matters.

Gay Ducey: A certain ability to let the story unfold without feeling you need to rush into the spaces in the story or that you need to overly entertain. In some ways, the performance technique I'm talking about is knowing when less is more. Part of good manners is to tell where you heard the story or how the story came to you. Now part of that's educational. It means that the audience can see that the story travels a certain journey, and the journey doesn't necessarily end with this particular storytelling. But it's also a way of linking yourself as a storyteller to the others. Linking yourself to the community and in some ways acknowledging to the audience that no storyteller ever works alone. We always owe a debt for every story we learn, and every story that we share. It's important to acknowledge the debt and the journey.

---

*The most basic thing is
that you have to be heard.*
— Michael Parent

Kathryn Windham: You see, you have used a word that I don't even like to associate with storytelling: Performing. I think there is a difference between telling stories and performing. I think storytelling is the most relaxed and personal and let's-all-get-into-this-and-have-a-good-time-together of all the arts. I think it's all right if you make mistakes telling stories. I think it's all right if you forget and have to go back and tell something. I think it's all right if you are enjoying it, and your audience is enjoying it. They will forgive you for any of those slips. I think we forget that our listeners want us to do well. They are not out there thinking, "I hope she forgets all her lines and falls flat on her face." They don't have that attitude. They love us and expect us and want us to do well. I think when you realize they are on your side you relax and enjoy what you are doing. That's one of the differences, I think, between performing and storytelling. You can change as the situation requires.

Carol Birch: What we all need is to better grasp what we do naturally to effectively communicate in our daily lives. For example, it helps to become aware of how you talk when you are not on the stage, so you can bring your abilities to the stage *at will*, yet *without effort*. What I often challenge people to do in workshops is to record three weeks of *their half* of telephone conversations. Call your mother, someone you are angry with, someone you need to console or have power over, someone you want something from and then listen, really listen, to all the voices you have inside you. We all have a multitude of voices inside which we readily, and usually rather unconsciously, employ. Only one person ever told me that she actually accepted the challenge, and she said she learned a great deal. To bring consciousness to what we do automatically is one of the most effective techniques I know. Only then can we hope to incorporate without effort on the stage the native skills each of us possesses.

Bill Harley: You can't deliver the whole story at an unbelievably fast pace or slow pace or loud volume or small volume. You need a sense of balance for all those things. This happens when you feel comfortable. There is not "one" technique that works for everybody. Everybody brings who they are to a story. The technique that works for me will not necessarily be something you need to emulate. You have to find what is *you*.

Beth Horner: It's important that the audience hear you. Actually, that is a big problem—speaking clearly and carefully into a microphone. The way one stands, the way one dresses, all of those things are important. Wearing high heels, for example, is not a good idea. One needs to be grounded whether that means sitting or standing. In using music with storytelling, I always recommend that whatever music is used in the story it should improve or blend with the story. It should not be used simply as a gimmick. That happens with beginning storytellers. There are times, however, when music—one note, one passage—evokes an emotion or tone in the story far more effectively than two paragraphs of words. Music should be included in your story when it enhances. It is important to know your

audience, scope them out, know a little bit about what they are bringing to the storytelling session. Usually the person who hires you can give you that information. If it's a group of women or a community group, ask what part of the country it is, so that you don't tell a story that would be offensive to them. Or maybe you know of something that has happened in the community lately.

For example, I did a program in a little suburb of Chicago. We started out with this ridiculous song, "Threw It Out The Window." At first they think you are being silly. Then they really like it, and I ask them for nursery rhymes, etc., etc. Well, someone suggested "Mary Had A Little Lamb," so it went, "Mary had a little lamb, Whose fleece was white as snow, She followed her to school one day, She threw it out the window." Everyone thought that was funny. Although I said, "Don't call in the SPCA."

Later on the in the program, I said, "Oh, I know about you people in Findley Park, you throw little lambs out the window, you have a murderous nature." It turned out there had been an awful gory murder lately. Big silence … well, I didn't know that it had happened. I think it is important to have known that ahead of time.

[How did you recover?]

Well, I didn't know why it fell flat, but I figured there must have been something. They told me later on. I just went on to the next thing.

Diane Ferlatte: I'm not a technique person. When I do a lot of workshops, they're into techniques and guidelines, but storytelling is much more than that. You can write notes for days, but if you don't do it, you'll never know it. You just have to do it. And once you do it, you'll learn the techniques and your own style. The more you watch other tellers and hear other stories, you will see things that work. I'm used to audience response that I get from church, used to that from storytelling around the house. We holler back. We say something back. I want the response.

Michael Parent: Vary your voice. Pay attention to the fact that you don't have to have acting lessons to modulate your voice. In normal conversation, we modulate our voices all the time. Storytelling is basically normal conversation elevated a couple levels for more eloquent communication. The most basic thing is that you have to be heard. You have to have variety in your communication, or people won't listen to you. If they won't listen, they won't hear you, and they won't get the story.

Margaret Read MacDonald: There are so many different styles and tellers. One person can sit perfectly quietly and not move a muscle and tell beautifully. Another person can jump all over the stage. What may be overacting for one individual is not overacting for another, if it comes from the heart to the audience and it works. So beyond the simple ability to speak clearly and get your ideas across, simple communication techniques to me are the only performance techniques that new storytellers need. I suppose being able to center themselves the way actors do is important, to be able to go into themselves and to become centered and then bring something out for the audience.

[What does that mean, become centered?]

To me it means stopping before I go on stage and being still and coming back inside myself and thinking of the audience and what I can give them, then going out there and responding to them. I'm like a still pool inside and I'm able to pour and direct my energy toward them in any way I want to.

Maggi Peirce: First of all, take your time. Nobody's wanting you to rush into your story. Be sure to make contact with your audience. Your audience are the people who are kind enough to come to hear you, and you should give them your all.

People always think that we who tell stories all the time never get nervous. That's a lot of baloney. We all are nervous. We all get an extra gulp in our throat sometimes that we didn't know was there until we start talking. Accept it. Storytellers are human, too. Accept that. Don't comment on it. Just start your story.

If you start being nervous, your audience starts being nervous for you. They worry about you, therefore you want to make your audience comfortable. They're the important ones, not you. What's important about you is your story, not you, and your telling of it.

Jim May: When you get out there, you've got about thirty seconds to a minute to establish something with the audience. So do something good in that first minute—a little joke or something humorous that just happened or maybe you could tag onto something the emcee said in introducing you.

Places that you don't know what the setting will be—a school, a church hall, a picnic, whatever—just take charge. They usually don't know what you need. Don't pay attention to what they think you should be doing or what the setup should be. Just get everybody as close to you as possible. Get the speakers where they're going to do some good. Take them off the shelf and set them up where they're closer to the audience. Set it up the way you need to do it because the setting can make or break it in one of those situations.

I've had times in a big auditorium where I've literally had the whole audience get up on the stage with me because the stage was so big, and I was so far from the kids. I just stopped because the kids were not connecting with what I was doing, I was so far away. The teachers were not taking responsibility. We got the whole group up on the stage where I was real close to them and that made a huge difference.

You have to be as clear as you can ahead of time but don't hesitate to change things when you get there, because you're the one who's going to be on the spot. You're the one who's going to be miserable for the next forty-five minutes or hour if it's not working, not the production person who is going to be in the back or out of the room. Get people close to you in a semicircle. Tell them ahead of time you don't want the kitchen banging around. You don't want the maintenance guy with a lawn mower outside the window. You can tell them these kinds of things ahead of time.

Doug Lipman: The first story you tell should be one you've told a thousand times so you can judge the audience by their reaction to it. If they respond in a way that surprises you, you won't lose the story. Whether it's a funny story or not isn't important. What's important is that it's a story that you know and love and can use to judge reactions.

Here are extremes: Warming up a preschool audience. You need a lot of your attention for that. Connecting to them, noticing where they are, what they can do. You need to tell a story that needs almost none of your attention. You need very little attention focused on yourself. There's another piece of your attention which I call your judgment. So it might be ten percent judgment, eighty percent the audience and ten percent for you and the story.

Other extreme: It's an adult concert getting toward the end of the evening. You're about to settle in for a twenty- or thirty-minute story because you've got them. Well, here you don't need much attention on yourself. You don't need much atten-

tion on them, because you are on the same wave-length already. So five percent of your attention goes to those three together and ninety-five percent of your attention is free to go into the story. Since you're so into the story, the audience will follow.

Len Cabral: Being sensitive to your audience is very important, as is realizing the time of the day, the space, and the age of listeners. Be aware of your environment. You know you don't want to perform with a window to your back. Is the sun better in your eyes or your audience's eyes? (Your eyes, of course.) I find audience participation a powerful tool in stories—either with songs or with poems—parts of the stories where they are participating verbally. Again that's another way of keeping the audience engaged in the story all the way through—a call-and-response type of thing.

I start off with a short story, because I want the audience to have some time to take me in. When you walk on stage, people are looking at what you're wearing—your shirt, pants, hair, this, that, and the other thing. They're not really listening for the most part. They're not ready to focus on that first story, so you should have a short first story. Let them get used to your accent if you're from a different part of the country, your timing and your rhythm, your pattern of speech. After they've taken you in, after they've heard your dialect or your accent, after they've understood your body language, after they've seen what you're wearing, they can now say, "OK, what's he talking about?" I always start out with a relatively short story and then work stories up in length as the program goes on.

Robin Moore: You need to have a variety of things you can do. If you have one story that is long and slow that really works for you, you don't want to continue to build a repertoire of just long slow stories. You've got to have a short funny story. You've got to have something with audience participation, so that when you get up there, you are changing textures all the time. When I did my first couple of paying gigs, I had only forty-five minutes worth of material. That's all I had, and once I went through it I was done. What I try to do now, when I'm learning stories, is think, what kind of texture is this story? When you have a variety it gives you a lot of confidence because you can change textures. At the same time, you are not locked in.

Somewhere in the program there has to be a really deep listening experience. What that means is a story with a lot of silence in it and a chance for everything to get very, very slow—you start to feel what I call "planet time." You go out of human time and start to feel the planet spinning. I usually like to do that first because if you start fast you have nowhere to go. If you start slow, you can build up from there. It helps if you can get people laughing early in the game. You are really unmasking yourself; you're disarming yourself when you are up there. Laughter is a great way to get your audience to do that. You open your hearts to each other. So I try to get some laughter in there pretty quickly and giving them a chance to participate, whether it's just as simple as asking a question or repeating something back. That's really important, so that they realize this is not just consumable entertainment. It isn't like a film. It's interactive. And in order to make the storytelling work, they are going to have to do their job as an audience, which in a lot of storytelling cultures means constantly prompting the storyteller and joining in the story. I try to encourage them to do that. You have to let them know when it's appropriate to do that and when it's not.

Heather Forest: Make sure that people can hear you and see you. From a technical point of view, you will want to know how to use a microphone. You want to make sure that the audience's ability to focus on you is unimpeded by a busy background behind you or from light glaring in a window behind you—various things like that. Performance techniques that come out of theater arts tend to apply to storytelling in devising an atmosphere for listening. Performance techniques where a person understands that his voice has to be relative to the room size: if a person is telling a story to twenty people, he might not need a microphone, but if he wants to tell to fifty or a hundred or five hundred or a thousand, he might need sound reinforcement so that his voice can carry in the same informal tonality as it would without amplification for a small group of people.

Susan Klein: Doing your homework is very important. If you are centered and you know, you simply know, the kind of material that works, it works for you. If you take the stage in a calm, open, loving way, the invitation is immediately clear to your audience.

I check to see what feedback I am gleaning from the group. If there is a part of the audience that I think needs a little more attention, I can focus something there. I check in constantly with my inner self to see what material would be most appropriate to do next. I generally do not decide what I'm going to tell until I'm standing in front of the audience and then it just comes. As a veteran of the stage, there has always been a wider knowledge of "I'm not the only one here. All these people in the audience have needs." I am somehow able to sense what people in the audience need and I surprise myself sometimes by the story I choose to tell. Someone always comes up afterwards and says, "You told that story for me tonight."

Connie Regan-Blake: Barbara [Freeman] and I usually have a listing of what we're going to tell, a set list. But we always stay open to what I call "the story tapping me on the shoulder to be told." I've had several almost mystical experiences with that, where I was not planning on telling a particular story, but the story kept coming to me and I ended up telling it. And something happened afterwards where it meant so much to a person in that audience. Who knows? How can that be? How could they have known? That happened once in the Philippines. We were telling stories on one of the bases and it was a fourth, fifth, and sixth grade group and "Oliver Hyde" kept coming to me. I don't tell it very much in concert. But it kept coming to me and coming to me, so I told "Oliver Hyde," about that fiddler and about how he cuts himself off from the community. A woman came up to me afterwards and said, "I am Oliver Hyde." I could see her face swelling with emotion. We stepped down the hallway and she said, "I have come over here, and I have cut myself off from everyone. I don't go out of my house, and I don't know what made me come to this performance today." It was the first time she had come out of her house in a number of months. She said she just didn't like it there, and she was afraid. Her husband was in the military, and they had been transferred there. We both sat there weeping because I knew I was supposed to tell that story. So I stay open. I think a lot of it has to do with being open to the energy of the audience.

Ed Stivender: Mime, ballet, puppetry, elocution, letting the audience breathe together.

Bill Mooney and David Holt: Only Jay mentioned vocal warmups. We both think they are very important. There are quite a few times when we perform four forty-five minute school shows in one day. That can cause a strain on your vocal cords if you're not prepared.

Here's our favorite: Pretend you are an owlet that has just been surprised. Start at the top of your vocal range and say, "Hoo-o-o-o-o-o" in a descending fashion until you get to the bottom of your vocal range. It should sound something like a bomb dropping. Try to blow air through your nose at the same time. Do not strain. Keep it all comfortable.

When we are nervous or tired, our vocal cords become taut and, as a result, our voices get higher. This startled-owlet exercise causes our vocal cords to loosen and start resonating properly again so that our voices can return to their normal pitches.

You can alternate the "Hoo-o-o-o's" with a lip articulator. Say: "The lips, the teeth, the tip of the tongue." Repeat it several times aloud, exaggerating the movement of your lips and tongue as you say it. Then go back and imitate the startled owlet several more times.

It may be a good idea to mention some physical things that you can do to help your stories be more effective. You can't always change the layout of the room where you are telling stories, but you can enhance it. If you're in a large room and you anticipate a small crowd, move most of the chairs away. Put out slightly fewer chairs than you think will be needed. Stack the rest at the back. This way, your audience will have to fill in the seats down front and latecomers will be forced to sit at the rear.

If the chairs are permanent like theater seats, carry some yarn or twine with you and rope off the rear seats so that your audience is forced to sit down front and close together. There is nothing harder than trying to move your audience as a group when they are seated far apart from each other. People *like* to be part of an audience. It makes them feel self-conscious when they are seated by themselves apart from their fellow audience members.

Work as close to your audience as you can. The closer you are to them, the easier it will be to move them into your story. Make sure there are no barriers between you and your audience.

Check to see that there are no entrance or exit doors behind you. If there are, change the seating plan (if that's possible) or arrange to have the audience enter and exit some other way and get those doors locked. Both of us have demanded that seats be turned around, that the seating configuration be changed, that the lighting be refocused.

Always keep in mind that it is your show. You are the writer, the director, the producer, and the sole actor. Most people that invite you to tell stories are lovely folks, but they may not always be savvy about setting up a space that serves you to your best advantage. It is not being pushy to demand that the hall serve you. Check the room temperature. If it's too warm, the audience will nod and droop. If the room is hot, fling open the windows. The audience is always perkier if the room is a little cool, say sixty-five to sixty-eight degrees. They also tend to laugh more if they are a little chilly.

Check the lighting. Make sure plenty of light is on the area where you will be telling stories. Comedy works better in bright light. It's hard to make an audience laugh when the ambiance is dismal. Bill likes to be able to see the audience, so he always makes sure that light is kept on them too. It's best to check on these things ahead of time. You might want to send a list of your technical requirements, including optimal seating arrangements and lighting suggestions, ahead of time. Most people will thank you for it.

Both of us have been plagued enough times by terrible sound systems that we now troupe our own. We both have a Gallien-Kruger 600, an amplifier with its own speakers and small enough to carry in a shoulder bag. We carry it right on the plane with us. We use a Shure hand-held cordless mike.

Respect your audience. Respect their intelligence. Do not talk down to them. This goes for school audiences just as much as for adults. Most audiences assemble with hope in their hearts. They anticipate the concert, the play, the movie, the lecture, the sermon, the storytelling event will be good. They are already on your side before you even open your mouth. Do not let them down. As Michael Parent mentioned, if you greet them at the door, you are even further ahead since you will be talking to friends, not strangers.

Generally you know a lot more than your audience about your subject (the stories). They already recognize that and expect you to be knowledgeable, prepared, and forthright. Speak sincerely and enthusiastically and look them in the eye.

A lot has been said about eye contact. We think it's very important. However, if your eyes light on a grumpy, sour face, don't let it affect you. Look pleasantly at it and move on.

Perhaps the best suggestion we can make is: Pay attention to The Golden Rule. Tell stories to others as you would like them told to you. Send out your energy and encompass the audience. Be their expert tour guide. Make sure their journey is safe and pleasant. They will thank you for it.

SUMMARY

» Enter the performance space, claim it, breathe, acknowledge the audience, start the story, stay connected with the audience, finish the story, acknowledge the applause and leave.

» Be present. Put your attention on your characters and your story. Really put yourself in the story. Know why you are telling it. Think about the images in the story.

» Make sure the audience can hear and see you.

» Work as close as possible to the audience.

» Trust yourself and who you are. Don't try to be somebody else.

» Let the story unfold without feeling you have to overly entertain.

» The audience will forgive slipups. They want you to do well.

» Posture and dress are very important. Do they make the statement you want to make.

» Have variety in your speech pattern or people won't listen.

» You have thirty seconds to a minute to establish yourself with the audience.

» Be clear about your physical setup ahead of time. Don't hesitate to change things when you get to the event. Make the room conducive to good storytelling. It is your show; demand the best.

» The first story told should be one you've told a thousand times before.

» Be sensitive to the time of day, the space, and the audience's age.

» The audience may not be ready to focus on your first story. Start off with something short. Give them a few moments to take you in and get used to you.

» Mix up the stories. Don't do three long, slow ones in a row.

» Create an intimacy with the audience, no matter what the size. The size of the performance should always equal the size of the audience.

» Limit the amount of introduction to a story.

» Make sure your voice is warmed up.

» Respect your audience and their intelligence.

HOW DO I MAKE A PROGRAM FLOW?

◆ ◆ ◆ ◆

Most of the tellers agree that the first story should be light and humorous. Bill Harley says that the first piece in a set is always just an introduction. Only after you have become acquainted with each other can you go to the meatier pieces.

It is necessary to snag the audience's attention immediately. It's a little like the man who bought a mule from a farmer with the understanding that the mule could understand everything. "You say 'Gee' and he'll go right. You say 'Haw' and he'll go left. You say 'Whoa' and he'll stop. All you gotta do is tell him." The man got the mule home and tried to work him but no matter how much he shouted and swore at him, the mule wouldn't budge. The man was angry and felt he'd been sold a bill of goods. He called the farmer. The farmer said, "Don't worry. I'll be right there." When the farmer arrived, he took a two-by-four from his pickup and walked over to the mule. The farmer reared back and hit the mule across the head as hard as he could. Then, he told the man, "I didn't cheat you. This mule understands everything allright. It's just that… first, you have to get his attention." An audience is like that—first you have to get their attention, and a short humorous story will usually do the trick.

Judith Black states the importance of effective bridges between one story and another, and how they can establish the theme and tone of the set. At the beginning, Syd Lieberman likes to give the audience a little taste of everything that's going to be on the program. Beth Horner relates a wonderful opening story about her father insisting on her wearing a life jacket at the lake. Milbre Burch suggests varying the humorous opening by substituting a story that has a surprise at the end. Jon Spelman notes the rhythm and shape of a concert. Michael Parent explains how he opens with a song and invites the audience to sing with him. But he cautions not to force them; rather, make it all so much fun that they can't help but join in. Bill Harley feels—like Will Rogers—that you need to know when to get off the stage, leaving the audience wanting more.

We begin with Elizabeth Ellis's description of how to make a program flow. We think Elizabeth's unique way of analyzing the shape of a program will influence a long line of future storytellers.

Elizabeth Ellis: Well, this is something I discuss in a book I've been working on about developing a personal storytelling style. There are four kinds of stories. What determines the type of story is the response the audience gives to it. So the first type of story would be:

Ha Ha. This is the funny story, from the most slapstick to the most subtle, from the noodlehead story to the sophisticated literary tale that is comic because of its plotting.

The next kind of story is:

Ah Ha. This is a story that has some element of surprise. It could be a story that explains where things come from, like a *pourquoi* story. It could be a ghost story. It could be a story like the ones O. Henry wrote. The broadest type would be the jump tale. The most subtle would be, "Oh, I get it! They're talking about why raccoons have rings on their tails!"

The third type of story is:

Ah. If you are telling to a large audience, you can physically hear that sound, "Aaah!" It may be a fairy tale, a personal experience story, or a story from the Bible. It encompasses a wide variety of tales. But the thing they all have in common is that "Ah!" reaction. It requires listening at a much deeper level of concentration than the "Ha Ha" or the "Ah Ha" stories. When the stories end, the audience is usually a long way out of their bodies, and it takes them a while to hike back.

The last type is:

Amen. Amen literally means "so be it." "So be it" is the response that is called from you and the audience. "Yes! Let my life be lived in that way." "This is the way life should be lived."

Occasionally you hit on a story that has each of these elements in it. If it is a long story, you would ideally want all four elements in it.

When I'm planning a program, I pick two or more stories from "Ha Ha," and one story from each of the other categories. It is a circle. It is my intention, if I can, to get all the way around the circle. I don't always accomplish it, but that's my goal. I go as far as the situation allows me to go.

At the point when I realize I have lost my audience or a significant portion of it, I drop back one category. If I see that everything is really falling apart, I drop back to the beginning again—to "Ha Ha." Say, for instance, I tell an "Ah" story and I see that this lovely thought-provoking story is falling on significantly deaf ears, I will drop back to "Ah Ha." Or maybe even to "Ha Ha" if it looks like I'm not keeping them with me.

It has been very good to have my stories categorized in this manner. It makes it easy for me to plan a set and think on my feet.

[Do you feel that audiences are so different? That some audiences will accept an "Amen" story and others will not?]

Sure. It depends on the situation. One audience might accept a story in one envi-

ronment where they wouldn't in another. If you're telling at the mall, how far you get to go around that circle is probably less than if the same audience were at a church supper on a Sunday night. If you're telling at an outdoor event with a lot of distractions, then the chance that you will get all the way around the circle may be quite slim. But some days you get lucky.

The relationship of the teller to the listener is a lot like a tourist and a tour guide. I can't get you to go with me unless you trust me. So I have to spend a lot of time at the beginning of our interaction together as teller and listener developing trust. If I can develop trust between us, then I can get you to go farther and deeper than if I didn't spend that time preparing our relationship. You're going to bail out on me if I try to take you farther than you want to go, faster than you want to go. But if I can really develop a bond of trust between us at the beginning of the teller-listener relationship, you will probably be willing to go pretty much anywhere I want to take you.

Bill Harley: I look upon the first piece as an introduction to the audience, so it's not necessarily something with a high amount of content. It's more just saying, "Hi, here I am and here's the kind of thing you might see." In the first ten or fifteen minutes, you have to introduce who you are and the kind of things they can expect to hear. If you use music, you don't want to get forty minutes into your set and then start singing. You let them know early on that that's part of your performance. Playing for a family audience, my first song is very simple. I usually ask something of the audience in that song, to let them know right away that they're going to be participating throughout the show. I might ask them to sing one simple phrase, or do a physical thing like raise their hands.

You don't start off asking everybody to stand up and do a big something. That makes them feel vulnerable. You ask them to do something small that doesn't draw attention to them. If you get them to do something physical, they are more likely to sing.

Most family audiences usually have a lot of three- to eleven-year-olds and then adults. You might have a couple of teenagers but not a whole lot. After about forty-five minutes to an hour, the younger ones are going to be losing it. Even though you are telling stories that have a point, the kids are probably going to need a lot of focus and repetition. You will have to begin winding things up.

I always want the audience to leave feeling that they have experienced something together. I don't want them to straggle out and say, "Yeah, the first twenty minutes were good, but then my kid began to lose it." I think the heart and gut of a storytelling session happens about fifteen to twenty minutes into it, once you have introduced who you are and the kind of things you do and have gotten the audience to participate.

The story that might have the deepest meaning to you happens once the audience has settled down and understands the range of who you are as a performer. If the story is being done well, the performer becomes invisible at a certain point. There is just the story. All the technique and things you are using are only to serve the story. Sometimes you see a performer with really good technique, but maybe that's all she has. She just shows off her technique, and soon that gets in the way of the story. You start saying, "Well, she has a really beautiful voice, but what was the song about?" "I can't remember, but she had a beautiful voice," someone responds. To me, that's a sign that she hasn't done her job.

At a certain point with good performers, *who* the performer is begins to take a back seat and *what* the performer is saying comes forward. That's where the heart stuff comes, a little bit later in the show.

Another thing to keep in mind (and it's really hard when you are having a good time): it's better to leave them wanting a little more. I remember reading a book by Will Rogers and he said the first rule of show business is knowing when to get off. Too many times we think we have to give them more. If your session is somewhere between forty-five minutes and an hour, you only go to that hour if you know the audience is really there.

For the last song I always try to find something that is easy to sing where everybody participates. If you are just telling stories, I think you need to find that one short, elegant story that makes a nice simple almost parable-like point and ties your hour together.

Syd Lieberman: I think you have to have a variety of stories. At the beginning of the program I like to give the audience a little taste of everything that's going to come: a little folktale, a little personal story. I like to keep it light and quick at the beginning. I think that they need to get a snappy start. I would never open with a long piece. That would be a disaster.

I'm talking about adults. I tend to be too crazy with kids. I tend to rile them up, rather than quiet them down. I don't know what it is they see in me that makes them do that. I actually like to start very quietly with kids, quieter than I think I should be, eventually involving them in audience participation. Otherwise, they're over the top by the middle of the program, then you're through and you can never get them back. I learned that through hard experience.

An audience really does like a laugh at the beginning. A lot of people come in and they don't even know what storytelling is. They are worried about what they've been dragged to by a spouse. I think you have to reassure them that it is going to be OK. It's not going to be a horror show. I think that's important to them, so they can start thinking, oh, it's OK, now I can sit back and enjoy the rest of this and not feel angry that I'm here. I think the beginning is really important to engage them somehow.

Once that's done, I like to do a variety of moods. I do something kind of sweet, nostalgic, and then something horrible to keep them moving. You have to have different moods for the audience. If you tell all the same kind of stories with the same feeling and the same kind of laughter, it's not going to work. They're going to get tired of that after a while.

The end is important too. You have to either end with a real powerful story or a laugh. You have to think about that last moment when they're walking out. I finish the first set with one of those "Aaah!" stories. I would feel funny about ending on a somber note. I think it's a little hard, too, for people to leave at that point. It's almost like a falling action after a climax. You need a little something to bring you back to reality and life.

Judith Black: We are so busy working on our stories we often forget that what makes an entire program flow are the bridges between tales. Pay attention to them. There is no one correct way to bridge stories in a program, but answer these questions when you consider how to do it:

What is the theme of the program, and how can I extend or emphasize it through the bridges?

Will listeners need the bridges to allow the stories to gently sink in or will they need to be physically and/or verbally involved during them?

How can your bridges offer variety and/or contrast to the stories?

Can you use the bridges to weave another thread of connection between you and the listeners?

Jim May: I always start out with humor. Although I try to stick with a set of stories,

I have alternatives. I always have an escape hatch. If something is not working, I always have more stories in mind than I have time to tell. So I have kind of a menu. I always think you need a menu and then you choose from that menu based on what's happening with the audience. I often end on a powerful note.

Beth Horner: I like to start out with something short, often with a song—something short and light and funny that brings the audience and teller together immediately. Something they can identify with right away. For example, I often tell a story of how I learned how to swim. I grew up swimming in a river and my father made me wear a life jacket. I hated that life jacket, because it was a hand-me-down. It was something from the Spanish Inquisition, and it was heavy. I would say, "I don't need this life jacket. I can swim, I can swim, I can swim." And my father would say, "Oh, but B Des, we love you and we wouldn't want you to drown," and he would put the life jacket on me. One day my dad was strapping me into the life jacket, and he noticed that it had some mud on it from the day before when I had been playing at the gravel bar in the river. He took it off me and started to rinse it in the river, but he got distracted by one of the other kids and accidentally dropped the life jacket into the river. It sank to the bottom. It turns out I had been holding up that life jacket for years, and that's why I'm such a good swimmer.

Well, everybody can identify with that story right away. I feel the audience is with me. So I always start out with something that any audience can identify with.

Michael Parent: Mostly I want it to be enjoyable for me and them. Since I mix songs and stories together, the way I generally like to construct the set is to start with a song. That relaxes me and usually relaxes the audience. Most of the songs I do are things they can join in on, if they want to. That's another thing. Don't force people to join in. Make it so much fun that they can't help but want to join in. Then I'll do a shorter story just to break the ice and get them in the world of stories, and then maybe another little song. Constructing your program is like modulating your voice. You modulate the set so that it has variety, varying the menu so that people can absorb it. If you don't vary the menu, pretty soon people are not really listening to you.

Milbre Burch: I consider some audiences "special-needs audiences": urban adolescents, teenagers everywhere, and almost all adult men. They are often the ones for whom the word "storytelling" translates as "baby-sitting." For these groups, I almost always start with either a funny story or one that has a surprise at the end. Once they laugh or are surprised, they relax a little, and everything—both telling and listening—gets easier.

I frequently start with something humorous whatever the audience, and then (with school children especially, though I also do this with adults) something with participation in it.

For a completely satisfying "listen," I try to make sure the concert has serious as well as humorous material. I hope to call forth from the audience a full range of human emotions.

If there's an intermission, I may end the first half with something I want the audience to think about; the same goes for the end of a show.

SUMMARY

» Open the set with a light or humorous story so that you and the audience can become acquainted. If you open with a song, invite the audience to join in. You can judge by how they participate the kind of crowd you are facing.

» The bridges between your stories can establish the tone and theme of the set.

» Make sure to vary the types of stories within your set. The stories you use should have different textures.

» Know when to get off the stage. Always leave them wanting more.

» We feel you won't ever go too wrong by following Elizabeth Ellis's way of putting together a set:

» Ha Ha

» Ah Ha

» Aaah!

» Amen.

INTRODUCTIONS AND THE ROLE OF EMCEE

We have included a few comments and tips on how to provide a good introduction at a storytelling event. The emcee, or introducer, is one of the most important roles at an event. The emcee sets the tone for the evening. There are so many thoughtless, inane, and downright bad introductions given to storytellers each year, we thought you might like to hear what three excellent emcees have to say about this aspect making a program flow.

Connie Regan-Blake: Your job as emcee is to help the audience welcome the storytellers. You need to open up the audience to be receptive to each teller as they come up.

I've heard some emcees use the introduction time to say other things. Certainly there are always announcements to be made, but make sure they are done before you begin the introduction for your teller. It is also your responsibility to make sure that the microphone is ready and that a chair and water are in place if they are needed. This should be seen to before you begin the introduction. It's not good to build up the audience's anticipation and then say, "Oops, we need to get some water up here!"

Your job is to set the stage for the best performance possible. So you need to find out ahead of time what it is that will make those performers most comfortable onstage. Interview them beforehand, and ask them what *they* would like said. I always ask, "What are some things that would help the audience know you and your stories a little better?"

It's always good to mention the teller's achievements—especially his recordings—because that's a way to help keep this profession alive. But it is usually better to mention the books and recordings after the teller finishes.

You need to find something specific and special to say about each teller. I think one of the worst introductions is the kind that starts: "Our next teller told me to tell you that she …" You should never put it back on the teller. Be sure you get the teller's name right. I think it is also interesting to know where the teller is from.

If there is only one teller for the full evening, your introduction will differ radically from the introductions you would give for seven different tellers over the course of an evening. If you are introducing more than one teller, it is important that the introductions be balanced. You should not introduce one teller that you know and love with a four-minute accolade, and then not say very much about the next teller whom you don't know so well. Give the same introductory weight to each teller.

When you finish your introduction, say something like: "Now join me in welcoming So-and-so." Cue the audience to applaud. Applause acts as a natural bridge to bring the teller onstage.

You should also be clear with the teller about time limits. I always ask if he would like a signal from me when they have five minutes left. If they want a signal, we agree on what it is to be—always something unobtrusive and discreet.

The emcee should never be the most important person at a telling. Many times the audience is given the idea that the spotlight shines brighter on the emcee than the teller. That should never happen. If you are a beginning emcee, it is always better to say less rather than more.

Donald Davis: I see the emcee's role as one of energy maintenance. The energy of the audience is the responsibility of the emcee. You must keep their energy up and directed all the way to the end of the evening. The evening should finish with the energy high rather than exhausted.

Many times people mistake being an emcee with being a warmup act. Those are very different events. A warmup act should be labeled just that—"A Warmup Act"—and it should have its own time slot. But to be an emcee, you have to be the policeman. You have to establish the rules in a polite gentle way, make the necessary announcements, and leave both the audience and the tellers feeling good about the event. And you must do it quickly.

You have to be able to grab the energy of the audience and hand it to the storyteller. It is important to not lose that energy. Whatever information about the teller you use should not be so long that it dissipates the energy the audience brings in.

My introduction should not only help the audience feel more excitement about what's coming, but it needs to make the teller feel better too. I want the teller to hear why I'm excited to be introducing him or her. I don't want the introduction to be merely a recitation of facts and figures. Certainly the audience needs to know enough about the teller so that they have a sense of anticipation and excitement, but as little as works is best.

I always ask myself these questions: Can the audience hear why I'm excited to be presenting this teller? Why I'm glad to be here and why I'm looking forward to hearing this person? Then I ask: Can the teller genuinely hear the same message from me? As I'm introducing you, do you sense that I'm glad to be doing it? My goal is always to leave the teller in a better starting place than I would have if I had tried to entertain and pull attention to myself, or told the audience my whole life story, or beat them over the head with the rules, or exhausted them so much that it's a relief to get me out of the way.

I also try, as I listen to the teller, to find a way to pop back up and put a period on the end of what the storyteller did. It's not that I'm trying to rescue an experience that didn't come off. But it is always good, in a multiple-teller evening, to build a bridge from one person to the next. The emcee is in a hard spot when he introduces someone and knows that the next person is going to be better. As I hear that first teller, I listen very carefully so that I will be able to tell the audience something really good that I got out of their story. It's like tying a little bow on the end of it. Then I move on to introduce the next person. That helps give the evening a more positive flow.

Advance preparation of introductions is very important, but listening to the teller is even more important. I was at a festival recently where the emcee's introductions were all canned—scripted prior to the event. There was no relationship to the festival audience in those events. So there were no smooth transitions. It was just chop, chop, chop … the next dog is … the next horse is … I began to realize how much an emcee has to listen, especially in a

multiple-teller program. You must be able to build a bridge from one teller to the next. Your job is not just to introduce the next person. You can't get ready for that ahead of time, so you have to listen.

[What do you do specifically when you are introducing a number of tellers and there is one you don't know and have never heard before?]

That's really hard. I try to talk with that person ahead of time. I try to be honest with the audience. When I was a minister, every time I moved to a new church, someone died the day I arrived. Even though I didn't know them, had never met them, I had to hold their funeral. This is what I learned to do: Instead of being dishonest and saying all kinds of things I didn't know—or instead of being crass and saying that I never heard of this person before—I listened to the dead person's friends and neighbors, and said back to them basically what I had heard. I apply that technique to introducing tellers. So now, at a festival, I can honestly say, "I never met so-and-so before this afternoon, but I really look forward to hearing him tell stories because my friend had him at a festival and the report of what he did has got me so excited, I can hardly wait." So I fish around and find recommendations or reports from other people. I have to find a way to say to the audience, "I'm excited to hear this person I'm bringing to you."

[What do you do when the teller has laid an egg? Do you still try to tie a bow at the end of the story?]

Yes, but it's tough. You have to listen. Really listen.

Nobody does everything bad.

I try to listen for one of three things. I try to listen to whether the teller has helped me through the story to meet *someone* I'm glad to have met (even if the story itself didn't succeed). Maybe it's a person who reminds me of someone in my life whom I haven't thought about in a long time. The teller may tell a story that makes no sense plot-wise but somewhere in the story they may have helped me meet a character that I'm glad I met.

Second, they may have taken me to a *place* I'm really glad to have been. In a workshop I was giving, a woman told about going to on a trip to try to find her great-aunt. The story amounted to almost nothing, but her description of market day in a nearby village was something I could come back to and say, "The whole time was worth getting to go through the market." That's what I mean by place. In stories, people may take us to a place of wonder. If I can remind the audience of that, it is helpful.

The third thing I try to listen for is *plot*. Did something happen in the story that I never would have thought of? Did something happen which reminded me of a time when ...? Either one of those will work. Maybe the plot took me through a happening that was totally new. "Boy that story really tricked me, really fooled me!" That's something I can pull out.

When I use those three guidelines (Can I see a person? Can I see a place? Can I find a little turn of plot?), there are very few times when I can't find something of value in a story. If I can focus the audience's last memory of the story on a particularly strong spot, they will walk away from the event with a better feeling about it than if it had just been left raw.

It could also be redemptive for the teller, especially if he comes off stage feeling that he hasn't done as strong a job as he wanted to. Or maybe the person before him got a better response. So I also try to say something to the teller about the particular aspect of his story that I liked.

One final note. It is very important that the emcee be the perfect role model of a good listener. Normally the emcee is seated where everyone in the audience can see him or her. If I'm emceeing at a festival

and I'm seated beside the stage, it's obvious to the audience whether I'm listening or not. If I'm excited about the story being told, it gives the teller a much better chance.

Susan Klein: The emcee is the subtle glue that holds a storytelling evening together. It's important that the emcee remember that his or her job is to introduce people. The emcee should not use the introduction time to promote her own career. The emcee is there simply to celebrate the people who are telling that evening. There are some storytellers who do just that. And there are some emcees who get a little muddy in their heads about what they are there for.

It is always the emcee's job to take care of the audience first. The audience needs to feel safe. Their role as listeners needs to stay intact. They must remain in a secure position. That doesn't mean that the emcee has to deal with the audience's psychic and psychological baggage, but the emcee needs to set and maintain a certain tone that keeps everybody in place. If a teller does material that isn't appropriate or doesn't know it's inappropriate or knows it's inappropriate and does it anyway, the audience and the other tellers always end up suffering. For instance, if the teller loses control of his emotions and starts emoting in a way that is not comfortable for the audience, then the audience loses sight of what their role is and feels that they must take care of that teller.

So the emcee has the responsibility for knowing what kind of material people are going to be doing. If you are one of those storytellers who happens to make those decisions just as you go up on stage, the emcee needs at least to know what to expect. The planned sequence of the evening's events needs to dovetail and roll in a way that the emcee can control. The emcee also needs to know what is coming next so she can balance humor and fright and poignancy and all the other aspects of storytelling. The emcee should always be chosen with great care.

I suggest to anybody taking the emcee position that brevity is to be celebrated. Storytellers should be introduced to the audience in as short a time span as possible. The emcee needs to make sure the storytellers are loved before they hit the stage. It's important that the language the emcee uses is inclusive rather than exclusive. For instance, you wouldn't say, "Well, So-and-so and I had a great time hanging out at the beach last week down in Virginia. We've been having this wonderful love affair forever. Now, will you please welcome my new best friend, So-and-so." That makes the audience feel like they've missed out on something lovely. It's not fair.

Rather than list all the places where the teller has performed or tell about every award she ever received or drown her in a long litany of accolades, simply speak about the fact that we're all in good hands with the next storyteller and then turn over the evening to her.

Recently, I was at a festival where the emcee was also a storyteller and basically forgot that five other tellers were there. He went on in his own way of telling stories about the storytellers and took up thirty-five minutes of the program to introduce five people.

The emcee needs to be vibrant and alive with eyes full of life, causing everyone to turn around and look at her as soon as she takes the stage. You want to choose someone who can command the situation, be-

cause if anything happens that gets the audience and/or the storytellers in trouble during the course of the evening—a fire or a medical emergency or somebody doing something inappropriate—it's the emcee who's got to be able to bring everything back on track in a subtle and firm way. It's a powerful position. You never want to irritate the emcee.

The good emcee also reserves the right to change the order of tellers if something goes wrong. For instance, if you need high humor to come in and save the day, and the next thing up is a ghost story or something a little more serious, you need to pull in somebody else. These things need to be spoken about beforehand. The emcee should always be in touch with the storytellers long before the fifteen minutes prior to the telling. She needs to have background material and know who she's introducing.

If you're introducing a single performer, do it succinctly and celebrate that person. Bring her onstage and let her do the work. If there are announcements or advertisements of upcoming events, they must be done before the introduction—not after the teller has been introduced. You never want to leave her or the audience hanging. The emcee needs to know whether or not to come back on at the end of a program and close the night, or if the last storyteller has in fact closed it and no one needs to hear another voice. It always depends on the material.

WHAT MISTAKES ARE FREQUENTLY MADE BY BEGINNING STORYTELLERS?

♦ ♦ ♦ ♦

It is difficult for a beginning storyteller when he or she first starts out. Mistakes are inevitable. A typical experience might go like this: A beginning storyteller designed a brochure and mailed out several hundred copies. A nearby elementary school responded and engaged him to tell stories. He was so excited! He had forty-five minutes of stories ready to tell. He arrived fifteen minutes before the assembly and was ushered into the cafetorium. The school cooks were busy preparing lunch, noisily banging pots and pans and gossiping. He assumed they would quiet down when he began his stories; the kitchen doors and windows would be closed.

The storyteller asked if there was a microphone available and was shown one that was attached to a lectern which rested on a table. The mike could not be removed from its holder. Soon five hundred kids trooped in, the kindergarteners sitting up front, the other grades behind them all the way to the fifth graders in the rear.

Our beginning storyteller started getting very nervous as he looked out at this sea of squirming humanity. He was introduced by someone who got his name wrong. He began with a long convoluted story that was one of his favorites. Oh, how he loved that story! And how he loved what he did with his voice in that story! He had practiced it leaping and prancing about his living room. He had a funny hat he put on in one section of the story. He knew the way he wore that hat would simply kill the crowd. And those funny faces he made! But he hadn't counted on being confined to the area around the lectern. He couldn't be heard without the microphone, and it couldn't move from the lectern.

The younger kids laughed at the first few funny faces he made, but they soon quit. The noise from the kitchen did not stop. The kindergarten and first grade students started wiggling, then talking. The storyteller began thinking, Mayday! Mayday! His delivery got faster and faster in order to get to the end of the story. He got closer to the mike, shouting into it to control the crowd. The louder he screamed the fuzzier the sound became. Now the entire audience was beginning to talk and wiggle. He saw teachers moving into the crowd to quell the unrest. Need we go on …?

Mistakes always happen when we first start out. Some of us choose inappropriate stories for the age level we are telling to. Others rush through the story at breakneck speed. If you begin to lose your audience during a telling, Bill Harley suggests slowing down rather than speeding up. Maggi Peirce cautions all beginners to simplify. Diane Wolkstein notes the importance of taking care of the space you are telling in and making sure you can be heard.

Most of the storytellers agree that you must tell stories out of who you are. You must never think that you are more important than the stories. You must guard against falling in love with the sound of your voice. You must, above all, take care of your audience and listen to them.

Maggi Peirce: One of the greatest faults with beginner storytellers is that they don't simplify. If a story is good, it will stand on its own feet. You don't need to make funny remarks or funny faces or things like that. I keep saying all the time it's the story that's important, and, of course, a lot of storytellers don't agree with that. They feel that there's a lot of mime, expression, gestures, et cetera. Look at your story and be careful that you don't put so much dressing on it that you can't taste the lamb chop. Let the flavor be the true sweetness of the story. Simplify.

Bill Harley: One of the more common mistakes people make is to speed up. If we begin to lose the audience, we need to remember to slow down, spend more time with the story images, and get back to trusting the story. Get back to the idea of emotional honesty. Don't tell the story if it doesn't ring true to you. It's like the old bar trick: You find two people who are listening and you play to them and hope that energy is something that other people will pick up on.

If I'm going to do a good show, I have to have several things. I need a place as free from distraction as possible. A beginning storyteller tends to get into bad situations—such as: "Just go over there under the tree next to the brass band and the Chinese acrobats." If you are going to make your seventy-five or hundred bucks and you don't care, then you just go do that and know that it's not going to feel good. But if you want people to listen to you and say you are really good, then you need to demand a place where good storytelling can take place. You need to say, "I can't work there."

Some people aren't going to want to hear that, and that's the hard part and you must deal with it. Environment is about eighty percent of good storytelling. Creating a space that is free of distraction is a great deal of the battle.

You develop a sense of "this story will work with these younger kids, or with these older kids, or this story has enough participation and enough to work on another level that both parents and kids will listen." A really good story doesn't necessarily work with everybody. We think that if we have one really good story, it will work anywhere. I don't think that is true. You need enough repertoire to be able to say "I know that story won't work here, but I know that this one will."

Beth Horner: I feel it's important to research a story before telling it. I am offended by some people who tell stories from cultures that they don't know anything about, and haven't taken the time to study them. At the same time, if a person has to do all that when he is starting out, he may never tell a story. So my advice for beginning tellers is just tell, just tell, tell, tell every opportunity you get. Then, when you get some confidence, learn some of the ethics. Learn to research cultures.

Many times, beginning tellers bring a lot of trappings with them to the telling— costumes, props. Recently I saw a storyteller who wore a hat and a greatcoat like they had in the West. He had a rope and he said, "I'm going to tell a story from the Old West." But he didn't use those things at all. They were simply distracting. I think that, with confidence, you can let that stuff drop away.

Jim May: Don't ever get ahead of the audience. Never act like you're more excited about, more in love with, the story than they are. Some storytellers come on so effusively and say how wonderful and funny this story is going to be. I've seen storytellers laughing it up more than the audience.

We all know people who tell stories like that in the parlor. They tell friends at cocktail parties something really adventurous that happened to them and it's something like having a lint ball in their dryer. It's not adventurous at all but they're acting like it is. And it's certainly not funny. I've seen this happen to a lesser extent with new tellers.

You ought to be a little bit behind the audience. You want them to think it's funnier than you do. You're always feeling a little bit surprised if they think something is powerful or wonderful. You always want to be a little bit self-effacing and behind them. So my counsel is don't get ahead of the audience. Let the audience pull you through the story.

Michael Parent: While you're on stage, ask yourself the same questions you would ask yourself if you were out in the audience. For instance, if people have been sitting for an hour and a half, it's OK to say, "How would you like to stand up right now and stretch for ten seconds?"

It's always important to remember there's an audience out there, and that's who we're doing this for. If people are squirming, it probably means they need to take a break. Pay more attention to the audience than to whether your tie matches your pants.

If you must introduce your story, make it quick. Get to the story. Remember that the audience came to hear the story.

Learn how to use a microphone. Practice. If you're going to take the mike out of its stand, know how that works ahead of time rather than fumbling around with it during the performance. Basically the audience doesn't need to worry about you while you're up there. So take care of business ahead of time.

If something's goes wrong, stop! If you're getting feedback and the sound system is messed up, stop! If a loud generator kicks on and nobody can hear you, stop! Wait for it to be corrected. Don't just plow through for the sake of getting through the story. Remember why you're up there—to communicate the story. Anything that gets in the way of your communicating the story must be dealt with.

Connie Regan-Blake: Don't tell a story that is too long. Lots of storytellers put too much into it, with their voices, faces, and hand motions. I was working with someone and she stood up and moved around a lot. I asked her to sit and tell the story simply without moving her hands. The story came alive. I recommend that tellers do less rather than trying to do more and thinking, I need to jazz it up.

Len Cabral: Sometimes a beginner tells a story that is too long. It is always best to leave the audience wanting more. Here's what I tell people: You have a ten-minute story, and if, as you tell it, your audience's attention starts wandering and the little ones are playing, then you know the story is too long. Tell the story again, but this time, make it a seven- or a six-minute story. Leave out some things. Streamline it. Make it a good six-minute story. Then when you tell it you will know it is a power-packed six-minute story. You can lengthen it by adding another few minutes and being more descriptive, maybe building it to a ten-minute story. Always have a short story that you can build on.

It pays to have lots of rapport, so that you can work in high schools and go into these audiences with confidence and know that they are going to enjoy *these* stories. They are already feeling put upon because "These people out here think we are little kids!" Yet in many cases they have never been exposed to storytelling. They don't know what it is. The job of a storyteller is to promote storytelling and make people realize that storytelling is not just for kids. People tell stories every day.

The power of storytelling leads to good listening skills and stimulates a person's imagination. It allows people to imagine things that aren't but should be.

Gayle Ross: They don't have faith in the story itself. They go at ninety miles an hour, because they think if they pause for breath, everybody will get up and leave. They also feel like they have to have incredible body, face, or eye gimmicks.

The story will guide you, if you trust it in terms of where it wants you to use timing, breathing, vocalization, and body movement.

All of those things should serve the timeless beauty and teaching of the story. The story doesn't exist to serve you. You exist to serve it. That's the big difference I see in people who are starting out.

A lot of people put more thought into the way they are going to print their first brochure than they do into why they should be a storyteller.

Robin Moore: Most stories can be improved by telling them at "half speed." The storyteller's world sometimes moves faster, but mostly, it moves slower than normal speech. So really slowing it down gives the audience time to dream the phrases.

Milbre Burch: Not knowing what to do with our hands; wandering around for no reason on stage; blaming the audience members who show up for the ones that don't; apologizing for our work in the introduction; and refusing to take the compliment that a listener gives us.

My students get only one apology per story in a workshop. We learn what we practice, so we need to practice being proud of our efforts. After a story, when listeners come to say how much they enjoyed the telling, rather than listing all the faults we felt were in the story, we must get in the habit of simply saying, "Thank you."

Pleasant DeSpain: One mistake is trying to repeat a memorized tale, as opposed to just being there to tell it. One of the biggest mistakes is using somebody else's story because you liked it or thought, gee, maybe

people will like me if I tell that story. It's a serious mistake. It never works.

The biggest mistake of all is when the beginning storyteller has a false concept of what storytelling is all about. I have often heard beginners say that storytelling is the answer to their problems, that it will provide a mask for them to be someone or something else.

Diane Wolkstein: The biggest mistake storytellers make is to tell a story they don't like. If they tell a story they don't really like, I won't like it and I guarantee no one else will either.

A second mistake is not to take care of the room. I think you have to take care of the environment and make sure that it's safe and secure. You must make sure that someone will be at the door. If the door keeps opening and closing, people get distracted. When people are beginning, they sometimes think that things will magically be as they imagine them to be, but they aren't. So I think a beginning storyteller needs to be certain there will be someone around who can help her so that she can tell stories in peace and create something magical.

The third mistake is not being audible. You have to be sure that you can be heard. Sometimes using accents is a mistake if you can't do them well. You can do it as a professional or not do it at all. You have to be consistent or the spell is broken and you're not believed. Not varying the pace—sometimes you have one pace the whole time. Often you're not really behind the story, because if you really have your heart in it, your heart will lead you in the direction the story is going.

Jon Spelman: One problem is thinking too much about the words and allowing yourself to worry too much about exactly how sentences are phrased.

Another mistake is not relaxing more into your mistakes. You're going to say a wrong word; you're going to leave out a plot element; you're going to call a character by the wrong name. This is going to happen; everybody does it. Just keep going. You will learn to judge whether or not to actually make a correction or whether the audience knows you made a mistake but they're still with you anyway. You called Jack "Jill", but everybody knows you were talking about Jack so there's no need to go back and correct it.

Steve Sanfield: They think they are more important than the story. Ultimately, the story is the most important thing, and we simply have to be vehicles conveying that story. Some people come to storytelling because they want to be loved and appreciated and because they think anybody can do it, but it's just not so. Once in the Old Gaelic and the Bardic tradition, there was a six- to twelve-year apprenticeship before anybody could call themselves a bard, which was the lowest of nine ranks in Ireland. Now there is nothing like that. There's no set of standards. And I'm not suggesting we start imposing one either. However, it's good to remember, especially for beginners, that such models did exist once.

Judith Black: Storytelling is a folk art, not a fine art. Your greatest success will come from telling out of who you are. Fake voices, pronounced unnatural movement, and a desperate desire to please are all kisses of death.

Tell out of your strengths. If you are a sitter, sit. If you are a singer, sing. If you are dramatic, act. If you are quiet and intense, allow your telling to be the same. Use your lifetime, not some imagined image, as the basis of your storytelling style.

Joseph Bruchac: Over-dramatizing. People who are not relaxing and who engage in far too much gesticulation. People who, in telling the story, forget the basic unity and leave out sections that make the story work, or emphasize the wrong things. Sometimes they simply hurry their way through the story. That's the most important thing of all—don't hurry a story, let it happen in its own time.

Jackie Torrence: They want to be too powerful. "Oh, I found this powerful story! It's about how the king saved the universe, and people in the universe will love this story, because they need to be saved." And they come up with this story that's so boring, because there are no new stories, there are only new storytellers. These new storytellers find these old stories that people have heard for hundreds of years, and they think they're putting new life to them. They may not have enough experience to put any life in them and then they become boring.

Some years ago in Jonesborough, a storyteller told a story and I was sitting near some friends from Indiana. The women are teachers, so they are sort of duty-bound to listen to these stories. But their husbands, who happen to love storytelling, get bored at the drop of a hat. They were sitting there listening and this young new storyteller was telling a story about a little girl jumping rope. The man seated beside me was getting further down in his lap. So when he's all the way down in his lap with a piece of string, sort of playing on the ground, he turned around to me and said, "If she jumps that rope one more time, I'm going up there and take it away from her." It was my sentiment exactly because the story was long and it was only interesting to her. Everybody there knew that story and it had probably been told every year. She thought she was doing a great job on it, but she wasn't even getting high enough to bring it over the top so that anybody would enjoy it. Beginning storytellers like the sound of their own voices, yet they don't hear themselves. I believe new storytellers should get little short stories and tell them and not jump into the big ones until they know what they're doing.

Susan Klein: There are a number of them. One is falling in love with the sound of your own voice and not knowing that an editor is a very, very advantageous person to have in your life, even if that editor is yourself. If it is yourself, you are in luck. Then you don't have to go too far afield to get someone to help you.

To tell the damn story is very important. Just tell it. Don't get involved with great long introductions and add on gestures. It makes me absolutely crazy if people think that they have to put on some kind of physical interpretation, or if they mime it and then they describe it rather than doing it all at once. For me, gesture is organic, and if your body happens to move in a particular way when you are speaking, then it's just perfect. But if you have to think about a million things to add on to it to try to make the story visual, you are missing the boat completely.

Another thing that beginning storytellers do that infuriates me is that they are not aware they have an incredible responsibility to take care of the audience. The audience has come and paid their money, and they are there to have a safe journey. If a new storyteller—and sometimes a not-so-new storyteller—gets up there and loses it, or starts to cry or emote in a way that is not moving the story forward and not taking care of the audience, then the audience has a horrible thing happen to them. They lose the sense of what their role is. They have to

deal with an untold amount of discomfort in not knowing what's going on or if they are supposed to take care of the storyteller.

Another thing that I've seen new storytellers do is to get preachy in a story. They feel that because they have the stage, their role as storyteller has now gone from being a dispenser of story to telling people how to live. I'll walk out immediately. It drives me crazy.

The last thing that new storytellers need to know is that it's a huge pie and there is a ton of material out there. They need to find new stories instead of just doing stuff you hear over and over again—"Wicked John and the Devil," for instance. I hear that at every festival I go to. Now that the art form of storytelling has taken hold in America and more and more people are coming to it, they have to understand the merits of doing their own research. They also need to know that it takes time to become a well-known professional storyteller. It doesn't happen by throwing your name on a brochure and calling up somebody and saying, "How do I do this?" There is a dues-paying process. They need to know that there is joy in making this investment and that the lessons learned will be incredibly valuable.

Carol Birch: Speaking with a voice that has nothing to do with the words you're saying.

David Novak: The most common mistake is that they don't listen to their audience. Maybe it's because they're nervous or they're wedded to the way they plan to tell the story. So they are not aware when the audience is beginning to get impatient, or lose interest or is ready for the story to move forward or end.

William Shakespeare: Speak the speech, I pray you, as I pronounc'd it to you, trippingly on the tongue. But if you mouth it, as many of our players do, I had as lief the towncrier spoke my lines. Nor do not saw the air too much with your hand, thus, but use all gently; for in the very torrent, tempest, and (as I may say) whirlwind of your passion, you must acquire and beget a temperance that may give it smoothness. O, it offends me to the soul to hear a robustious periwig-pated fellow tear a passion to tatters, to very rags, to split the ears of the groundlings, who (for the most part) are capable of nothing but inexplicable dumbshows and noise. I would have such a fellow whipp'd for o'erdoing Termagant. It out-herods Herod. Pray you avoid it.

Be not too tame neither, but let your own discretion be your tutor. Suit the action to the word, the word to the action; with this special observance, that you o'erstep not the modesty of nature: for anything so overdone is from the purpose of playing, whose end, both at the first and now, was and is, to hold, as 'twere, the mirror up to nature; to show virtue her own feature, scorn her own image, and the very age and body of the time his form and pressure. Now this overdone, or come tardy off, though it make the unskilful laugh, cannot but make the judicious grieve; the censure of the which one must in your allowance o'erweigh a whole theatre of others …

That's villainous and shows a most pitiful ambition in the fool that uses it …*(Hamlet, Act III, scene 2).*

SUMMARY

- » Simplify. Simplify the story and the telling of it.
- » If you feel you are losing the audience, slow down.
- » Make sure your telling space is free from distractions.
- » A really good story doesn't work with everybody. Know where it *does* work.
- » Know about the culture the stories evolve from.
- » Make sure you know who is your audience. Know how they are feeling when you are telling.
- » Don't ever get ahead of your audience. Never act like you're more in love with the story than they are.
- » Don't give in to the tendency to overact.
- » Learn how to use a microphone.
- » If you must introduce your stories, make it quick. Get to the story.
- » Do not ever be condescending with your audience.
- » Learn how to pare down a story to its bones, so that a flabby fifteen-minute story becomes a lean seven-minute story.
- » Good stories never need a lot of gimmicks. Have faith in the story. Let it dictate the way it should be told.
- » Learn how to control your flyaway hands.
- » Don't worry so much about the words or sentence phrasing. Just tell the stories.
- » Remember that you are never more important than the story.
- » Tell stories out of who you are. Fake voices, unnatural movement, a desperate desire to please are all kisses of death.
- » Don't fall in love with the sound of your own voice.
- » Take care of the audience. Make sure they have a safe journey.
- » Be careful not to become preachy.
- » Listen to your audience. They will tell you how you're doing.

HOW DO I CONTROL STAGE FRIGHT?

◆ ◆ ◆ ◆

Stage fright has been labeled the number one fear in America by a number of different books, including *The Book of Lists.* It ranks higher than the fear of war, disease, or snakes. Most people are more afraid of speaking in public than they are of death.

What exactly is this fear, this stage fright, that strikes such terror in our hearts? Perhaps we're afraid that we will fail or seem inadequate to our peers. Maybe we fear being exposed as not very bright, knowledgeable, or talented—or all three. Maybe we'll be called ugly and stupid. A lot of us simply fear that we will forget what we're supposed to say.

How do I we get rid of this stage fright? And if we can't get rid of it, how do we control it?

We can't guarantee that we can rid you of your butterflies, but we can help you train them to fly in formation. Nearly all of us get nervous before telling stories. Just remember that your audience is just as preoccupied with their fears, doubts, and needs as you are. Therefore if you focus on their needs and not on your fears of inadequacy, your nerves will be rapidly forgotten.

A number of the storytellers make the same point. Bill Harley says, "The audience is on your side." Milbre Burch and Len Cabral remind us that the audience wants you to do well and succeed. Robin Moore suggests that we keep in mind that we are telling stories to individuals, not just a great mass of bodies. Margaret Read MacDonald counsels to always put the audience first and to ask, "What do they *want*? What do they *need* from me?" Michael Parent usually goes out beforehand and talks to people in the audience so that he feels he has some friends out there.

Another important deterrent to stage fright is adequate breath. Most of the tellers consider proper breathing to be the biggest help in controlling fear. A highly effective breathing exercise is near the end of the chapter. Gay Ducey recommends starting your story after you have inhaled deeply and then exhaled most of the air. Pleasant DeSpain offers a good suggestion about how to use mother's breath.

Jay O'Callahan controls his fear-monkeys by thinking about the characters in his opening story. Gayle Ross and Bill Harley both open their sessions with stories they feel comfortable with and can immerse themselves in so that all their excess energy is absorbed in the telling. David Novak talks about muscle relaxation, and Penninah Schram describes her rag doll exercise.

As you read this chapter, you will realize than no one, not even professional storytellers, is immune from stage fright. We face it at virtually every telling. Our methods of dealing with stage fright may vary, but they are effective for *us.* We hope that these suggestions will be just as helpful to you. You may even come to agree with Jackie Torrence's grandfather that a little bit of fear helps keep us from getting The Big Head.

Bill Harley: You have to remember that the audience is coming to your house; you're not going to theirs. They are coming into your world. If you anticipate being uncomfortable with that, then it's a good idea to get there early and walk around the stage. Get to know that space, so that by the time the audience arrives, it's a place that you own.

The opening story is actually a kind of handshake. It should be one that you feel comfortable with so you get your grounding in that place. Don't assume the audience is your enemy. They want you to succeed. They're not looking for you to make a mistake. The only place that happens is showcases. The audience has invested time in you, so they're going to give you every chance to succeed. We too often forget that the audience is on our side.

Michael Parent: It's important to remember that nervousness—stage fright—is natural. Everybody feels it, even seasoned performers. The difference between people who get swallowed by it and people who are successful is that the successful ones know how to overcome it and use it. So if you get nervous and you've been doing this for a long time, you probably do something to channel your energy. It might be something physical. Maybe you practice your guitar. If I'm "afraid" of the audience, for whatever reason, I've found that, rather than run away from them, the best thing is to approach one or two audience members and talk to them. Have a conversation. Ask questions. That levels out the fear. If you talk to one or two of them and they don't actually bite you, then it really helps.

Having a ritual can also be helpful. For instance, you might make sure that you are there well ahead of time. Make sure the stage is set up the way you want it, the chairs are set the way you want them, and the sound system is working well. You can make sure they have water or tea for you, whatever you need. Even if all those things are taken care of, just checking on them becomes part of your ritual. You look over or think over your stories, or play through the songs you're going to sing. Perhaps you know some breathing or physical exercises that relax you. Going through the ritual prepares you to do the performance. It also gives you something to do other than just sitting there and getting nervous.

In storytelling, the advantage is that you are not going onstage in character—as a character—so you can show up beforehand. You're not going to be dressed in a costume, so you can more easily go into the audience beforehand and talk to people. For instance, with junior high students, I've found that the best thing for me to do while they're filing in and I'm waiting for the program to start is to go to the front row and talk to some of the kids. Just ask some questions. You might ask them questions about something that would be helpful for you to know. For instance, ask how many assemblies did they have this year or how often do they have assemblies. If they tell you that last year they had one assembly and it was The Dancing Bears of Bulgaria, you have some idea of what they've been exposed to. You can also refer back to it in your show and make a connection for them.

Margaret Read MacDonald: I just stop and say, "What does this audience need from me? How can I serve it? How can I give them what they need?" I think of them, not myself. By thinking of the audience and putting them first, it changes the way you approach them. You approach them with a giving, outgoing feeling instead of a worried "I'm in front of them" feeling. You reach out to them. Once you approach it in that way, you drop yourself. You become a nurturer and you're thinking of that and the self goes away.

Len Cabral: Everybody wants to hear a good story. Nobody wants you to fail. When you are up there, everybody is on your side. They want you to be good. The experienced tellers want you to succeed, and people want to hear a story they haven't heard before or they want to hear it ended differently. Nobody wants to be bored. No one is sitting there saying, "I hope this fellow tells a boring story." They want to be entertained, so they are already on your side. They are cheering you on. You have to be aware of that and have the confidence they have in you. You can steer the ship, but they have come along for the ride and to help out wherever they can. So I feel that they will help you overcome the fear of it. Then have fun.

Doug Lipman: It has been said that fear is excitement, minus breath. That means that fear and excitement are similar. The big difference is: Have you decided that it's not safe to breathe? The biggest piece of advice when you feel afraid is: Look around and decide if you are in danger. If you are *not* in danger, say, "What I'm experiencing—the racing of my heart, the sweating of my palms—this is my body getting ready for an exciting, wonderful event. As long as I keep breathing, giving myself oxygen, and keep inhabiting my body, I can use this excitation to be even more present and perform even better."

It's important not to fight it, because that just sets off a whole downward spiral of "Oh, my God, I'm going to be scared! Oh, I'm getting more scared! Oh, now I'm really scared."

Be aware that if you are actually experiencing fear, as opposed to excitement, and you've decided that it's safe, then what you're experiencing is not about the present. It's about the past. This is reminding you of some humiliating, fearful times. At this moment you can say, "OK, I'm safe now. I don't feel like it, but that's about the past. I will act now in the knowledge that I am safe and that I have a gift to give these people and they're hungry to receive it."

Jon Spelman: I value stage fright. It's useful. It raises your level of attention, gets you focused and gets you revved up and ready to go. I get a little afraid if I don't have some stage fright. One way I control my fear when it gets really strong is to tell myself that in a certain sense I'm over-valuing myself; that my being frightened of what people are going to think of me gives me more power than I really have. I'm not

the major force in their lives. They're just going to spend an hour or two with me, and they're going to forget, or not even notice, any mistake I make. So in that way I'm over-valuing myself by allowing myself to get too scared.

At other times, though, I want to be careful not to undervalue myself. You have to talk yourself up to yourself and remember how good and how interesting you are and how hard you've worked and how good your story is and how much the audience is going to enjoy it.

The most useful way of avoiding stage fright is to really give your mind something to focus on besides your fear. You can choose what to focus on. We can all do that even in moments of extreme emotional distress. You can focus on the images of the story and the more you've worked on the story the richer those images are. The images are your friends; you put your attention on them and they carry you through.

Beth Horner: Well, just remember that life is really hard, and this is not the be-all and end-all of your life. If you can get your taxes paid, you can make it through this night. This is only one experience and usually everyone out there is rooting for you.

Robin Moore: I try to find some people in the audience who seem open-hearted and try to make eye contact with them and realize that what I am really doing is telling the story to a room full of individuals. I'm not telling it to seven hundred people or three hundred people. I'm telling it to individuals, and I make that connection with them. What I have found works well for me is to do the opposite thing and really slow down almost to a ridiculous point so that I have a lot of silence and a lot of pausing in the story. That seems to help bring me back to the reason I am there. It's not for everybody to look at me and pay attention to me, but for us to all be held in that story together. If you let the silence come into your tale, that will start to happen.

Ed Stivender: I carry a magic cloth from Botanica Jugadores. When I have it with me, all I do is say a few Hail Marys and my system calms down. Drinking before a performance is a serious mistake in my tradition.

Steve Sanfield: I think any performer worth his salt has stage fright. But if instead of being frightened or nervous, you say, "Oh, I'm excited." It's the same feeling, and it only adds to the dynamics of the telling.

Before I go on stage, I need time alone. I use basic meditation techniques and some deep breathing to calm and settle myself. At those times right before going on stage, I never think about the stories at all. I just trust that the stories will be there when I get on stage. I read somewhere what Jaesha Heiftz, the violinist, used to do before a concert. He spent the day thinking about what he was going to sound like, but he didn't pick up his violin. He just thought about it. I try to approach a telling in the same way.

Penninah Schram: I remember to breathe when I feel tension or nervousness. A slow breath in and an even slower release are the keys to relaxation and control over stage fright. I still experience it. Breathing, yawning, humming and stretching are great ways to help relieve it. I love the rag doll exercise, which is really like all exercises that achieve relaxation, because you are adding and then releasing tension consciously. It's an exercise where you imagine a puppeteer controlling strings from each part of your body, stretching you higher and higher, then cutting the strings and letting you fall over and dangle. Finally, when you come up slowly and

evenly to a standing position, you are alert, relaxed, and ready to tell.

Milbre Burch: I try to take care of myself. I remember to breathe from the diaphragm. I like to pace before a performance, keep moving if possible, or bounce on my heels. I also tell myself things will be OK, that I will perform to the best of my ability.

If I'm tempted to be intimidated by my audience—say it's junior high schoolers with a clear love-hate relationship with their principal who's going to introduce me—I stay out of the space until they're in their seats to avoid the heavy "I can't believe we have to do this" vibe. When I enter the space, I make a clear decision not to take any generalized negative energy personally.

For the most part, audiences want to support us; they want us to succeed. My job is to get out of the way of my fear, do my work, and be prepared to forgive myself for my mistakes. The audience is usually more than willing to forgive our occasionally tangled tongue; let's take our lessons from them.

Jackie Torrence: My grandfather used to tell me that it's good to have a little fear. It can keep you from getting a big head. When you lose that little tiny bit of fear that controls and humbles you, look out. No matter how good you are, no matter how long you've been in the business, or how good people tell you you are, somewhere down the line somebody's going to dislike what you're saying and doing, and it's going to burst your bubble when you find out. If you keep that little bit of fear, you'll always know, I need to please this audience, so I'm going to have to do this, I'm going to do that.

Gay Ducey: You can define stage fright either as a dread enemy or a comprised friend. If you define it as a dread enemy, then you're going to subject your audience to a pitched battle between you and them. If you define stage fright as a comprised friend, then you can take what you need from that fright, and some of the things are good. Fright gives you an adrenalin rush that is useful. Sometimes it gives you a heightened state of awareness that is good. If it's debilitating, then you need to do some physical work, not just emotional work.

Take a deep breath. Then instead of starting your story with the breath held, start it on an exhaled breath. Always. Take a moment, hold that breath one second past when it's comfortable, then exhale it and start the story.

Sometimes people are helped by taking ten or fifteen little dance steps (out of view of the audience), as fast they can do them, which drains off some of that energy.

Susan Klein: You can't operate on the stage as a creative force if you think the audience is not going to appreciate or like you. You have to be beyond that. You have to take the stage with the intent of winning them over immediately, knowing that you have the power to create something so wonderful that they will clamor for more. You need to know what you wish to make happen during that hour or that fifteen minutes or whatever time you're given. When you know that, you can rise to that position and do your work, and they will love you.

Gayle Ross: I tend to let stage fright have its way up until the moment I actually take charge of the stage. I let myself get as nervous as I want. I pace. My stomach flutters. I gulp gallons of water. Then of course precipitate a near crisis by wondering, as this woman is introducing me, how much time is there? Do I have time to find the bathroom or not?

If it's a really high stress situation, then you can almost guarantee that I'm not going to waste much time on pleasantries to start. I immerse myself in the story, because that is where I am the most confident and comfortable. I get a really good powerful story started right off the bat that will take all that energy. By the time that story's over, I can start the visiting, relaxing, talking, and getting to know people. When you're really nervous, the last thing you want to do is try to make chitchat. I'm much more comfortable introducing myself and making the kind of small jokes and patter and things that usually go between stories if I am not in the flush of that total terror. Then it's likely to be disastrous.

Jay O'Callahan: When I get very nervous, I try to think about the characters. For instance, if I'm really nervous and I'm about to do *The Dance*, I think, I'm going to meet these people. They're all going to a party. That might be enough to excite me. Or I'll think, well, I'm giving them a gift, and that might calm me down. That's very helpful. I consciously try to take the attention off my nervousness and put it into the character. That is, I think about one image or one character. Before doing *The Dance*, let's say it's a difficult situation or I'm just plain nervous. I'm waiting backstage for twenty minutes, and I'm thinking it's not going to go well tonight. I'm beginning to think about myself and my own worries. Well, I try to switch that. I see the character who is about to open the show. He's up on the roof. It's night. I try to think about him and what he's feeling up there. I try to get inside him. I actually pace back and forth and walk just as he walks.

I also do breathing exercises to try to relax my face and do a little Chigong, an old Chinese exercise, by lifting my arms up and bringing my hands down very slowly in front of my chest and belly.

The idea is to bring the energy down from my head (my worries, my fears) into my feet, to really ground me. I do not simply go back there and pace. I never do that; my mind and my heart are very actively involved in thinking about the scenes and characters.

Pleasant DeSpain: It's not fear for me; it is energy. It's intense. Physiologically, we know what is released in the bloodstream, but what happens essentially is that there is more oxygen in the blood. If we don't use that oxygen in a way that we can control it, it will control us. Fear is holding and what I know I have to do is surrender. By surrender, I do not mean give up. I mean let go. I mean surrender unto what *is so*. I am going to be the focus of the energy, and I have a job to do.

I do some basic practical things. One, while I am being introduced I reflect. I say, "Am I ready? Yes, I have done my homework and I'm prepared. Do I want to be here?" That's a valid question that I have to answer for myself, because if I don't, I shouldn't be there. But if I do, and I get that feeling, then I do want to be there. "Who's here to listen? Why are these people here?" I admire their willingness and their generosity to be here to give me their time, their energy, their imagination. With all of that, I do "Mother's Breath."

I inhale to a count of seven. Seven heartbeats. I hold it for one heartbeat. I hold it for one heartbeat. I do that three times around. It puts me into my center. I walk up on to the stage and the first thing I do is let my breath go. Then I inhale my audience, if you will … and I begin to tell.

Carol Birch: I think the way to control stage fright is to have your energy focused *out*, not *in*. When I've had stage fright, I was worrying about the wrong person. The storyteller's job is to be concerned about the audience, about the audience members making their way safely across the bridge into the story and back again. You're not supposed to be worrying about whether they're going to like you when they come back across the bridge. I've found that as soon as I stop worrying about myself and start focusing on others, my energy goes out and with it goes stage fright.

David Novak: Muscle relaxation. Do a little warmup. Loosen up. Good deep breathing. Good mental preparation. Before a concert, I lie down, visualize myself telling all of my stories, and I visualize everything going very well. When I finish, it's as if I've already done the concert, and I have a greater sense of ease or confidence.

Laura Simms: I acknowledge it. I lean into it. I say to myself, I'm terrified, and then I lean into it so I can reap the harvest of the tremendous energy that's there. I never fight it. I don't try to conquer it. It is my friend. Be willing to say, I'm really nervous right at this moment, then stand and feel the nervousness. By doing that, it very often turns into energy. If you push it away, it will come back. I try to befriend it. I think stage fright is part of the package, something to be admired and respected because it means that you're alive.

Bill Mooney and David Holt: The best antidote for stage fright—by far—is to be prepared. Remember the old Boy Scout motto? *Be prepared.* Not bad advice regardless of what you're doing. The best way to be prepared is to rehearse. Nothing—absolutely nothing—helps calm stage fright more than being well-rehearsed. Athletes know this. Why do football or basketball teams spend so much time rehearsing basic plays? Why do golfers and tennis players work endlessly to perfect their swing? Musicians and dancers know this too. The more you practice the better you become. Also, if you are well-prepared, you will spend less time thinking about what is coming next in your story, and pay more attention to your audience and their wants and needs.

Sometimes you have to sit around and wait before you begin telling stories, and your butterflies may start getting feisty. There are several physical ways to help harness them. The most effective way is deep diaphragmatic breathing. Oxygen is an excellent calmative. Inhale deeply through your nose into your belly as you count to six, hold your breath for six counts, then exhale through your mouth as you count to twelve. Be sure to push all the air out of your lungs.

1. Inhale-2-3-4-5-6
2. Hold-2-3-4-5-6
3. Exhale-2-3-4-5-6-7-8-9-10-11-12

Keep doing this breathing pattern for a few minutes. Make certain that you are using diaphragmatic breathing. If the area just below your rib cage swells out when you inhale, then you are breathing correctly. When it's done right, your chest doesn't expand, just your belly. Think of breathing all the way down to your toes.

You can do a couple of isometric exercises to get the blood flowing again. They are unobtrusive enough that you can do them even if you're in full view of the audience. If you're sitting, reach down on either side of you and grab the chair seat. Pull up as hard as you can for ten counts. Let go and feel the blood flow warmly into your hands and arms. Scrunch up your toes as tightly as you can. Hold them that way for ten counts. Let go and again feel the warm blood flow into your feet. You can do the same exercise for your hands by making tight hard fists and holding them for ten counts.

We have had varying degrees of success with visualization. These days, visualization is at the cutting edge for a lot of competitive athletes. Swimmers visualize every stroke, tuck, and turn at the end of the pool. They see themselves winning in record time. Slalom racers visualize themselves skiing perfectly through every gate on the downhill course. They visualize how good their form is, how much faster they are skiing than ever before. Try visualizing your opening story. Hear yourself telling it. Notice the rapt attention of the audience. Visualize the standing ovation and the *bravos* at the end of your telling.

SUMMARY

If you remember nothing else from this chapter, remember to *be prepared!* If you are well prepared, stage fright will vanish as soon as you begin your first story.

» Do deep regular diaphragmatic breathing, breathing all the way to the bottom of your belly and then expelling all the carbon dioxide.

» Go through exercises that help you release your tension: the rag doll exercise, isometric contracting and releasing.

» Start with a story that you feel comfortable with, or a powerful story that you can immerse yourself in, so that the story absorbs all of your excess energy.

» Think more about the audience than you do about yourself. Put the audience first. Realize that they want you to succeed. They come with hope in their hearts. They want to hear a good story.

» Give your mind something to focus on besides fear. Visualize your artistry, effectiveness, and success.

» Create a comforting ritual before the telling.

» Get comfortable with the area where you will be telling stories.

» Go out and talk to members of the audience before the telling.

WHAT ARE THE ETHICS OF STORYTELLING?

• • • •

When the storytelling revival started in the early 1970s, only a handful of professional storytellers were on the circuit. We consciously agreed that we would not "steal" or use each other's material. In principle we decided that whoever worked up a traditional tale first could lay claim to it and the rest of us would not tell it. We also recognized that part of the job of a professional teller was to continually find or create new stories.

Now storytelling is a national movement involving thousands of people, and it is no longer possible to claim or "own" a traditional tale but only your version of the story. Yet one of the first tenants of ethical storytelling still remains. Each storyteller needs to find his or her own material so that we can extend the boundaries of our craft. If we only raid the repertoires of fellow tellers for new material, it won't take long for the whole storytelling movement to collapse. We'll all be telling the same "popular" tales.

Traditional stories are for all of us to share. It is inevitable that many tellers will discover the same folktale. Does anyone "own" them? Who has the right to tell these stories? What is our obligation to the culture that created them?

How we address and answer these questions can either undermine or strengthen the sense of community for storytellers. Ethical treatment of tellers, stories and other cultures is part of the foundation of the movement and will help keep the revival growing and flourishing in the future.

Michael Parent: It boils down to common sense. Let's use a car analogy. If my car is sitting in the driveway, it's clearly my car. If you want to use it, you ask. If that car is community property, and if there is an accepted procedure for sharing the use, then you follow that procedure.

Folktales are, to my mind, community property. If it's clear that a specific version of a folktale belongs to somebody, then you should ask that person about using his version. If it's an original story and you want to tell it, well, that's like using another person's car. Would you go to that person's house and take his car and not say anything? No, of course not. If something clearly belongs to somebody else, it's just common sense to ask if you can use it and on what terms you can use it.

I think it gets tricky in the case where people take folktales and make them their own. Tomi DePaola took the "Clown of God," a centuries-old story, made up his version and created a successful book. Now people want to tell *his* version of the story. Well, that particular version is his, but it's an old story. So in that case, I'd say either find out the terms under which you can use his version, or go back to the original source, the French folktale, read that, and come up with your own version of it. Then you've got no argument with the other guy, because you have basically taken the same raw materials that are community property and built your own version—your own car, so to speak.

Beth Horner: I think of three things: cultural ethics, community ethics, and audience ethics.

Cultural ethics mean learning enough about the culture that the story comes from so that you aren't treating the culture or the story incorrectly. The clearest examples in the United States are the many Native American stories that we tell without really knowing what part they play within their own culture.

Community ethics are the ethics within the large national community of storytellers. It is ethically incorrect to steal a fellow storyteller's stories—particularly his signature stories. You must always ask that person if it would be all right if you told his story. Many beginning storytellers, myself included, become excited when they hear a good story told well, and they want to run right out and tell the story themselves. But once you begin to make your living by telling stories, it is important to look at your repertoire and make sure that your stories are not the ones you heard from another storyteller. Or if they are, then your version must be significantly different.

Once, when I was a librarian, I heard Laura Simms tell the story "Henna." I loved that story. I got a grant to put together a series of stories about women from Radcliff College. I wrote to Laura and said, "I would like to tell 'Henna.'" She said, "Fine, here's the source that I worked from." I went to it, read it, and got a lot of other sources and read those versions and then I put together my own version. Later I learned that "Henna" was, at the time, her signature story. That story meant a great deal to her. It was improper of me to ask her, and I felt bad about it later. But she never said a word to me.

I feel it's your job as a professional storyteller to come up with your own material. You have to find new stories. You may be a late arriver in the gold rush so you might have to dig a little harder, but the gold is still there.

I think there is a way of telling a story that you have heard from someone else in a way to honor that person. I do that with a story that I learned from Elizabeth Ellis. In fact, there were four of us, Dan Keding, Elizabeth Ellis, myself and Gil Ross, telling at a festival. We all told the same story. All of us had heard it from Elizabeth. We started doing tag-team storytelling. One person would step up to the mike and start telling the story and someone else would tap him on the back and he had to step back and the next person would come forward and continue with the story. The funny thing was that we all had four radically different versions of the story, which was "Jack And The Haunted House."

Then there are audience ethics. You make sure that you are not offending anybody in the audience. You try to understand the experience they bring. Early on, I recognized this when I was telling what nearly everybody else told when they started out, "Wicked John and the Devil." Then I realized there was this wife-beating theme in it, and I was telling stories at a battered women's shelter. Well, I started the story and I just stopped and said, "I don't think this is an appropriate story, and I'd like to tell another." I think you have to take care of your audience in that respect.

Laura Simms: I don't tell other people's stories without asking permission. I also usually don't tell stories that people make their careers on. If I hear somebody and I really see that this is their signature story, I never tell it, because I feel like they should be known for that. Besides, there are enough stories in the world that I can tell as mine.

Sometimes, if people really love my stories, they try to copy my sounds and gestures and pacing and words. But that has everything to do with who I am. So if they ask my permission, I will say, "Well, go ahead. I give you permission to learn that story, *but* do your own research and make it your own and then say you heard a version told by me." But to memorize what I do—… it's like stealing my life. I feel like I'm a protector of the story and to tell a story that's just memorized the way I tell it is dishonest.

Bill Harley: The first thing is to find your own voice. I think it's OK to try on other people's stories if it's in search of your own voice. However, if you are performing in a venue with another storyteller and you are using her material, something very close to her, it's better to not do the story there. Stories from other storytellers are fine to tell in a classroom, in a safe setting, in a place that is not a broad public market. If it's in quest of finding your own voice, then I think it's OK to do that. Quite obviously, what is completely unethical is recording a story that you got from somebody else.

If you are telling a story you have heard from somebody, you owe them a debt. You must acknowledge it. You must say,"I owe this person a nod for introducing this story to me." That's bottom line stuff. It's a little bit trickier when the story is traditional and there are a number of different sources. I think that when a storyteller puts something out in the universe, he has to let go of it a little bit.

I think beginning storytellers sometimes delude themselves into thinking they can tell a story better than the person they first heard it from, so it's OK. Or they think that they have made the story their own. But when you hear them, you realize that all those phrases were really developed by somebody else. You constantly have to challenge yourself. Is this story mine? What debt do I owe to the people who told it before me?

I tell mostly original stories. Sometimes I get people calling me up saying, "I want to tell this story of yours," and it's one of my original, first-person stories. I say, "Well, if you have to tell this story, OK, but I want you to know that it is not your story and your job is to find your own stories." It feels very strange to me. I have to think that maybe they're not doing a lot of work on their own stories.

Milbre Burch: Honor your ancestors; cite your sources.

Like many in my generation of revivalist storytellers, I started out blissfully unaware of the need—both legal and courteous—to get permission to carry copyrighted material into the marketplace. But as they say, "Ignorance of the law is no excuse." And that veil has been lifted within our community.

Since my enlightenment, I've had numerous interesting encounters on the trail of permissions. Although it can make for a time-consuming journey, it has been, by and large, a very positive experience.

Having learned that a story isn't finished until it's told, I continue to introduce new (copyrighted) stories in some settings before I have sought permission to work with them. I have enough modestly paid classroom and library gigs to feel some confidence that I'm in a legally defined "safe harbor" doing this. I consider this the early courtship of a story.[Editor's note: See "What are the Copyright Laws Concerning Storytelling?" chapter in this book.]

After a few tellings, it becomes clear whether or not there's a fit between me and the story. If there is a fit, and I'm ready to commit myself to the story in a wider range of settings, then it's time to make my "honorable intentions" known.

If, for example, I am engaged enough by the story to want to take it to a festival, it behooves me to "ask for its hand" from the writer, publisher, or other legal guardian.

Usually, I make my first inquiry directly to the author or his or her heirs. After all, the writer is the person I most want to convey my excitement over a story to. The writer, however, may not be the sole owner of the copyright.

I have never had a "no" so far. Arrangements vary by author, publisher, and circumstance. The agreements range from letting me tell the story for free in live performance, to paying a reasonable fee for each use, to paying a flat fee for a certain number of years' use on a recording. The most I have ever paid is $300.00 for a five-year license to both perform and record a story.

In some cases, I have verbal permission from an author regarding free use of the story in live performance. But *always* when it comes to a recording, everything's in writing.

Jon Spelman: There are stories in the public domain, and stories that are owned, legally and/or morally, and I think that's how things operate in the world right now. But I also think if you start dealing with oral histories or stories you've collected or stories other people have collected orally, or a mixture of stories you and other people have collected, it's a whole different game from literary stories, or stories identified with only one teller. Take Vietnam oral histories. Who owns those? That's a very murky question, even legally. My copyright lawyer says he's not even sure that the person who collects oral histories in a book can own those stories, because it's not clear that anyone from whom he collected ever signed over rights to the stories. Where's the copyright? The person that has copyrighted that book has copyrighted that series of stories or that set of oral histories, printed in that order with that title. But who owns an oral history if I go out and get it, if somebody has told me something and I tell part of it?

Jackie Torrence: In my mind it's all very clear. I love music, and I think music's wonderful. I love storytelling and I know it's wonderful, but there is a difference. When you settle down and you write a song, a song that comes up out of your heart and mind and then you put the music to it, that's very special. When you do the same thing with a story, that's special because nobody has told the story before. If it's my story, give me credit for it. If you use and record it and get money for it, then pay me for figuring it out.

Steve Sanfield: A lot of it is very clear because of copyright laws. However, I think it basically comes down to kindness and good manners. You don't borrow your neighbor's rake, or shovel, or tractor without asking permission.

Margaret Read MacDonald: I feel that, throughout the ages, stories have flowed from culture to culture and from teller to teller. If the stories had not kept flowing around the world the way they did, we wouldn't have all these stories today. That's why we have so many variations, so many wonderful stories, and why they're still here. People have felt free to share them, and if someone heard a good story, he went off and told it. This has gone on since the beginning of time.

Right now there's a very strong sense of ethnic groups and individuals clutching stories and saying, "Don't touch, it's mine, you can't have it." I don't think that's for the good of the world or for the good of the story, or for the good of the world of storytelling. I think we have to share stories. They have to be passed on. They're a very special part of our culture and ourselves and we can share them. I think we have to let go.

Gayle Ross: If you learn a story from another storyteller, it's a matter of courtesy to acknowledge it. I sometimes sound like a name-dropper, especially in my school performances. I try to do a wide variety of stories from many different cultures, so I'm always dropping names.

I always mention other tellers and their impact, if they played a part in the way a story evolved through me. I try to always credit my sources.

The thing that bothers me the most is when people with no experience with a particular culture try to learn and tell stories from that culture. It can lead to tremendous blunders. I'm hyper-sensitive to nonnative people telling Native American stories, because the opportunities for screwup are legion. There are many things about traditional Native American culture that you couldn't possibly know unless you had experience in the culture. It can lead to brutalizing the stories which, to me, are living spirits. It also perpetuates more misconceptions in stereotype, which none of us needs. I hear the argument a lot from tellers, "Well, I need to tell Native American stories because the children have so few opportunities to know and learn them. I want them to experience that culture." What they're learning is worse, since a non-Native American is telling the story.

I guess it boils down to the Hippocratic oath. First, do no harm. The first thing you should think of when you are telling a story from outside another culture is to not make things worse. For teachers and librarians and anybody who takes the little extra effort to do more in their job by learning and telling stories, I cut them a lot more slack. I do like to steer in the direction of collections written *by* native people as opposed to *about* native people, but I cut them a lot more slack. But somebody who is a professional storyteller, somebody who is joining the ranks of these generations and generations of people who have been charged with carrying on tradition, they have a much bigger responsibility and I don't cut them any slack. I don't just brush it off when I hear somebody take a story that they've learned from me and then turn it into an absolute travesty because of their ignorance of the culture. For me that's the biggest ethical issue that a professional storyteller can face. How well are they managing to represent cultures outside their own? How well are they living up to those responsibilities?

Doug Lipman: There was something that came out of the St. Louis Congress (a precursor to the National Storytelling Conference), where we all went at each other. There was a sub-group of librarians and the librarians said, "Before the workshop we agreed on three things. We agreed to learn the sources of our stories that we tell and credit them where appropriate, and obtain permission where appropriate." In my view, that's the best that we can do right now. *Where appropriate* covers a multitude of sins, and that's going to be an individual decision. We're not as ready to agree on what *appropriate* is, but I think we are ready to agree to those three things. We need to know where our story is from, and if the story has a single source, does it make sense to ask permission? If the story is a single source we need to ask permission if we're telling somebody's personal story or a story they created. At the very least we need to ask them for permission. If they have contributed original elements to a story they didn't create, e.g., they've made this song to go with "Red Riding Hood," or they have this great characterization of the wolf, that also needs to be treated as something that we need their permission for.

There's another level which isn't even ethics anymore. It's what Donald Davis called "the politeness level," which is what I ask of people who want to tell my stories. First of all, I say, "I'm thrilled. Please tell my stories. All I ask is if you're going to publish it or make bucks off it some way besides performing it to get my permission again—a separate permission for that." Also be thoughtful about shared audiences. For example, if you and I are both at a festival and you're going up right before me, please don't tell a story you learned from me without checking that I don't want to tell it then. We can share stories without making each other's living hard.

> *Honor you ancestors;*
> *cite your sources.*
> *— Milbre Burch*

Joseph Bruchac: I have no objection to Anglos telling Native American stories. My objection is to people not recognizing that the words "Native American" encompass in North America alone more than four hundred different cultural traditions. So I object when people don't give the kind of acknowledgment or respect that certain stories need. In many of the cultures of native North America, if you tell a story that someone else told you, you are honor bound to say who gave you that story. If someone says, "You do not have permission to tell this story," then you are honor bound not to tell it. It is a form of copyright within the tradition.

Traditional copyright is very much alive in native North American cultures, in some cases more than others. That is where I have problems with the mis-telling, mis-attribution or the lack of attribution and acknowledgment that sometimes occurs. People say, "Well, I'm going to tell an Indian story." They tell a Cherokee story but don't say who they learned it from or where they got it from. Or they tell it in such a way that you clearly know it is not a Cherokee tale.

I believe that all native stories are sacred stories, in one way. You have to understand that all breath is sacred to native people. I've been taught this again and again, so they are not meant, any of them—even the funny ones—to be taken lightly.

I say to non-native people who are telling Native American stories that they have a couple of responsibilities. The first responsibility is to know as much as they can about the people and the tradition and where a story comes from, preferably through some contact with knowledgeable contemporary native people from that tradition. That means not thinking that every Indian knows everything about every story, which is a common mistake people make. "You are Indian. You are also spiritual, tell me about Sundance."

The other important thing is acknowledgment. Certain stories that I tell were taught to me by particular people. I'll mention their names, and say when I was taught the story and that they gave me permission to tell that story. There are a lot of stories that fall into the category of what we could call traditional copyright. Those stories are not to be told without permission of the people, the families, and the tribal nation that is taking care of that story. Stories are alive, not just a collection of words put together.

David Novak: When you're working with other storytellers in an olio situation, a difficult thing is respecting time and respecting the fact that you are not alone. Remember you are sharing the time with other tellers and that the story you tell is going to fit in somehow with the story that was just told, or is going to leave the stage open for the next person to follow you. It's hard on the teller who follows you if you tell a story that is too long or a story that is abusive or too confrontational. You're leaving a difficult situation, and the next storyteller is going to have to pick up the pieces. That's part of the ethics of sharing the stage with another performer.

In terms of the story itself, it's important to respect the story and have a clear sense of what you've done with that story if you change it. I'm constantly changing stories. I don't want to abuse the story, but I do want to interpret it. It's a fine line.

Ed Stivender: A responsible-, responsive- and respectful-to-the-Siblinghood-of-all-Performance-Scientists person always gives credit before or after, always pays royalties, always asks permission, first sneakily then directly, and follows the code of International Workers of the Word, Jonesborough, Tennessee.

SUMMARY

Barbara Griffin, Olga Loya, Sandra MacLees, Nancy Schimmel, Harlynne Geisler, and Kathleen Zundell compiled this etiquette statement. They encourage others to pass it out or read it aloud at storytelling events. Their statement does a good job of summarizing the views of the storytellers we interviewed.

» Stories are to share and tell. While we encourage the art of sharing stories, we want to encourage respect in our community. You deserve respect. Respect others.

» A storyteller's personal, family, and original stories are her/his copyrighted property. It is unethical and illegal to tell another person's original, personal, and/or family stories without the permission of the author/storyteller.

» Folklore and folktales are owned by the public, but a specific version told by an individual teller or found in a collection is the author's or teller's copyrighted property. If you like a folktale a storyteller has told, ask that teller for a reference or where it can be found. Research the story by finding other versions and then tell it your way.

» Published literary tales and poetry are copyrighted material. They may be told at informal story swaps, but when you tell another's story in a paid professional setting you need to research copyright law. (If you record an original story you need to get permission and pay the author.)

» When telling anywhere, it is common courtesy to credit the source of your story.

» Pass stories, share stories, and encourage respect within the storytelling community.

HOW DO I MARKET MYSELF?

• • • •

A unanimous agreement exists among our storytellers. Word of mouth is by far the best way to market yourself. Having good word of mouth also implies that you are a good storyteller with good stories to tell. Therefore everyone agrees that no matter how many fancy fliers and snazzy brochures and flashy business cards you print up and send out or how much money you spend on a media blitz, if you are not a proficient, engaging storyteller, those marketing tools won't help one iota. Therefore it's a given that you need to become a good storyteller with a full bag of stories before you ever seriously begin to market yourself.

Donald Davis suggests that you "tell every time you're asked to tell" and just let your craft grow. That way your reputation will proceed you. Jay O'Callahan talks about how media publicity has been important to his career. Jon Spelman explains why the secret of marketing is simply "being out there and continuing to be out there."

Michael Parent adds another aspect of marketing. He thinks you need to look not at how you are similiar to other storytellers, but rather how you are different from them. Then, base your marketing strategy on that difference. Gayle Ross tells about the "pony system" in Texas public schools, and how she uses this free inter-district delivery service to send out her brochures to principals and PTA chairpersons.

Connie Regan-Blake suggests arranging a free performance and inviting all the people who are in positions to hire you. Jim May warns about limiting yourself to just one kind of audience, while Doug Lipman entertains us with the story of Perrier's marketing strategy and how it may be analogous to opening up new markets for storytelling. Bill Mooney concludes the chapter by describing what marketing methods he used when he first started telling in New Jersey schools. We think you'll be able to pick up some good tips from these tellers, which will help you sell yourself and your services better.

Donald Davis: This is a personal belief of mine, but I don't ever want to go anywhere that I am not wanted. So if somebody calls up and says, "We've seen your name in the *Storytelling Directory*, or so-and-so said you might be a good person for us," I almost say, "I better not go there." But if somebody calls me and says, "I've heard you at three festivals and now I'm planning an event, and I want you to come," then that's the place I'm going. Those people know why they want me to be there. They know what I can do, and I know the preparation is going to be good.

I have a reverse feeling about marketing. I avoided being a professional teller for as long as I could until the demand was such that I really couldn't avoid it any longer. That took twenty-three years. Not twenty-three years of telling, because I've been telling all my life, but from the first time I got paid for telling a story. Twenty-three years later, I started doing it full-time. I wanted it to grow so that anytime I went somewhere at least the people putting things together knew why they had me there. It's very awkward to walk into a place and have to sell yourself on being there.

[Yes, it is. But for a mid-level storyteller ...]

Just keep telling and doing what you are doing. And tell every time you are asked to tell, every chance you have. Let it grow. Part of what you need to find out is, "Is this what I ought to be doing or not?"

One of the hard realities is that being interested in something and being competent at it are two different things. I can be very interested in something and not be good at it. If I plan to do this, then I need to be harsh with myself and say, "OK, I've got to find out whether I'm just interested or whether I'm good, and I'm not the one who can say whether I am good or not. This is a buyer's market, not a seller's market." You can talk somebody into hiring you once, but if you're going to go back and go back, it has to be because they want you to.

I'm almost shy about marketing. I'm almost standoffish about saying, "I'll help you know how to find me and then I'll help you know some of the variety of things I do." I want that to be after someone knows something about me and my work. Everything I do comes about because the person who calls is a person I've met somewhere along the way. The few times I've been sent somewhere by a booking agent or an event planner of some kind, I've had negative experiences, because the people were saying, "Who is this?" and the person who was organizing it was saying, "Well, I don't really know, but I have heard you'll like him."

Robin Moore: The first couple of years in the business were pretty rough. Fortunately I had some good advice and plenty of encouragement. They pulled me through the tough spots.

When I went to my first National Storytelling Festival in 1979 and realized that storytelling was a viable profession, I felt as if I had found my niche in the world. At that point, I was working as a journalist and felt restless and unfulfilled. I knew I loved stories, but I needed to be convinced that I could realistically leave the nine-to-five world behind with the expectation that storytelling would be more than a pipedream. I needed to know that I could support my wife and children by being a storyteller.

When I went to my first National Storytelling Festival and realized that people were doing just that, I said to myself, If they can do it, why not me?

Fortunately, my wife was supportive of my dream and encouraged me to "go for it." We sat down and worked out a plan and a deal.

The plan was that I wouldn't quit my journalism job for a year. I vowed that by the next National Storytelling Festival I would be a full-time teller. I went to the office for a full year knowing the day I was going to quit but keeping it a secret. Having this inner goal was important and helped me to pull through some of the rough times at the office when I might have been tempted to bail out early.

I did as much work on weekends and evenings as I could, slowly building my clientele. My goal was to book performances a year in advance so that when I got to my launch date, there would be work there waiting for me.

I started out with a market I knew—my old friends the Boy Scouts. I charged a very low fee, reasoning that what I most needed was exposure, not cash. It worked. Soon word of mouth allowed me to fill the calendar with Boy Scout meetings, campouts, and dinners. But I knew I would need more than evening and weekend work to survive.

I knew that word-of-mouth advertising is the hardest to get, but it's also the best. I also knew that I would have to build my reputation one performance at a time. Satisfied clients would recommend me to others. I also tried advertising. I made up a simple brochure and mailed it out to local schools, offering a program of stories related to frontier America with demonstrations of old-time living skills (my old Boy

Scout routine with an educational twist). This was to be my bread and butter for years. I took time off from work and did school performances when I could.

Meanwhile we saved our money so that we would not be destitute when October 1981 rolled around. My wife was in the throes of starting her own business as well, so we were both "taking the leap" at about the same time. I wouldn't advise doing it that way, but in our case it worked. Both of our businesses have survived and prospered over the years, thanks to the burst of entrepreneurial energy we put into our lives when our businesses were young. It was an exciting time, but it was exhausting. Fortunately we only had to work at that pace for the first couple of years. After that things leveled out and we were able to lead saner, slower lives.

The deal I made with my wife was that if I couldn't match my journalism earnings with income from storytelling in that first year, I would go back to my nine-to-five job comforted by the fact that I had given it my best shot.

Today I still make most of my living by storytelling, but I have branched out into a few other areas. Over the last ten years, I have written six children's books and have been lucky enough to have them published by HarperCollins and Random House. The income from book sales has amounted to perhaps twenty-five percent of my income, leaving me free to follow a more relaxed performing schedule. Now I spend approximately seven months of the year performing and teaching storytelling, mostly at schools. I spend the remaining five months at home, working on books and recordings.

One final point: Notice that I said you can make a living by *traveling* around and telling stories. Travel is an essential element of the business. I drive between thirty thousand and forty thousand miles a year, and I know there are other tellers who do

much more. When people ask me what I do for a living, I sometimes say, "I drive around the countryside in a van, picking up checks. I may have to tell a few stories before they will give me the check, but mostly I get paid to travel." A large part of the business is just getting from point A to point B on time.

Some of my storytelling friends spend a lot of time on the road away from home. That idea never appealed to me. I have a busy wife and two active kids and a piece of land that needs constant attention. I wasn't willing to give up these things. So I have basically opted to be a regional teller. I work in Pennsylvania, New York, and New Jersey. I usually leave home early in the morning, go out and do a day in the schools, and return by dinner.

I also do a limited amount of week-long tours in the tri-state area. We call this "going out on a raid." After I've been out on a week-long raid, I have made enough money so that I can relax a little bit and not worry about working so hard the rest of the month.

This has meant doing humbler gigs and not getting the higher fees that might be available if I traveled more, but I feel that I've made the right choice. If you don't have time to take your kids fishing or prune your apple trees or work in the garden, I think you need to stop and ask yourself how successful you really are.

Of course, this plan is only possible if you are near your storytelling markets. My approach has been to locate on the rim of a large metropolitan area within an hour's drive of Philadelphia. This way I can live in the country and have peace and quiet and a good quality of life, but I can also join the rat race when I have to. I need to be near my kids. We live in Montgomery County, which is a nice country area, and it's only an hour from Philadelphia. I found that if I could get about one hundred to one hundred fifty schools a year to have me in, I could go out, do a day's work, and be home in time for dinner. I didn't have to go on the road. That was real important tp me especially when my kids were younger.

I had a dad who traveled a lot. So I made up my mind, especially when my kids were very young., that I wanted to be there. I wanted to be able to work in the garden, work on the house, do all that and be around the house. I was able to work out an arrangement so that I could go out and do local gigs and be home like a regular dad. Of course, I have every summer off because there is no school in the summer. I have more than a thousand public schools within an hour's drive of my house. Within two hours, I can reach kids in New York and Baltimore.

Everyone needs to find their own way. I can only offer this as something that has worked well for me. I find it takes a year for word-of-mouth to work because people plan their schedules annually. So, if Joe Smith, the principal, has you at his school this year, he is not going to have you again until the following year. But if Joe liked you this year, he'll tell Fred and Sally and all the neighboring principals. They all talk to each other. The word-of-mouth has really been a blessing for me, because I haven't done any advertising in five years.

The first couple of years I distributed a lot of brochures. I had a brochure that really worked for me. I sent out mailing after mailing. Then, as the bookings came in, I went out and did the best job I could performing, trusting that when you do good work people are going to recommend you.

Jay O'Callahan: The most important thing about marketing is word of mouth. The second most helpful thing is media publicity. I learned right away to always be polite and encouraging to reporters. If one phoned, I always made time. It could be the smallest paper in the world or the tiniest radio station. The media is a great ally.

It's also important to be dependable. That's stretching marketing a bit, but if I made an appointment as a storyteller for a school or an interview, I was always professional. I showed up and did my best. I think that sense of being extremely professional is important.

You can expand on being professional by having a business card. You should have an answering machine with a good clear message and respond right away to calls. You can expand on your marketing with a publicity kit. A publicity kit needs to be interesting, so I would take odd jobs that still had wonderful names because I wanted those names on my resume. If I was at the Smithsonian or I was sent to Africa (that was early in my storytelling career), I would make sure that they got on my resume right away—anything impressive. Including those names broke down walls very quickly for me. People didn't know me and they didn't know my name, but they certainly knew the Smithsonian Institution. They certainly knew the Library of Congress. Those places built in a safety level.

Be aware of where you perform. Those places can cause people to think, I can take a chance on this person because of the names they've got on their resume. You have to be totally honest, of course.

Jon Spelman: It has always seemed to me that one of the secrets of marketing is just to be out there, and just continue to be out there. About eighty-five percent of marketing success is showing up, showing up a lot, and showing up on time.

If you have brochures and they're out there and you're getting them in places where they should be and where you want them to be, and you're sending out mailings to people and you're calling people on the telephone and you're turning up at showcases and you're good, you're going to get into the marketplace. A lot of success comes from being good. The first thing you want to market is something that is really good. A lot of people who complain to me about their lack of marketing success say, "I don't know why your brochures work and mine don't. Is it the way they're designed and printed?" And sometimes you really feel like saying, "No, it's because right now I'm doing better work than you are. You're not yet working hard enough on telling your stories." There aren't secrets, just little tips, but there aren't secrets of brochures, marketing, or which venue is surefire, or if you can only get a review in this certain newspaper. It's all cumulative and takes place over a long period of time. Mostly it's just working hard to be good, being out there a long time, using your head, and keeping your eyes open.

When I'm in a new town, I go through the newspapers, all kinds of newspapers, and look at who's presenting what and what kinds of venues exist in that town. I'm always taking little notes and then firing off a brochure to somebody. And there are places where you have to send brochures year after year after year after year. I get a surprising amount of work from people who say, "We've been wanting to have you here for five years." You never knew, because they never told you that. They've just been talking to each other about you for that long. I also do what a lot of what other professions call trade shows—showcases, regional arts meetings, conventions.

Connie Regan-Blake: Be sure you're at a certain level. You don't have to be perfect at storytelling to start marketing yourself, but be sure you're good enough for people to hire you. So get that kind of experience first. Once you feel you're ready to start expanding and maybe to start charging, I recommend that you offer to do a free performance—but as part of your "pay" they invite five people that are in a position to hire. You might go to a school, tell them you'll do two performances there if they'll invite an arts council person or people that you know can hire you. That's one of the best ways to start on a grassroots level. Then invite more and more people to see you who are in a position to hire you. You can send out eight million fliers but if people haven't seen or heard of you, the chances of them hiring you are slim.

Bill Harley: Word of mouth is the major way. When you first start, nothing beats word of mouth. You need to remember that. There are no shortcuts as far as that goes. I think there is intelligent word of mouth, which is when someone says, "I like you, I'll have you come to our school." Then you, being intelligent, not pushy, say, "Give me your phone number, or who can I call at your school?"

Collect letters from people who say they really liked you and find ways to incorporate them into your press kit. Of course, at a certain point, you do have to work up your first brochure. Once again, you have to find your own voice and what makes you different. You need to look for your own voice from the very beginning.

How can I put out a brochure which says I'm not just another storyteller? The way I did it and the way most of us did it was to work for a long time for little or no money. I would go to the libraries and say, "Can I do some shows in the afternoons for you?" People also see you in elementary schools. Once you get that brochure together, you can get a mailing list of all the libraries in your state from the Department of Library Services and send it out with a return card. There are a lot of mailing lists. A lot of your time is spent on the phone, especially in the beginning. You've got to do it yourself. You have to divide yourself into thirds. One-third is the performer; one-third is the creator—the person who does the work before he gets to the stage—and one-third is the business person. If you are not willing to give all three of those parts their equal due, then you are not going to make it.

A lot of us get into performing because we don't like the business world. Although we hate it, we are in business, even if it's just a matter of sitting on the phone for an hour, and calling. "Did you get my letter? Are you interested in hiring me?" And asking for your fee.

Marketing is word of mouth. If there are twenty really good storytellers in your area, you've got to do something to kick your marketing up a level. If your promo, video, and tape are all really good but you're not doing good shows, it's not going to make any difference. People will say, "Yeah, we hired him because we loved his promo material, but I wouldn't have him come back. He just didn't hold the kids' interest."

Beth Horner: The best marketing tool is to be good, so that everything you tell is an advertisement for yourself.

In some areas of the country there are showcases. For example, in the area where I live, there are now four different showcases for school and park districts and libraries. It's essential to audition and to get into one of those showcases to get a lot of bread-and-butter business. So finding out about those showcases and doing well at them are essential. Otherwise, you need a good public relations packet with audio tapes, photos, a lot of letters saying how great you are, a brochure and one or two good videos showing your versatility.

Michael Parent: The issue boils down to this: How are you different from the thousands of other storytellers in the country, and who are the people who might want to hear about you? For instance, one angle I pursued with some success is that I am bilingual. I grew up in the United States

speaking French and English, so I've had some work just because of that. I'm invited to multicultural festivals, asked to tell French-Canadian related stories, and sing French-Canadian songs. The simplest way I can put it in terms of marketing is: What is your special feature or your special commodity, and what is your market? Who would be really interested in it?

I also found that making yourself more available to people seems to help. If you say, "I'm doing this new program, and I'm going to be in your area on such and such a date," it's a good way to market. Or you could say, "I'm going to be in your area doing this program in Biloxi, and if some people in Mobile would be interested, I'd love to leave complimentary tickets for you so that you may consider having me come to Mobile some other time." But you've got to get the word to people that might be interested in hiring you, either by mail, by phone, or by getting them to a show. You may even propose doing a program for a reduced fee at a conference where people who could be interested in hiring you later would be present. You could say, "I'd do this for the Alabama librarians if you folks will make sure that the people who might hire me next year are there." You make it part of the deal that they invite those people.

Gayle Ross: Many school districts have what they call a *pony system*. Wonderful devices. These are inner-district mail services. If you have completed your addressing, you can go to the district headquarters and drop off stacks of brochures that will then be sent to the memo boxes of principals throughout the district. It saves an incredible amount on postage. The list of schools in any given district is easy to find.

These days, because of the kinds of stories I tell, I guess I tell at three or four other kinds of events for every elementary school I do. I still keep my elementary school prices low compared to what I make in other venues because I never want to be out of that market. It's the way things come along that dictates where you'll go and what you'll do.

Jim May: If you're going to say, "I'm only an adult performer; I only want to work in theaters," or "I'm afraid in front of adults," you've got a much bigger marketing job than if you see storytelling as a pretty pervasive human need and you're willing to talk to everybody from kindergartners to university presidents about the needs for storytelling in their environment. That's going to make a big difference. Now I'm not saying you have to be that broadly based to make a living. You can find a niche. The school job is a perfect example. You can make a living at schools or you can make a living being a keynote speaker. However, if you're just starting out and you're looking to get something going, you need to explore all possibilities.

Doug Lipman: There are two basic approaches to marketing and they depend on the audience you're going after. One is to go after market share of an existing audience. This was Perrier's strategy going after a ten percent share of the bottled water industry.

The other marketing strategy is to find new markets. This was Perrier's strategy when they went after a one-half percent share of the much larger bottled beverage business and that's when they became a household name. They went from 10 percent of something small to one-percent of something much larger.

Right now in storytelling, you can market to existing markets. You can try to say that you are the newest, latest person for schools or libraries or other venues that already know about storytelling.

To me, though, the real opportunities are in finding new markets that don't

know about storytelling yet. The disadvantage, of course, is that you have to educate them. Instead of saying, "Oh, you're a storyteller, line up over there," they say, "Why would we need a storyteller?" The advantage is that once you succeed in that market you are Scotch Tape, Xerox, Kleenex.

Len Cabral: Do a good job. The proof of doing a good job is getting callbacks to a festival, school or library. That's a good sign that you're hitting the mark.

You never know who's out there. There was a coach who used to say, "Come on now, hustle up, hustle up, you never know who's looking, you never know who's looking!" And when you're performing, you never know who's looking. You might get a job in a library, but a principal or a parent is there who happens to be the chair of a PTA for a whole region. So you never know. One job leads to another.

Collect your own mailing list. Don't say, "May I have your mailing list?" Start your own mailing list, collect addresses of people who were at your performances. They saw you perform. They know your work. The next step is a brochure. A nice brochure. Don't put your prices in your brochure, because that limits how long you can use it. I send my brochures to libraries, schools, PTO groups, and I leave them behind when I perform at different places. Then I pick up addresses of different festivals from magazines, like *Storytelling* magazine.

Heather Forest: The first step is to tell stories and people will find you. When I first started I didn't have a brochure but people found me because every time I told stories, there was someone there who invited me to tell stories someplace else. It was by word of mouth that I found myself telling stories as a full-time job. I don't think it's appropriate for someone who is just starting out to make themselves brochures. There may be nothing to write about yet.

At a certain point, there were enough experiences and thank-you letters and references that I could create a brochure to let people know that I was available and these are some of the places that I've been. But mostly I let people know where I was telling so that they could come and see for themselves. In the very beginning stages of developing a repertoire, it is important to have many performance opportunities in order to shape the tales and learn how the stories affect people. If there aren't enough settings to tell for pay, then tell for free. It's the telling experience that makes a teller improve.

Bobby Norfolk: I market myself by means of brochures, press kits, and follow-up calls. The brochures I developed had to go through many evolutions before I was satisfied. I finally got busy enough to warrant having an office manager. He got ideas from talking to other more successful tellers and observing the various styles of brochures in order to finally come up with a satisfactory product.

You need to decide if you want smooth, slick paper stock or recycled, more subdued stock. This paper can be used to create a two- or three-fold brochure—the number of folds is determined by the amount of copy you want on your brochure. Don't be too wordy and avoid redundant material, as well as information that is unrelated to your storytelling background.

It is important to insert photos in spaces between your copy. You must be the judge of what photos you use (i.e., head shots, action shots, or both). Color photos can run into serious money, and you need to build to the point of including color in your brochures. Remember, it's all part of the evolutionary process.

Milbre Burch: The new vaudeville circuit was one of the first venues for my storytelling in my early days of "recovery" from being a mime. I worked in a trio called the Heart of Gold Vaudeville Company, doing schtick, singing songs, and telling stories. We'd hammer out all our press materials in committee, rehearse and throttle one another within an inch of our lives over conflicting artistic vision, then duke out our next week's rehearsal schedule. Finally, we'd load the van for an hour to head to a twenty-minute gig at a mall.

Leaving Heart of Gold after three years was bittersweet, and going solo was scary. On the other hand, it was a great relief to think that I never had to stroll—wander through an uninterested or over-stimulated crowd—and tell stories at an outdoor festival or a fair again as long as I lived. It was a breakthrough for me: realizing I didn't have to be all things to all sponsors. Clearly, it was time to produce my first solo brochure.

Everyone has seen fantastic press materials for performers who stank onstage and terrible press materials for folks who really shone in performance. I knew you couldn't always trust a good brochure to be attached to a quality performer. So in those early years, I figured my best marketing ploy was to convey something about my personality through my brochure. I included various pictures of me as a debutante, a mime, a nerd, a dog! I tried to convey a sense of humor and play. I also included, "The Truth Is …" And on the next page, "Milbre Burch Tells Stories."

Now, with many more years of experience, I've added professional accomplishments as well as personality to the mix. I work with a designer to tie all the ideas together into a handsome package. Even so, I suppose most of my jobs really still develop through word of mouth.

Also, over the years I've spent a good bit of time, money, and energy working on audience development, co-producing concerts as a member of the Spellbinders back in Providence, Rhode Island, and producing six years of BY WORD OF MOUTH, an adult storytelling series in Pasadena. Creating and sustaining a performance venue over time helps get the word out about storytelling in a pretty concrete way.

Pleasant DeSpain: First, every program I do leads to at least one more program. That, to me, is the best marketing tool I have ever come up with. It requires that every program be the best job I'm capable of doing. Our best marketing tool is always our last program.

Second, print a good brochure. Often, I am called by people who do not know me and have not heard me, but they have heard *about* me. They want a little more than my promise of "Yes, I can do this for you." I ask for their address and tell them I'll send a brochure. I don't mean slick, but I do mean professional.

Third, follow through on jobs. I'm professional in my correspondence, basically polite, with a note. I always call ahead for programs—a week ahead—saying I will be there as promised. I always show up. I always write a thank-you note, politeness at the end after they have done so much for me.

It pays off in so many ways. Good marketing is having a professional attitude and following through. If it is a profession, then it must be done professionally—no shortcuts.

Jackie Torrence: If you want somebody to know that you're telling stories and you want to be hired, let it be known. Put an ad in the paper with your telephone number and/or a post office box and ask if somebody is interested in hiring a storyteller for an adult party. Put an ad in church bulletins to advertise entertaining at children's birthday parties. Volunteer at the public li-

brary and church functions and different things in the community. Don't become a nuisance, but let people know. Then make sure you say, "Now, I'm giving you this free, because I want you to see what I do, but I do charge, because I have to eat."

Have a brochure or a card. If you haven't done enough to have quotes and so forth from newspapers and magazines then a card is sufficient. You can put your picture on a piece of paper and state your intentions. Then wherever you are you'll have something to hand out. Maybe you'll be on a bus and overhear a conversation, "You know, Irma, I'm having this party tomorrow night and I don't know what I'm going to do. You know that band that my husband hired last year? They all died last week and we don't have anybody to play." Well, as you're getting off the bus, you can hand them your card and say, "I'm a storyteller. I can entertain your party for you."

David Novak: I rely heavily on word of mouth. For me, the best jobs come because somebody heard about me and was interested in my work. So because of that, I have hustled less and less over the years. I got tired of hustling. Acting, for me, was all about hustling. That was not a happy lifestyle and it was not productive. As a storyteller, I was being sought out because people heard me and somebody recommended me to somebody else, and they called me up. Now I need to be ready when the word of mouth is there. So it is important to have photographs, clearly printed material, biographical information.

Bill Mooney: I'll add a few thoughts since I am a new face to this generation of storytellers. I started telling stories in the 1960s to adult audiences. I toured all over the world telling stories of nineteenth-century American frontier humor in the format of a one-man show called *Half Horse, Half Alligator*. I became busier and busier in New

York theater and television and didn't come back to storytelling until the latter part of the 1980s.

When I returned to full-time storytelling, I decided to start by marketing myself to schools, since they are primary places where storytellers are engaged. I live in New Jersey. We have more than two thousand public schools in our state and not one of them is more than a two-and-a-half hour drive from my home.

I first made sure I had plenty of good stories. I cannot emphasize this enough. You have to know your craft. You have to have good, appropriate stories, and know that they work. It's not good enough that your mother or your boyfriend likes the way you tell stories. You have to try them out in front of kids, and you have to try them out over and over again.

There's an elementary school right around the corner from my house (my sons went there), so I called them and asked if I could tell stories for free. I told in classrooms so that I could try out the stories more than once or twice. When I had exhausted that school, I called another one close by.

When I felt reasonably secure with my stories (and knew I had a good variety of them in my pocket), I contacted Young Audiences of New Jersey to see if they would be interested in my becoming one of their storytellers. They asked, "Where are you performing? If it is close by, we'll come and watch you in action." I was not performing anywhere. But I called several schools near the Young Audiences offices and asked if they might be interested in a free storytelling session. They all said yes. I then called back Young Audiences and told them I would be in their neighborhood on such-and-such dates. Young Audiences liked what they saw and included me on their roster.

After being booked by them for a couple of years, I decided I could no longer remain with them on an exclusive basis. I was grateful to them for having given me paying opportunities to hone my skills, but I was not getting booked as often as I thought I should be. We worked out an arrangement that I would tell a specific set of stories for them exclusively, and I could do whatever else I wanted on my own.

I had pictures taken. I contacted a graphic artist whose work I liked and told him the kind of brochure I had in mind. I wanted something eye-catching, something that would stand apart from the hundreds of brochures that schools receive each year.

The brochure was designed in the shape of a folder. It contained only pictures, a few quotes, a short bio, along with my name, address, and phone number displayed prominently. It did not include my prices, since I wanted to use the brochure for six to eight years. Being a folder, it could easily include newspaper clippings, letters of praise and recommendation, photocopies of my books and audio-cassettes covers, pricing schedules, and simple fliers announcing special Halloween, Christmas, or Earth Week programs.

I next went to the post office and purchased a bulk mail number and rented a post box. I then called the New Jersey Department of Education and found out how to buy their school directory. It lists the name of every principal in every school in the state, along with their addresses and phone numbers. New Jersey supplies not only a written directory but a computer disk of every school and its principal in the state. After the graphic artist had created a flier that I liked, he designed stationery and a bounce-back card for me. Now I was ready to begin my mail order business.

I knew that Sears and many of the other large mail-order companies consider themselves lucky to get a three percent return on their fliers. Three percent of two thousand schools is roughly sixty jobs. Yes, I would be pleased with that kind of return. My first mailing went out in September, arriving the third week of school. The mailing included my brochure, pages of quotes, newspaper articles, etc., and a cover letter addressed to each principal. I had entered the principals' names, along with the school addresses, into my database and then mail-merged them with the cover letter.

My initial mailing drew a little over three percent in bookings; not bad for the first time out. I followed the first mailing with another one in January and a third in May. These two later mailings were not the folder brochure, but a little one-page flier that I created on my Microsoft program, Publisher.

For the next two years, I kept to that schedule, making three mailings a year. The January and May mailings cost me much less. The postage was basically the same, but I had the little one-page fliers duplicated for two cents a page at a local office supply store.

There are two reasons for the three-times-a-year mailing. The main one: You need to keep your name circulating in the job pond (i.e., schools). It never hurts to remind them that you are out there, that you are still out there, still alive and kicking. There is another important reason. I found that principals and PTA program chairpersons kept moving and changing. They would be replaced by someone who knew nothing about assemblies or storytelling or, more specifically, me. It's a little like throwing pebbles into the pond. The ripples those pebbles make keep going out and out and eventually they hit something. I no longer send out three mailings a year. Word of mouth has kicked in and that, of course, is the best way of booking jobs.

In order to generate printed articles about me, I would call the newspapers in the town where I was performing to let them know what school I was telling in and the hour. Half the time the papers would send over a photographer or a reporter or both. The paper was happy, the school was happy, the parents were happy, and I was too.

It's extremely important to maintain good booking records. I have a month-at-a-glance calendar that lists my engagements and the performance times. I keep a separate notebook that contains the Letters of Agreement and the travel directions. I do not set aside a date until it is actually booked. Then I mail out two copies of a Letter of Agreement and a request for travel directions along with a self-addressed stamped envelope. All your good marketing practices will sail right out the window if you don't keep accurate records of your bookings.

One last thing: I always call a school to confirm that I'll be there. And I always, always, always write a thank-you note to them afterward. It is not only polite, but it allows me the opportunity to suggest a new program to them for their assembly next year.

SETTING YOUR FEE

One of the most agonizing aspects of becoming a professional storyteller is deciding what our fees should be. There comes a time in every storyteller's career when we feel we have paid our dues and have presented enough free programs. It's time to start making some money.

How much are we worth? This question touches a deep nerve in all of us. How do we put a dollar value on all our hard work and creativity? We tell stories because we love doing it. No one becomes a storyteller for the money. But to really devote our full energy to our love, we need to be paid. Here are some ideas on helping you decide how much to charge.

David Holt: Deciding what to charge for your storytelling programs is a grueling process for many. You have to decide what *you* are worth. Since you are not selling a product but rather a service, your worth is fairly subjective. But supply and demand will influence your fee in the same way it controls the price of tomatoes.

I am a strong believer in having a set fee structure. Once you decide what to charge, it will relieve you from panicking every time someone asks your fee. Having a set fee means, of course, that you will be too expensive for some jobs and not charge enough for others, but in the long run your business and your nervous system will be less upset.

You need separate fees for schools, evening concerts, festivals and workshops. How do you set these fees?

First, find out what other storytellers charge both in your area and around the country. Then honestly evaluate your experience, your ability, and your level of success so far. Where do you fit in? Be realistic. If you are as good, and experienced, as the people in your area who are charging $500, then it is likely that your fee should be the same. If you are just as qualified, but are unknown, then your fees should be lower to reflect this. (Notoriety is always worth money in this society. Just ask Michael Jackson.) If you are in great demand and are working more than you desire, then raise your fees a little. If you don't have enough work, try lowering your fees. It is a matter of supply and demand.

Storytellers are in the entertainment business. Throughout this business you will find people charging similar fees. Fees between $25 and $800 usually move up or down in increments of $25. So, typically, you find people charging $50, $75, $100, on up to $800. In other words, you never see anyone charge $67.50 for a show. You might as well set your fees this way too. It sounds professional and you can round your charges up a little bit higher as well. At about $750, fees start to move in increments of $250. You will, therefore, see fees of $1,000, $1,250, $1,500, $2,000, $2,250, et cetera.

Decide beforehand if your fees include your expenses (i.e., travel and lodging) or if expenses are additional. This can be a point of negotiation with the sponsor.

Schools always have less money than most other sponsors. They can only raise a limited amount. Your school fee will probably be lower than your concert fee. It is part of our work as storytellers to spread the word to children. Moreover, schools are reliable, gratifying places to work.

Generally, sponsors who hire storytellers have the money to pay you before you arrive. In other words, the money for your fee does not have to be collected at the door. In situations in which you are paid from the proceeds collected at the door, you need to negotiate your payment well before the concert. There are several ways this can work:

You get a guaranteed fee. No matter how much or how little money comes in, you get that money. No more, no less.

(Note: If the sponsor loses money, you will never be back.) You and the sponsor work out a split of the proceeds. Perhaps sixty percent for you, forty percent for the sponsor (this is always negotiable). I still like to have a guarantee, even if it is low. Otherwise the sponsor might get lazy and not do the publicity and other legwork since they have nothing at stake. You take the first (say) $500. The sponsor takes the next $500 to cover expenses and profit. Anything over $1,000 goes to you (or perhaps you split the money). The percentages are always negotiable.

There are four factors to consider when taking a job.

1. Fun: How much will you have?
2. Exposure: How much will you get?
3. Altruism: How much do you care?
4. Money: How much?

One would hope that there are at least two of these factors present when you take any engagement. Sometimes you have to consider exposure or altruism if you especially believe in a cause. Fun is worth money to me. If I get to see all my friends, or I get to go to a place I've always wanted to visit, I will consider taking a slightly lower fee. Real exposure is important. This is why people are happy to play at the National Storytelling Festival. It certainly isn't the money. Television never pays much, but the exposure is worth the extra effort and lower pay. If you really believe in a cause, you may be willing to work for free.

I bring this up because many times sponsors will try to get you to lower your fee without really offering any perks. Let me give you an example. A renovated "artsy" section of a city a few hours' drive

from me called and wanted me to perform for their street festival as a benefit (i.e., no money). I said I only do benefits for charitable organizations. The sponsor told me I would get lots of exposure. I wanted to tell him that people die from exposure, but I politely said that I get this type of exposure all the time from my regular paying performances. Then he told me how much fun it would be. Perhaps if his festival was being held in the Caribbean I would have been interested, but I knew his street festival would be fun only for the spectators. Finally, he asked how much I would charge, and ended up paying my fee. In essence, keep your eyes open and know what is important to you.

When you finally set your fees, do not print them in your brochure. You want this promotional piece to last a long time, and your fees will probably change. Print your school, community concert, and workshop fees on a separate sheet that can be inserted in your brochure. You don't need to print your festival fees. Most festivals have a set fee that they pay all the participants. You just need to decide what your bottom line will be.

Your prices will change over the years. The economy will be better or worse, and you will get more experience and become better known and more in demand. Fees need to be re-evaluated every year or so. But it is not that gut-wrenching process you go through the first time you decide your charges. The most important thing to keep in mind is that you are deciding only what you are worth as a performer, not as a person (which, of course, is priceless).

FINDING AND USING AN AGENT

Storytelling is a creative occupation. We all want to concentrate on the creative, nurturing aspects of our work. But storytelling is also a business, and the business has to be attended to diligently. All performers would like to have someone else do their booking, so they can work on being great storytellers. But finding an agent can be a thorny problem. Here's why:

David Holt: In a perfect world we would only have to work on our art, give performances, and have fun. An agent would do all the rest: write the letters, make the calls, seek out the interesting high-paying jobs.

Dream on. It doesn't work that way.

Performers ask me at least once a week, "How can I find an agent?" The chances of finding an agent who will do most of the booking for you are very slim. Here's why: Agents are supposed to find you work, but like everyone else they are trying to make a good living for the amount of time they spend doing their job. Since they get a percentage of your fee (ten percent, fifteen percent, or twenty percent ... usually twenty percent these days), it stands to reason they are going to work a lot harder for an act that brings in $5,000 than for one that brings in only $500. Most agents have a stable of performers, but actually they work hard only for their top money-makers—the acts that are always in demand. The agent needs to make only a few phone calls to find them work. Often sponsors will call the agent to book these headline acts. Of course, any good agent will occasionally find work for his other acts, but it simply takes too much time to ferret out every little possibility—particularly if it doesn't pay well.

In general, you need to be making $1,000 or more per engagement on a regular basis before an agent will get interested in you. The agent will probably want to have an "exclusive" with you, meaning all your work (no matter how it comes to you) will funnel through the agent, and he will collect twenty percent on everything. If you are in demand, the agent will be de-lighted. All he will have to do is answer the phone and negotiate fees. This makes his job a lot easier. If you are not in demand, he may have a difficult time booking you. He might work hard on your behalf for a while, but agents tire easily if demand isn't brisk.

If you are in demand, on the other hand, you can answer the phone yourself, or you can hire someone to do it for you. (Re-read this chapter.) The reality is that you will probably have to book yourself forever.

Sometimes you can work out an arrangement with an agent to represent you in a specific area. I have an agent who books only storytelling symphony concerts, another agent who books only international children's festivals, and another who books only Texas schools. Bill uses an agent just for his bookings on cruise ships. This works well for all of us. The agents know how to focus on particular venues that we do not have the time or knowledge to handle. Our agreement is exclusive only for the specific type of job. The agents represent me at conventions and showcases and include me in their mailings. I could not do this for myself because I don't know these particular niche markets. None of the agents find me a lot of work, but they do find me jobs that I could not have secured in any other way.

There are some wonderful agents out there but not many at the level at which most of us work. So get your business organized and do it yourself until you can hire someone to help you. Agents can be a help, but they will never relieve you of being the one in charge of your career.

SUMMARY

» Again, the Boy Scout motto becomes prominent. Be prepared!

» Make sure you are a seasoned teller with a large repertoire of stories before you begin to seriously market yourself.

» Word of mouth is by far the best marketing tool you can have.

» You need a brochure that explains who you are and what you do. It does not have to be expensive, but it should be eye-catching to separate it from the hundreds of others that people receive. Until word of mouth kicks in, your brochure may be the only thing you have working for you. Make sure your name, address and phone number are prominently displayed on it. Business cards are useful. Personalized stationery generally makes a good impression.

» Make photocopies of articles about your storytelling. Save and duplicate all congratulatory letters. Send them as part of your publicity packet.

» Get a bulk mail number from your post office. If your state school system has a "pony system," find out how to use it.

» Have an answering machine with a clear pleasant message to take your calls when you're away.

» Continue to let people know you are out there. We are bombarded daily by all types of advertising material. Advertisers know that we need to be reminded that they are out there wanting our business.

» Remember that every program you do can potentially lead to another. After you finish a program, let your sponsors know that you have another program that you think would be perfect for them next year.

» Look at how you might be different from the thousands of storytellers across the country. What makes you unique? Use that in your marketing.

HOW DO I RECORD AND MARKET AUDIOS?

• • • •

At some point in your storytelling career people will start asking if you have recordings for sale. It will occur to you that if you had an audio tape, you could sell a lot. This is the time to start thinking about making a tape or compact disc. A good audio tape can help you build a larger audience—all those who do not have an opportunity to see you perform live. An excellent tape can work for you as a demo and audition tape as well. Tapes help you keep a higher public profile, working to remind listeners of who you are and what you have done. Producing an audio tape, however, is not a project you should rush into. You will need time, money, and good advice.

David Holt says that "for most storytellers, the largest sales of tapes will be at performances. There is no reason to make a recording unless you can sell it."

Jim Weiss talks extensively about recording and marketing your tapes. He also explains how he and his wife, Randy, went about establishing nationwide distribution.

Virginia Callaway explains why "the most important part of any recording project happens long before you enter a studio." Doug Lipman reminds us that an audio tape is a completely different entity from a live performance.

Carol Birch cautions us to have someone in the studio who can say, "That doesn't sound right to me." And Diane Ferlatte tells how, without knowing anything about it, she produced and recorded her first audio tape.

Doug Lipman: The first thing to understand is that you are now in a different medium. If you're making an audio tape you are no longer in person rolling your eyes and hunching your shoulders. If it's video, you have to understand the difficulties and limitations of that medium as well. When I go into a studio to make a tape of some kind, I have spent a while practicing in that medium. The first time in a studio I thought, oh, I've told this story a thousand times. I'll just go in and tell it to the microphone. That didn't turn out exactly as I had hoped.

The second most important thing is when you are actually recording, have someone there whose judgment you trust. Someone who can say, "Yes, that's great, go on, "or say, "No, you need to do that over again." Ideally, someone who can

help you know how to do it over again. It's very, very difficult to record at your best and also decide if it's good enough.

When you first say, "I'm ready to make a tape," you have to start with: Who is this tape for; why are you making it? You have to decide: What's my intention for this tape? If you're making a tape to make a little extra money at your performances, or so that people will have something of you to take home, then that's going to add a lot of implications to what material goes in, how you record it, whether you record it live or in the studio, and what you put on the cover. All those things are going to come from your initial intention about what it is.

On the other hand, if the reason you're making a tape is because you hope that some mail order catalog will carry you, then you've got to design everything from that point of view. If you're making a tape because you want people to hire you for more gigs who haven't heard of you before, haven't heard you perform, then that's going to color what should be in there.

So before you decide to make a tape, you need to decide why you're making a tape and be ruthless about following through.

David Holt: There is no reason to make a recording unless you can sell it. If you need a recording to help you get bookings then make a high quality demo. Your best bet is to hire someone with good portable equipment to record two live concerts. Mix down the best fifteen to twenty minutes of the live program and voila! you have an inexpensive little recording that shows what you can do.

Most of your sales will be at your performances. Make sure the tape includes a few stories that live audiences really enjoy and request. This will motivate them to buy the tape. You want this recording to have a long shelf life and be sold for years. You don't ever want to be ashamed of it. As has been said many times in this book, it is all word of mouth. Your tape will be out there promoting you while you are somewhere else. That is why it needs to be very high quality.

Hire a professional designer for the cover and find a good printer to print it. Use a professional recording studio and hire a producer. A producer will help you think through your material and see if it fits together in a package. In the studio, the producer can tell you when you need to do another take and when you nail it. Basically, he will help you focus the project and will represent your best interests in the studio.

You can do a lot of pre-production work at home on a portable tape recorder.

Work over the stories until you can do them easily, until you like the way they sound. Decide what their order will be. Pass this work tape around to friends in the business and prospective customers. Ask for honest opinions. Listen to what people say. There is no reason to make a tape that won't sell. You are the artist and you have the ultimate decision about what goes on your recording, but it would be foolish to make a commercial tape and not consider your market.

Lastly, make a tape that will add to the world of storytelling. There are lots of mediocre recordings available. Make yours exceptional. A really good recording will have fans and a life of its own.

Virginia Callaway: As you become known as a storyteller and develop a devoted following, your fans will want to buy every recording you put out. But until that glorious day, it's important to help buyers, whether they have heard you or not, know what your tapes are all about and to be pleased with what they buy. There are a number of ways to make this happen.

The most important part of any recording project happens way before you ever enter a studio. It is essential that you know who you want the end listener to be before you ever set up a microphone. Are young kids the target? Adults? What's the theme? Animal tales? Ghost stories? True-life adventures? If you can state the focus of your tape in five words or less, you're on the right track. A hodgepodge is harder to sell and promote, particularly in the retail marketplace.

Well thought-out packaging is the next critical aspect of marketing if you are putting recordings out on your own label. Packaging is not the place to scrimp. Look at each title as a take-home extension of you and that will help you remember to keep the quality high.

As a consumer, if you were shopping for a record and you saw one titled "Blue Sky, Green Tree" by someone you had never heard of, what would that title mean to you? Would it entice you to buy it solely on that? But if you were going to be spending a quiet evening at home with your honey and you saw "Blue Sky, Green Tree: Romantic Piano Love Songs," you might give it a try. Always ask, "What's the point?" Always tell the prospective buyer about your recording. They'll be much more inclined to buy what they can understand. A title and subtitle or theme can make all the difference.

The art work should be eye-catching and tell even more about what's going on inside. Again, art work is not the place to cut corners. If you've been into a kids' store or a bookstore lately you know how many zillion other tapes are on display, each hoping to catch the consumer's eye. How will yours stand out? The title? The theme? The art work?

In designing your cover, remember you're hoping for lots of reviews, so make sure your artwork on the cover works well in black and white, too. This will encourage reviewers to use your cover alongside your review.

On the back of your package, include a list of the stories, their times, and a brief description. Radio deejays rely on this information. Teachers like it too. You may be thinking that there's not much room on the back of a cassette for all this info. Look at popular music records and you'll see that they all use U-cards instead of J-cards. Those are the cardboard inserts that wrap around the cassettes in the plastic box. When looked at from the side, they either resemble a "J" or a "U," the latter having more space. They can also have numerous foldout panels and can be printed on both sides. Why, you can include your life history!

The majority of storytelling cassettes, compact discs and videos are sold by the performers at their concerts. But if you are interested in placing your products in stores or in working with distributors, it's important to provide an order number. For example, if Suzy Q. puts out her first tape on Suzy's Records, she could number it SR001. How you number it is up to you, but keep it simple.

Just as important is adding a bar code. More and more stores and distributors are using computerized ordering and inventory systems. If your product does not have a bar code, they just can't deal with it.

Storytelling is hard to market. If your titles are for children, the job is somewhat easier, but much more competitive. SILO Distributors and Rounder Kids carry children's titles, but getting picked up by them takes perseverance. (Being a touring artist can make a big difference in their decisions.) They also carry some adult storytelling titles, but there is less demand for these on the retail market. Record stores have not warmed to storytelling as a whole, so don't waste a lot of energy there.

The most effective marketing strategy for beginning tellers is to develop a strong following locally and approach your local bookstores and children's stores about selling your products. As your touring area expands so will your market.

As your touring and success in the marketplace expands, you're going to arrive at an interesting crossroads. At some point, the "business" of running a record label and being a creative performing artist is going to wear you out. You'll need to decide if you are going to seriously pursue promoting your label on top of touring. If the answer is yes, you can't do both by yourself. Since your strength is as a storyteller, you need to keep your energy focused there. Hire someone else to assist you or to run the record label altogether. You may think you can't afford to, but you can't afford not to.

If you do decide to really promote your label there are several professional organizations that can help you tremendously. The first is The National Association of Independent Record Distributors (NAIRD). This group will teach you everything you need to know about running a record label, introduce you to people who have done it successfully for many years, and let you meet "new-timers" like yourself. There is an annual convention in May that is outstanding and will help your label immensely.

A second group is the Audio Publishers Association, which only specializes in spoken audio. They have recently instituted a new membership category just for small labels. It offers great services and is worth looking into. (Addresses for both these organizations are in the back of this book.)

There are a lot more ways to market, such as trade shows, advertising, in-stores. Get to know other storytellers and talk about how you can work together to cut corners and still be effective. Co-oping a booth at trade shows or sharing the cost of an ad in a publication with others can actually work better for tellers with a small number of titles, and the overall impression is stronger.

The only limit to marketing is your own creativity and hard work. The rewards are well worth it.

Diane Ferlatte: I didn't know anything, but I did it. When you don't know, you ask somebody. I went to a studio and asked, "How do you make a tape? What do I have to do?"

I knew I wanted music in it.

"What do I do?"

"Call musicians. Ask the people at the studio. They deal with musicians all the time," they said.

"You know anybody who plays the banjo?"

"Oh, yeah," they said.

I call the guy, a young student who plays good. He came over to the studio, and I told him what the story was about. He picked out a few little things. He played in the back of the story, worked out fine. Just made it up as I went along.

For the next story, I needed a drummer.

"Got a drummer? How much would you charge me to do this? Oh, good price."

I just did each story as I went along and got the backup behind it that I wanted. Then, once it was all together, the engineer told me what to do, how to put it together. It had several tracks. I just learned by listening to the engineer and getting to know what I wanted. I knew the story, that's it.

Then I said, "Uh-oh, J-card. What's a J-card? How am I going to do that?"

A friend of mine does drafting design. I called him up and asked how much would he charge just to drum me out a little J-card. He asked what I wanted on the front.

"Just my name, some kind of little design, and my picture, something that says 'Diane Ferlatte,' and I think I'm going to call the tape *Favorite Stories* or *Stories That I Like.*"

He did that, kind of scratched it out, what it might look like. Then I talked to another storyteller. You ask other storytellers who've done it. She found a good place somewhere in New York where it's really reasonable.

I don't have a distributor. The only people that distribute them now are people that know about them. These tapes won awards—they both did—the ALA Notable Recording and the Parent's Choice. So they're in this magazine that goes all over the country, and all these libraries are ordering the tapes, because it's in this book. Advertise in the National Storytelling Directory. People read that a lot and they look in the back, and they might want to order it. But usually I take them with me, when I go to performances or festivals and that's where I make my big sales, you know, just taking them with me. Lately the libraries are making big sales, and re-ordering, so that's good. Two people who have catalogs want to put them in their catalogs, so I'm in two catalogs now and they keep re-ordering for their catalogs.

Bobby Norfolk: The investment for recording can be somewhere between $2,000 and $3,000, depending on your product. Studio time needs to be figured in as well as the cost of materials, printing, manufacturing, and distribution. If you can't get satisfaction from a recording label, invest the money yourself, but make sure you get all you can for your dollar. Shop around for the best deal (as always), and try to get a studio with good quality reproduction capacity. You don't want to sound like you recorded in a giant soup can.

You can pay someone on consignment to handle your cassettes, and pay somewhere around fifteen to twenty percent of the total cost of the tape, or sell your cassettes in bulk outright at the wholesale price to a bookstore or music store that carries storytelling cassettes. It is much more difficult to get your tapes on consignment at the larger book chains than in the smaller "independent" bookstores in your immediate area.

Jim May: You get real good professional technicians, not just somebody who's a good hacker with his own hi-fi or something. You'll always get a lot of people like that who will want to do it for you, but you want someone who has recorded people already, who is a good editor, good technically. Once you do a tape, you want it to endure. You want to sell that tape the rest of your life if possible. You don't want to have to redo the cover and the inside. Get a brochure. Work on your stories. And kind

of relax about the tape, and wait until you're sure you can do a tape that you're going to like for a long time. Then once you have done it, forget about it, because all the stories will get better as you tell them over and over again. And you won't be happy with that tape anyway probably. However, once you've got all those things down, there will be many occasions when you'll earn more money selling tapes than you will on your fee. It will all supplement your income. You can't really go wrong with having a tape.

Len Cabral: I probably sell most tapes from the stage—from a performance. Sometimes stores will call me directly and ask me to send them tapes. Sometimes tellers have their tapes for sale at festivals but they had to buy them from the company that made them, and then they don't make any money from them. The festival wants twenty percent or forty percent and the storyteller ends up making $2. I think it's a better investment to produce your own tape if you can come up with the money to do it—that is, if you're going to be working a lot, and you have a lot of opportunities. If you're not working a lot there's no sense in having the tape because you're not going to have a lot of opportunities to sell it.

Jay O'Callahan: I started putting out my own tapes because my first one was with another company and I wasn't happy with it. I was making very little money, and feeling I didn't have the artistic control, so I made a conscious decision to control my cassettes. The second decision was to make sure that they were professionally done, very carefully done. I rented a WGBH studio in Boston and got one of the best engineers in the city.

I found it was important to build up a mailing list. My mailing list is made up of people who have seen me and want to be on my mailing list, so they're behind me. I find it's important to put out a mailing a couple of times a year to let them know I'm out there and this is my newest release or newest book.

I found it is important to have new cassettes, to vary things a bit, so when they get a brochure, they say, "Well it's going to be something new. It's worth opening it. It's not the same old stuff." I found it's very important to do it as carefully as I can. I want the brochure to look good. I want it to look professional. I want it to be very easy for people to order. That gets into small things like having an 800 number. But these are my allies here. These are my little babies. I want people to be interested in them and find them as easy as possible.

Pleasant DeSpain: In my package of materials I send to the school once I am hired, I offer several masters of materials they can print out, including an order blank master for books and tapes along with a little note to the parents on it. Now the school must agree they want to do it. And I give them a discount depending on the price of my books and tapes. Right now, the discount is between ten percent and fifteen percent, but I am giving reduced fees or prices on the product. I autograph them while I am there.

[Very clever. So they already have them in hand when you go to the school?]

No, I have books and tapes that I send ahead of time as loaners—and I pick those up when I arrive. I also send a gift set of books and tapes autographed for the school. That way I don't have to autograph pieces of paper. I won't do that in a school. I say, "No, I have autographed one set of books." I will autograph all the books and tapes that they buy from me. I have to get cooperation and help from the teachers or the PTA. It's amazing how much more I earn. Often I match my program fee for the day.

Jon Spelman: I think it's difficult. I just have two tapes of my own out now. One is a live performance for which I hired a professional sound technician; and the other, the same professional technician and I worked in a booth that we rented from a small business that does recorded books. I think it cost us $100 for the booth and the equipment. It's high quality broadcast sound. I think when you're just doing voice the problems can be vastly simplified. I don't think you have to spend great amounts of money to make basic storytelling tapes.

Carol Birch: You need someone in the studio with you who knows you and your storytelling style really well. Although I've helped people record stories, I am not the important part of the equation. You don't need me or anyone else who has directed other recordings. You need someone who is a good enough friend so that if he says: "You're sounding awfully teacher-ish now," or "You sound like you're imitating So-and-so here." You will heed their advice. He needs to have a well-developed sense of you and your way of speaking.

I also think it is imperative that while you're actually recording, whoever is helping you *just listens!* Literally. They need to have their back to you or their eyes closed so they are not affected by your eyes, your facial expressions, or any of your body language. They need to *hear* the nuance in your voice, not see the raised eyebrows that communicate those feelings along with what you say. The only thing on the tape is your voice—*the way you say the words*— so you need an aural mirror. It is nearly impossible to watch someone, especially people you are fond of, and divorce yourself from their gestures and their expressions.

The person also has to help you stem the tide toward jazzing up the tape with effects and extras. So often, engineers in typical recording studios are frustrated rock stars. They are used to layers of sound— they want reverb—they want music—they want bells. You need help remembering what *you* want in the face of persuasive people in what is, for the storyteller, a foreign environment.

Beth Horner: One warning about recording: I recommend always making sure that you get your copyright and royalties straightened out before you make your recording—certainly, before mixing, editing and marketing a tape. You cannot sneak around.

Heather Forest: I don't market my tapes. I record for recording companies and it's their responsibility to do that.

[How do you talk them into recording you?]

I send them demo tapes. Usually, I make a sketch of how I want the tape to sound. Before I submit the sample, I know which stories are going to be on it and I know the order of the stories that I think would work. I call this a "scratch tape," but it's a very well done tape. I have a four-track recorder at home and I carefully design the tape and then I send it to various recording companies that I think might be interested. At this point, I have recorded six albums of storytelling.

Jim Weiss: Recording and marketing are quite different. Let me begin with recording. First of all you have to find the right studio. There are lots of recording studios with lots of different prices and lots of different areas of expertise. Find a studio that has had experience recording the spoken word. Call the local ad agencies and say, "Where do you record your voice-over work?" Talk to each studio and ask for samples. Then choose one where you like the people and the pricing is competitive.

Second, you must realize there are always costs above and beyond just recording the story. Everything from the cost of tape to additional hours spent editing, mixing, mastering. You need to go in with questions like: "What are these costs?" "How much more is it going to be?" "Can you give me some idea of what it'll ultimately cost?"

When I do a one-hour recording, Randy (my wife) and I estimate that it will take at least twelve hours of studio time. Usually it takes more than that. And studio time gets longer as we get pickier about the quality with each succeeding tape.

As a storyteller, I don't like to use a script. I don't memorize the story. I memorize what happens. I go into the studio only with notes that tell me the chronology of the story, the names of the characters (particularly if they are names from some other culture), and maybe a few key phrases that I really like, that embody a whole section of the story. But other than that, I don't have a script. So what I end up doing is recording and editing.

Sometimes I will record a twenty-minute story and the only thing I have to edit out will be the couple of times I stopped to drink some water. Other times, it might take weeks to make a one-hour recording— lots of takes and lots of editing.

I always make home recordings first to test out my stories. Then I play them for my wife and my daughter, who are my editors. They are officially called my Ruthless Editors. They are honest and they know what I'm after.

I can't emphasize enough that you must do your work ahead of time, before you go into the studio and start paying by the hour and watch the meter ticking. I know a lot of tellers who go into the studio and tell their stories just the way they do them in performance. I guess there's some value in that. But personally I don't find it valid, except as a way of preserving the material.

I think you owe it to your listeners to give them the best you can do. Recording a story is not the same as telling it live. If you bring some other people into the studio, as I have done on occasion, it can change the energy to make it closer to a live experience. But it still isn't. Being behind that glass wall, talking into the mike alters everything. You have to be aware that's going to happen.

When I'm in front of a live audience, I select my material based partly on who is there. I have the opportunity to add things or make comments or shape the story as I go, as I see people reacting. The phrases you usually finesse with a facial expression now need verbal explanation. That's part of the joy and the interaction of being a live storyteller; in the studio you lack that. You have to create it for yourself. You have to think about who your audience is and what you want to give them. I want my stories to go out there and walk by themselves.

You have to be aware that anybody can pick up your tape and play it. That has particular ramifications for stories with a lot of violence. In my case, I record a lot of the classics. I know many of my listeners are children. I am very cognizant of that. There are things that I can explain and soften in a live telling, but I don't know who is going to buy my tape. I don't know how old the person may be. I don't have the same opportunity as in a live performance to soften it. So I need to think about the content of the story. Some stories just don't work as well on a recording as they do with a live audience.

[Have you ever found that once you got into the studio the story wasn't working?]

Oh, yes. I did one-half of a recording. I was going to do two different stories, one on each side. The first side was wonderful, one of my favorite stories to tell. It simply poured out. I said, "Boy, this tape is going to be great!" But when I got to the second side, that story had very heavy, dark energy to it. I recorded it about six different ways over two and a half recording sessions and still couldn't capture it. At that point, even though I had a first side (one of the best things I've ever recorded), I shelved that whole project. I spent a lot of time, money, and thought, and I said, I'm not going to force this thing. I hope to find another side B at some later point. Instead I thought, what do I know that I can tell? That I really love? And I recorded *The Jungle Book*, which I've wanted to tell for years. It came out wonderfully and we just received our fourth ALA Notable Award for that recording.

[You started Greathall Productions with your wife, Randy, didn't you?]

If people compliment me on the recordings, I always say, "Thank you. If you loved the stories, you're complimenting me. If you heard it in the first place, you're complimenting my wife, Randy." She runs the business side of our production company.

We started very ignorant of what was out there. And in 1989 there wasn't as much out there in storytelling, in the recording field. At that time most tellers tended to go into a studio and record three or four or five of the stories people liked in their live performances. They made up a tape and sold it following their concerts. A lot of tellers still do that. We didn't take that approach.

We wanted to be able to distribute our tapes and get them into stores and have people hear them. There is a tendency among some elements of the storytelling community to look upon this as commerce, and to look upon commerce as something untouchable. I disagree very strongly with them. I believe that if you have some art to offer to the world, and something you find sufficiently valuable that you're going to tell in the first place, then you want to get that out to people. The reality is, you're going to reach a lot more people this way than you are in individual performances. So you should be doing both. That's what works for me.

We had the idea for Greathall Productions in June. By Labor Day, I was holding in my hand five one-hour recordings ready to sell. Today I probably wouldn't move that fast, because I'm pickier and slower with the process. Yet some of those five are still among our top sellers and I still love the vitality of the recordings. Two of them won national awards right out of the gate. We were very lucky.

We followed our own instincts. We decided that the art work on the covers was very important. We knew that, unlike a book that can be picked up, thumbed through and the author's style seen immediately, you couldn't do that with a recording. You have to give them something visual on the cover. You have to think about what stories you're going to tell. You have to ask yourself, are they marketable to a fairly wide group of people? Maybe you are willing to market to a specific group of people, and that's fine, too, but you need to decide that. It has a lot to do with your expectations. You need to think about what stories you're collecting on a given recording.

We have found that if we group the stories thematically—like Greek myths, for example—that tends to work very well. People can say, "Oh, here's a whole subject I really enjoy. I'll take it." If you had only one Greek myth on a tape of five stories, they may not want to spend the $10 to get just that one story. It also makes it possible—in a case like Greek mythology—for you to record things without having to explain each time about the gods, for example. You do it once in the first story and the whole thing's covered. The stories build on each other. These are marketing as well as artistic decisions. I may not tell an entire

concert of Greek mythology, but on a recording that's the approach I'll take.

Once I have an idea of the kinds of stories I want to tell, I'll do a series of rough drafts at home. That's both an artistic and a marketing decision. You have to know before you go into a studio that the story that works well in a live performance also works well as a recording. You may need to adapt your story to the new medium. It's perfectly legitimate. It's like a painter who says, "I'm painting in oils today. Tomorrow I'm painting in pastels. So I have to vary my technique. I'm still Monet. I'm still following my own artistic vision. I'm still painting the same garden. But this is the medium I'm going to use for this picture. The other one for that picture." You have to be willing to make those changes.

Your most valuable tool will be to find somebody whose opinion you really trust, and whose ego is not involved, to help you listen for those things. Although, in the end, the decision is always the teller's.

We put together a brochure. We've got all the cassette art work showing. We started with black-and-white but we're using a full-color brochure now. If you have any quotes from people who have heard you, if you've won any awards, if you've performed at any particularly prominent places (the Smithsonian, Jonesborough, or have a thank-you letter from one of these places) put that on the brochure. This is how store owners or individuals or librarians or whomever are going to realize that there is something worth paying attention to.

We began by going out to stores and playing the store buyers bits and pieces. I figured out what was a good episode from *Hercules* and a good episode from *The Arabian Nights*. I had the tape ready right at that point. I'd say, "Would you like to listen to a little of this?" Two minutes later, they would say, "Wow, I really like that.

How many titles do you have?" I'd say, "Five," and they'd say, "OK, I'll take them."

There are distributors of spoken word for children. There are catalogs all around the country that carry the spoken word. Probably the most important thing I can emphasize to a teller is don't be surprised if you get a "No." Just keep asking politely.

We're carried now by virtually every major distributor in the United States. I think every one of them said "No" the first time we applied. We're on some of their bestseller lists now, but they didn't know that was going to happen. They said, "You have to win some awards first."

We didn't know there were awards.

Randy said, "What awards are those?" They told us and we applied. We got a couple of those awards, and *bang*, that distributor picked us up. But it took a year to do it. The awards like the American Library Association ALA Notable and the Parent's Choice Gold are invaluable as a means of legitimizing your work. If you get a letter of recommendation with a pungent phrase, use it.

The distributors are a big key. We sell directly to individuals. We sell directly to stores. But most of our sales come through our distributors now. They are the ones who will go out to the stores for you. It means you get a lower percentage of the profit, but you more than make up for it with volume. It gets your recording into more hands. Catalogs are another way to go.

One other thing that is absolutely essential: your attitude in dealing with people. Some artists don't have business experience, so it helps to talk with someone who

does. More than that, you have to be polite. You have put your ego aside at the beginning. You've poured your heart and soul into a recording, you contact somebody, you play it for them or send it to them, and they say "No." How does that affect you? Well, you can't let it stop you. You have to understand you are going to hear "No," especially at the beginning, more often than you hear "Yes."

Remember, first, that person is not the only contact in the world. Second, that one person's opinion does not necessarily reflect the opinion of 999,999 other people you're going to contact who may love the tape. Third, you have to be able to go back to that person and say, "I appreciate the fact that you listened to it. Can I send you another tape, or can we talk later?" It may be that right now they're not carrying this kind of tape. Maybe they will a year from now, or there may be somebody else in that job a year from now who will love it. You can't just write off that company or that person. You have to keep plugging. There are more potential buyers and listeners out there than you will ever have time to reach.

The last thing is that you have to be organized in shipping to them. You need to be able to manufacture your tapes and have them on hand, then promptly and efficiently get them their recordings and their invoices, particularly when you are dealing with distributors and catalogs. They do not want to deal with people who can't keep their commitments. That's the fastest way to lose a big customer. So there's a business sense involved in this too.

ADDITIONAL RESOURCES

National Association of Independent Record Distributors and Manufacturers (NAIRD)
P.O. Box 988
Whitesburg, Kentucky 41858
(606) 633-0946

◆

National Academy of Recording Arts & Sciences
3402 Pico Boulevard
Santa Monica, California 90405
(310) 392-3777

◆

2 Music Circle S
Nashville, Tennessee 37203
(615) 255-8777

◆

157 W. 57th Street
New York, New York 10019
(212) 245-5440

◆

Audio Publishers Association
2401 Pacific Coast Highway #102
Hermosa Beach, California 90254
(310) 372-0546

SUMMARY

» There is no reason to make a recording unless you can sell it. It is foolish to make a tape without consulting the market.
» Decide beforehand who the tape is for. Children? Adults?
» State the focus of your tape (animal tales? ghost stories? true-life adventure?) in five words or less. Every tape should have a coherent theme.
» Since most of your tape sales will be at performances, include stories that live audiences enjoy and request.
» Studio time costs money. Do all your pre-production work before you get to the studio.
» Record a scratch-track (work tape) first at home. Pass it around to your storytelling friends, librarians, and prospective customers (young children, teenagers, adults) and ask for their honest opinions. Then *listen* to what they tell you. There is no reason to make a tape that won't sell. It is easier to sell a children's storytelling recording than one for adults.
» Rent a professional recording studio and hire a producer. You don't want to sound like you used a string and a tin can to record your tape.
» Call a number of recording studios to compare prices. Ask what they normally record. You may want to steer clear of studios that specialize in rock bands and are big on reverberation. Choose one that has a respectable voice-over business.
» Realize that a recording is quite different from a live storytelling event. Always keep in mind *who* will listen to the tape and *where* they will be hearing it.
» Hire a professional designer for the cover and find a good printer for the J-card.
» Since most stores and distributors have computerized ordering and inventory systems, it is a good idea to get an ISBN number and add a bar code to your cassette.

WHAT IS THE LIFE OF A PROFESSIONAL STORYTELLER LIKE?

◆ ◆ ◆ ◆

Have you ever daydreamed about becoming a full-time professional storyteller? Do you want to throw off the chains of that nine-to-five job and be free and creative? Do you long for the carefree life of a roving teller of tales? Well, maybe it is time for a reality check.

While telling stories for a living can be a most rewarding career, it can also be extremely nerve-wracking. On the positive side, you can be your own boss and do things your way. But, as Michael Parent points out, "The self-employed have the most demanding boss of all." Motivation for your career has to come from within. No one will push you but yourself. You have to stay inspired year after year.

Making money doing something you love is everyone's dream. But the dream can become a nightmare when there is no regular paycheck and you have a month or two with little work and bills due. As Robin Moore reminds us, you have to work hard to make a living as a storyteller. You can't be lazy.

Working at something creative is truly a joy. Finding, creating, and sharing stories is the high point of the storyteller's job. Most of us would do this work for free. But in order to have the time to pursue our interest, we must make money at it. Much of a performer's time is spent keeping the business alive, getting bookings, making calls, writing letters. You have to attend to the business even when you are on the road.

If you like to have a regular schedule, forget the life of a performer. One day you are a secretary, the next traveling to a gig, then you are center stage and everybody loves you, then you are back at the hotel by yourself watching TV, then you are back home, your own secretary again. But for many of us the variety is the spice. As Jim May says, "I like doing something different every day."

Perhaps the greatest pleasure in being a storyteller is the feeling that you are making a difference. "I'm in a position where I can promote reading, justice, and understanding among people," says Len Cabral. The storyteller has the power to lift the spirit, move, and inspire. It is a great reward. Jay O'Callahan says, "Storytelling is inviting and personal. It's human. It deals with language and life and emotions. It deals with the reason why we are all here."

To carve out a niche making a living by your creative wits is a great satisfaction. It takes a lot of work and perseverance, but to stand before an audience and see the look of enchantment in their eyes and feel the power of a good story makes all the struggles worthwhile.

Beth Horner: If you are an organized person (which I am not, but I try to be), you begin by looking at the creative and the business things you have to do that day. I try to handle the business things as quickly as possible. Then I create. In a typical day, you are bouncing back and forth between the business side and the creative side of your job. You have to be a travel agent and book your tours and get the right flights, et cetera. Then, of course, you have to be a chauffeur and get yourself to wherever your gig is. You have to pump yourself up and get ready for a performance. You have to be a hair and make-up artist and try to look halfway decent and get your clothes ironed. Then you have to go out and perform. Afterwards, you have to be gracious and talk to people about how your stories hit them and what they meant to them. Then you have to be your own roadie and pack up everything and find a place to sleep. Sometimes I can't find a hotel and end up living in my car.

Michael Parent: I would say forget about being a performer for a living—storytelling or otherwise—if you don't have a high tolerance for insecurity. Otherwise, performing for a living will drive you crazy. You've got to be flexible. You've got to be willing to sell your car or your house, if it comes down to that, if you want to keep on performing for a living. If you're not willing, you could tell stories part-time and support yourself doing something else— keep your day job, so to speak.

If you want to get into performing full-time, you should realize that you'll have to give up some things. You won't get the corporate insurance plan. You won't get the regular paycheck. It boils down to weighing what is important to you. If you're just starting out and financial security is important to you—if you're really going to miss your regular paycheck and that's more important than being a performing artist—I would say, "Don't try to make a living being a storyteller or any kind of performer."

It will likely take a few years to get yourself established. Even then, you're going to have some cyclical periods. I sometimes have the feeling that I don't work at all. Other times, I have the feeling I'm working all the time. You're always hustling. You always have things to do, people to write, follow-up calls to make. You need to put together a new program or a new brochure, or new stories, or new songs. Then there's the creative aspect.

You've always got some ideas for a new story or for getting into a new performance venue. You're always trying to find time to create the work or create the material or create engagements. When you're on the road, the performing aspect is quite exhausting. So a lot of times when you're out there thinking you're going to have all this time to work or create, very often all you've got the energy for is to just do the performances and do those well.

The biggest factor in the performing life is that you're completely in charge of your own time. I find that being self-employed, the boss can be as much of a jerk as when you're employed by somebody else. I think you can be much harder on yourself than any boss would ever be. It's very difficult to keep that balance of working well without driving yourself into the ground.

Jackie Torrence: I remember years ago the first time I met this one storyteller and I said, "Tell me about yourself."

He said, "I've been a storyteller for so many years and I try to work two weeks a month. That ought to be enough to keep me happy, because I have a family. I want to see my family and so I work two weeks on and two weeks off. I don't want this business to take over my life."

I thought, well, that's very nice.

About two years later after he had made it into a national magazine, I said, "Ah, how are you doing?"

"Oh, I'm so tired I don't know what to do," he said. I said, "Why?"

"I worked a month, I'm so tired."

I said, "You're not working two weeks on, two weeks off anymore?" He said, "No, I had so many requests I had to fill them."

If you are a good storyteller and you want to work, if you want to continue working, you have to fill some of those appointments. Sometimes you can't work two weeks on and two weeks off. You have to work for people when they ask for you. Sometimes it doesn't run two weeks on, two weeks off. You work four weeks straight and maybe you have four weeks at home.

My family life suffered a great deal. I took my daughter a lot of places with me. We traveled a lot together. I lost my husband completely, because I could not support a relationship and be on the road every day. That suffered. The only real relationship that I've been able to keep up with is the one between me and my daughter, and that's because I could take her with me everywhere. It's not easy being away from home. It's not easy being on the road, but it's most satisfying to me. And if I had it to do all over again, I would select the very same way I came to be here.

If you are a good storyteller, you will want to work. And if you want to continue working, you have to work. Sometimes you can't work two weeks on and two weeks off. You may work four weeks straight and then you have four weeks at home. You have to work for people when they ask for you.

Jim May: Being a storyteller means having to thrive despite not being on a regular schedule, not being home, not having your slippers on at five o'clock every night, not being able to watch family relationships blossom and grow over a long period of time. And the people around you, like your family, need to be able to forgo those things also. Otherwise they will constantly bug you about why you're never home and why you can't plant the crocuses on November 15 at four o'clock like the family's been doing for years.

It's an exciting life. You never know what the next phone call will bring or where it will take you. You have to be able to see the romance of getting up at four o'clock in the morning, getting in your car, and heading off somewhere. Often you are alone a lot.

First and foremost, I like the variety. I like doing something different every day. I like that I have the time to be alone to think. I like that when I return to my family, it's a homecoming and a honeymoon rolled up in one. I like those moments of excitement, those ups and downs in my life, more than a lot of people. It's not a very steady or predictable kind of life, but there's a lot of variety and excitement. You're always working with ideas and seeing where those ideas will lead. And of course, that moment when you're in front of people, telling them a story, and having them really connect with the story, is one of the great highs of human experience. It's as good as anything I've ever experienced as a human being.

Doug Lipman: In order to be a storyteller in our society, you have to be an artist and a business person at the same time. Being a professional storyteller involves all the things that are true of any small business. You spend a lot of time communicating via phone, fax, mail. Because you're a small business, you need to get help with that part as well as with your storytelling. You need to find somebody who can look at what you're doing, what you're investing in, and what you're getting in return. Business is a whole other world. People spend their lives just on that part and you might as well get help from them if you don't know it already.

Another important thing to think about is your failures just as much as your successes. There was a time when my school work, which had been going up and up and up, suddenly went down to zero. I said, "OK, I've got to do something else. What am I going to do?"

I came up with coaching other storytellers, which I'd been doing, but not pushing. I wrote an article on coaching and got a number of responses. Then I said, "OK, I'm going to devote more of my advertising, attention, and resources to developing the coaching." For the past several years, that's what I've been putting my energy into, and it's very gratifying.

Susan Klein: You are going to be putting up with irregular meals, an absolutely rotten knot between your shoulder blades from driving too much and sitting on airplanes, the need for a masseuse at all times trying to sleep in foreign beds with foreign pillows until you start to bring your own pillow on the road, having to buy things that you forget to pack, being late to places because your airplane didn't get off the ground on time, having to deal with that racing feeling of having to get someplace and then, of course, they can't start the show without you, not always having enough time to rest, being chronically tired on the road, coming home to mountains of mail, needing to do a lot of office work on the road, strained relations at home, and an erratic cash flow—it comes in gobs, sometimes great huge gobs, but not in a regular pattern. There are times when it's flowing like water in the springtime and other times it just ain't there.

You have to have great discipline if you are going to be a touring artist because you have to carve out times for your creative work; it simply is not there. You actually have to make time and yet you have to continue to make a living. I find the fatigue the hardest to deal with. I'm beginning to have this idea about airplanes. Sometimes we get off an airplane feeling real raggedy, and we can't quite get it together and we don't feel centered. I think that our souls tend not to be able to catch up with us when we take flights. They keep trying to catch up with us on some other plane.

Len Cabral: I love what I do. I'm really pleased to be able to make a living doing something that I enjoy—working in schools and having young people look at a storyteller and say, "Now, here's somebody who really enjoys what he does." To

have a career that you feel good about and make money doing it!

It's a real learning experience for young people to see an adult in a career that appears to be fun for him, yet he's making his living at it. Kids are always under pressure. "Come on now, your Mom wants you to be a doctor, your Dad wants you to be a lawyer, an accountant, you're going to take over the family business ..." Kids always have to deal with the pressure of "What am I going to be when I grow up?" It helps them to meet adults who are doing positive things and enjoying them.

I meet lots of people. I find out a lot about the country, and about other people. I'm in a position where I can promote reading, justice, and understanding among different people. That's probably my strong point. I feel glad to be in the ranks of storytelling. I don't know if there's the same camaraderie in other trades—if people are able to share the way storytellers do. I don't know how many lawyers share accountants or marketing expertise, or if advertising people get together and say, "I do it that way or this way." Storytellers can get together and share for the good of society, and us all. When we work in schools, we're promoting reading, writing, listening skills, and we're promoting humanistic things.

Robin Moore: It's a great life. But ... if you want to make a comfortable living at this, you need to work a lot. If you are used to getting a paycheck every Friday, you can see by just laying out the fee structure of storytelling that it ain't going to happen from here on out. In order for money to come into your house, you're going to have to go out and get it. For me, what that's meant is a lot of driving—thirty thousand or forty thousand miles a year—and between three and four hundred performances a year.

I like working a lot. But it's a real humbling profession in the sense that you have to walk into the arena day after day after day. You can't rest on your laurels, because the crowd next week doesn't know anything about the crowd that you had a great time with last week. You have to go and re-create that all over again. But if you have that fire in your belly—the kind of thing that feeds and nourishes you—then you'll be really happy with storytelling.

The other side of the coin is there's a real high burnout rate. After my fifth year, I got so burned out on storytelling that I was going through performances like a robot. I didn't know what I was going to do. The only way my system could keep going was by disconnecting—going somewhere else where other performances were on. I overcame it just by chance. The book business kicked in about the time that this was happening. So I not only knew that I had some other ventures out there, other pots that were cooking, but I also knew that there was something else to take up my creative energy besides the oral tellings.

I don't know very many professions where you do best if you just be yourself. A lot of times people call me up and say, "Oh will you come and tell stories?" I say, "What kind of stories do you want?" They say, "We don't care, just come." That's incredible to me. When I worked as a journalist, I worked in organizations where you were expected to mold yourself to the organization. In storytelling, I feel that the older you get (if you are really doing the soul work that goes along with this), the more like yourself you become. It really encourages you to be an individual.

Milbre Burch: For me, the hardest part of juggling motherhood and my life as a working artist is carving out time for *me* to have some solitude in which to slow down, relax, and create. That quiet time or private time has always been the first to go and the last to get back when things get hectic. Now it's even harder, but still it's worth the struggle.

Jay O'Callahan: My days differ so much. If I'm performing in a theater, it's very regimented work. It's like being in the army. If I'm in a theater, I'll get up and have breakfast. Then I will stretch for half an hour. I do some tai chi and yoga. Then I'll do a half-hour of voice exercises, and I will do maybe fifteen minutes of scenes. All day long I'll rest or walk and think about the scenes. I'll get to the theater an hour and a half ahead, and I'll do the same regimen. I'll do several of the scenes and then finally do the show. So that's really like the army, but I enjoy being in that army.

If it's performing in a school, it's different because that's early. I get up and drive off. I do schools usually in New England, and hopefully Massachusetts near my home.

The day varies. In the summer, I often go to a secret barn, an ancient piggery, where I write. There are no more pigs there—just a spider's web and me and a pen and a pad of paper. I'll just sit there and write and get up and pace.

Sometimes a day for me is sitting on a plane. Last year, it took thirty-six hours to get to New Zealand. Thirty-six straight hours. I got to New Zealand and there was a reception for storytellers, then the festival began, just like that. That's a real part of my life, just sitting in an airport, sitting in a plane.

The work is unusual. We're swimming against the great tide of television and the movies. These are wonderful entertaining things that involve billions and billions of dollars. Storytelling is just the opposite. Storytelling is inviting and personal. It's human. It deals with language and life and emotions. In that sense, it deals with the reason why we're all here. But it does so in a personal way and that's unusual.

Storytelling is not sitting in a study. Storytelling is being with people. It's a wonderful thing to do. If you become a storyteller, you'll meet some very strong and some very unusual and some very wonderful people around the world.

Gay Ducey: I think I represent an odd amalgam. I'm the kind of storyteller who also has another job and it happens to be walking a spider's web in between both of them. I'm a children's librarian half the week, and I'm on the road half the week. I teach to bisect those two jobs.

You have to not mind drinking really bad coffee. You have to be willing to perform in auditoriums of any size and nature, anyplace in the world and still find them home. One of the reasons I'm still doing both is that when I walk into the library, I know that I'm a part of a community. It stays there and waits for me to come. When I walk into a storytelling performance, it's to create a community and to find the difference between the two. When I'm at the library, I know that I am the center of children's lives. I can't walk down the street without having a number of young people talk with me, which is a great pleasure. When I'm on the road, there is a certain wonder in anonymity, of going in and doing it. Leaving that contrasts nicely with being in a community where being known is part of your job. It's like the stealth bomber of art forms.

Pleasant DeSpain: It's the life of a juggler. I'm juggling several careers at once: storyteller, author, salesman. Story is at the heart of all my work, so it's a life that nurtures instability. I never know what next month's income will be or where specifically I'll be because the phone has yet to ring. From the inside, it is a life of stable growth. Each year in this profession has led me to more and more awareness of who I am as a human being. It's also pro-

vided me with more stories to tell. It's an extremely satisfying life—the writing, the telling, working with adults, working with kids. When kids ask me at schools, "Are you rich?" or "How much do you make?" I tell them I'm a rich man because I'm wealthy in what I do.

You have to not mind drinking really bad coffee.
— Gay Ducey

Jon Spelman: The last nine-to-five job I had was the summer I was seventeen. I feel as if I've controlled much of my own life, which I like very much. That's worth lots of hassles, and a lower level of income than in many other professions, and fear about not having steady work and all those kinds of things. Freedom has its prices, but it's worth it.

Right now, particularly since I have a five-year old child, being able to work at home is a real bonus. On the other hand, working out of your home also means that your personal life and your business life get really mixed up. I've created two rooms with two desks to try to keep those things separate. But it doesn't really work, because you have to write that letter about that person who overcharged you on your tires while you're sitting at your desk also working on a story, and answering a phone call about next week's bookings, and another phone call making some arrangements for your child. A lot of things are always going on at once, usually at least five, and you have to be able to compartmentalize your mind and work on just one thing for ten minutes, if that's the only time you have.

I couldn't construct a typical day. One of the things I love about my life is that there is not a typical or average day. I might stay up until three in the morning working and not get up until ten or eleven. Or I might have to get up really early and be at a school at 7:30 in the morning, and then have the rest of the afternoon at my desk. I might travel for fifteen days in a row and perform in rural and urban, formal and informal settings, different places, every day. I might be in residence at a theater or in a community for two to three weeks.

I would rather describe what would be one version of an ideal week. The week might be this: Tuesdays and Thursdays, daytime or evening, I would have some kind of nearby community storytelling event. I'd be telling stories, or doing a workshop, or sharing stories with a special group. I'd be going to a community center, or a church, or a private occasion of some kind, or a local community college or something like that and doing an hour concert or two forty-five-minute back-to-back concerts. The other parts of those two days might be used for phone calls and getting out contracts to people. Going through check lists making sure I got back the contracts I sent out. Doing the business of talking with the woman in Texas who does my national booking, setting those things up.

In an ideal way at least two of the other days, Monday and Wednesday, would be devoted to working on new material and preparing for performances that are coming up. I now have about eighteen hours of narrative performance material available. Someone says, "We want you to do *Frankenstein* on Friday night." Maybe I haven't done it for six weeks, so I have to spend some time going back over it. That's mostly pleasurable time, and the best time is working on new material. Then, on Friday or Saturday night I'm going to perform for adults in some place that's further away. It's maybe an airplane trip away. If things are really ideal, it's an interesting place and I can take my family and I'll perform on Saturday night and on Sunday we'll go to some fascinating place together.

Carol Birch: In terms of finances, my life was often unpredictably lean and fat. In terms of inner personal stuff, it's sometimes seemed too isolated and then too overwhelming. From 1975 to 1986, I worked alone, traveled alone (which I found exhausting), and then experienced a rush of intimacy and energy with a whole bunch of people, only to find myself alone again. It was probably exacerbated by not having much of a home base. For me, there is no way I can minimize how positively being happily married and having a home have affected my life as a storyteller. I didn't enjoy years of mostly freelance work as much as I now enjoy juggling five areas of storytelling interests.

Now I work as a storyteller on the road and within a library, teach storytelling at Wesleyan University in Connecticut, produce storytelling recordings, and write about storytelling. It feels as if the gifts of storytelling now surround me, rather than feeling like I only have one way to travel on the very narrow path towards becoming "a household name." I'm so much happier since I gave up the familiar passions of "fame and fortune!"

When I started working at a library again eight years ago, the plan was to get out of debt the first year, save the down payment on a house the second, get extra savings in the bank the third year, and then quit. But working at the Chappaqua Library (New York) satisfies me in ways I never expected. It provides a deeper sense of community than I've ever known. My job there is to be part of a team and that provides a daily, and healthy, dose of ego checks. My colleagues don't need a star; they need someone to share the cycles of pleasurable and less-than-pleasurable tasks.

But I fortunately also have the freedom to work as a storyteller on the road, and my sense of community has increased there as well. The storytelling community feels like family to me—I mean with all the attendant problems *and* pleasures of an extended family. Sometimes someone is walking towards me at a festival and I swear it's just like thinking, how can I get away before he starts telling me all he's done since the last family reunion?! Or I hear someone tell a story and feel that mixture of pride and pleasure at his achievement like I felt when a niece invited me over to her apartment for the first time.

I love teaching storytelling, producing storytelling tapes, and writing about storytelling because each of these perspectives forces me to think conceptually and practically about stories and storytelling as both processes *and* products.

David Holt: I love the life I live, but a professional storyteller's life is not for everyone. There are a lot more things involved than getting up in front of an audience and performing. Here are some things you may want to think about:

You need to be self-motivated. No one is going to push you to create new material or find work. It is all up to you. You have to have that spark year after year to be successful, but that's all part of the fun.

You have to keep yourself entertained and involved, or you burn out. In my work I am always adding new material or creating a new project. That keeps me out of a rut. In my travels I explore the places I visit and try to come away with a story or song to remember the place.

Being a full-time storyteller is a business. For almost twenty years I have answered my own mail and handled most of my bookings. When I am not on the road, I'm probably at my desk. Now I have an assistant, but it still takes a lot of time negotiating, returning phone calls, juggling my schedule. It is endless and not easy to stay organized.

For most of us, traveling is part of the job—perhaps the hardest part. I bet I spend more time in airports in a year than many

people spend in a lifetime. Most of the travel time is spent alone. You must enjoy your time alone because there is a lot of it.

On the other hand, you must sincerely enjoy being around people. You'll meet lots of folks on the road. These relationships are friendly, but somewhat superficial, because you never have much time with anyone. Be ready to answer the question, "How did you get into this line of work?" about a million times. If you have a tendency towards loneliness you should consider another job.

Families can handle a traveling father or mother (if the trips aren't too long), but almost every homecoming takes some adjustment. Get used to it and don't make a federal case out of it. The traveler comes home either elated or burnt out. It is his job to fit back into the family routine. (Most travelers I have interviewed agree that there is usually a day or two of sexual awkwardness too. It part of the price you pay. Marry an understanding spouse.) If a storyteller's life still looks good to you then let me offer a few simple but very important tips:

Always keep improving. My motto is, "Be good and get better."

Be easy to get along with and not overly demanding. Promoters and presenters share information. The fact that you are flexible and enjoyable to work with will help keep the work coming your way.

Be able to do a lot of things—workshops, schools, studio work, or wait tables. If one part of your career starts to slide, you can fill in with something else. Never become dependent on one organization or one type of job.

Keep the same phone number and P.O. box address throughout your career. Make yourself easy to find.

Be available.

Get a good travel agent. It will save you a lot of time.

Find a good accountant and keep all your receipts. Almost every move you make is tax deductible. Get office help; even a part-time worker will be a great help.

Stay healthy. Being on the road is hard on you. Exercise and avoid fried food.

Never eat in a place named after the animal you are about to eat: "The Happy Cow," "The Friendly Fish," "The Perky Pig." Keep a sense of humor.

Call home every night.

WHAT WAS YOUR WORST PERFORMING EXPERIENCE?

♦ ♦ ♦ ♦

If you perform long enough, you will have a bad experience. It's guaranteed. In fact, you may have many of them. They are always painful but sometimes they are valuable in teaching us our limits. "I'll never do that again," we come away saying. Sometimes you just have to smile and perform for yourself because the situation is so horrible. At times, that doesn't even work.

David Holt says, "I have had a lot of unusual experiences but one of the weirdest and worst was a job for the tobacco industry. I was hired to play for an annual meeting of one of North Carolina's major cigarette companies. As I entered the dining room where I was to perform I noticed thousands of packs of cigarettes piled two feet high on tables around the room. Each of the five hundred guests picked up a couple of packs before they went to their table to eat.

"Everything was fine until the meal was finished. Then every single person lit up and started chain smoking. Within minutes, the room was filled with a smoke cloud, which quickly became a dense fog. By the time the performance was to start, I literally could not see the other side of the room because of the smoke. It would have been funny except that I had could hardly breathe and had to cough every few seconds. I sang "Cigarettes and Whiskey and Wild, Wild Women, They'll Drive You Crazy, They'll Drive You Insane," just to poke a little fun at them. I did a short performance out of necessity, got my check, and ran out into the fresh air. What a nightmare."

Don't let stories like this scare you, particularly if you are new to the art. Use them, instead, to help you prepare for what you may encounter. Awful things happen to everyone, from the beginner to the old pro. In fact, it is the difficult experiences that teach us the meaning of professionalism. Unless real danger is involved, we do our job to the best of our ability, giving one hundred percent every time. These true stories were terrible when they happened, but looking back they become a great source of comedy and comfort. Nightmares happen to everyone.

Donald Davis: The worst performing experience I ever had was for drunk Republicans at the Washington Hilton. After a two-hour cocktail party, about an hour-long dinner, and an interminable master of ceremonies, who spent forever introducing everyone's spouse, partner, friend, and girlfriend until at 10:30 p.m., after people had gotten there at 6 p.m., I was now supposed to be "the program." It was a killer.

What that taught me, which is important, is never to ask anybody how long I should tell, but always ask them when is this supposed to be over. Don't accept, "Oh, it doesn't matter," as an answer. It taught me to say, "Yes it does. When do the people expect to be leaving? If you don't know, let's figure that out right now. If they expect to be leaving at nine o'clock and you want an hour show, then you better have me on at eight o'clock. If you mess around, recognizing this person and that person, and giving door prizes and piddling the evening away, and you don't get me on until quarter of nine, you are going to get fifteen minutes, and you have paid the whole price."

I found that does more than anything else to move an evening along, and to really make it work. People have a tendency to let time get way out of control, and I'm surprised at how often bad experiences come from people just being worn out before it starts.

[What happened that night?]

Well, I did the best I could. But all the way through, I kept having to say to myself "I am getting paid for this." I got it over with and got out of there, and had some kind of a sense that the people there had no idea what went on. When I got up there, I thought, this is gone before it starts. It's way gone. I mean, they had paired up and made friends and were ready to leave way before I ever started. It was a killer.

Beth Horner: I was once booked for an outdoor community affair and performed on a small stage right next to a rock band. I said, "To hell with this." I finally didn't use the microphone anymore and they were mostly children, and nobody could hear me. Nobody even knew I was there. I just had a few children and kinda pulled them up on the stage with me, and I sat down and told the stories. I didn't know what to do. Those are the places people think storytelling will work and it doesn't. It doesn't work when there are so many distractions a person cannot concentrate. The difficult venues are those which have incredible amounts of distractions, like the outdoors. Give me a nice intimate theater every time.

Jackson Gillman: As any performer is well aware, there are times when a performance environment is less than hospitable. Depending on the particular piece and situation, one can absorb a varying degree of disruption. There is a certain piece in my repertoire of which I am very protective. It is an hour-long story called "Hard Knocks," which portrays a feisty adolescent and his deaf sister as they try to cope with their father's increasing alcoholism. Due to the sensitive nature of the program,

when I perform it in high school assemblies, I am very particular about trying to prevent any potential distractions.

I had occasion to perform this piece at a special school which serves as a kind of last resort for troubled youths, from elementary age on up. I am reluctant to present this program to younger children, but the administration insisted on including the lower grades. The students were a relatively wired group but as they got interested in the story, they became respectfully attentive. In the delicate parts of the story, you could literally hear a pin drop, but in this case it was a dime which rolled from the front row. It was a minor distraction, but I was glad when it finally stopped, far from its young owner.

When the boy, perhaps eleven-years-old, got up to retrieve it, however, it took a little more discipline to ignore the disturbance. But now that he had his dime again, that was the end of it—or so I thought.

To my chagrin, he dropped it again a few minutes later, shattering a dead quiet. Again the retrieval, a bit more distracting than the first time. This occurred several more times during my presentation, which was intense enough, thank you. At each drop, roll, and stop, he would stop, drop, and crawl after it. This boy wanted his dime, but not badly enough to put it in his damn pocket and leave it there. I quietly prayed that each skirmish was the last.

The story I was performing generally takes all the concentration I can muster, but this time a massive number of my brain cells were working overtime, pondering what to do the next time this "dime bomb" exploded on the floor. Try a quick, icy don't-even-think-about-it glare at him? Casually stop, drop, and crawl, and pocket it myself? No, this was just one of those supreme tests of professional mettle which I had to pass in order to receive my storytelling medal of honor. Then, after I displayed my steely cool under fire, I can take the kid backstage and execute him.

I owed it to the performers who followed me and to the boy who was simply unaware of the distraction his behavior caused, and to myself, to speak to him afterward, as tactfully as I was able, though the backstage execution idea still had its appeal. The easiest thing, of course, would have been just to forget about it and not say anything. It was over, after all, and it went very well, considering. Why bother? Because I knew I'd kick myself soundly on the way home if I didn't.

I hated this but I was going to make myself do it. I was going to approach him. No, he approached me. He was smiling. He told me he really enjoyed the show and he took my hand—to shake, I assumed. No, he gave me something. It was a dime. It was the dime. I tried refusing it, but he was insistent. He wanted me to have it. Not to have accepted it at this point would have been ungracious. My rehearsed words of reproach had no place. He was probably holding it, or trying to, the whole time to give to me afterwards. This is not a Purple Heart for injuries received in the line of fire. It was a boy's dime, made of some silver alloy, but to me, it was my battle pay and it is pure gold.

What could I say? Words failed as all I could think of to say was a very sincere, "Thank you."

Diane Ferlette: The nightmare job, or so I thought, was at a conference in San Francisco after brunch. They had a speaker before me, a woman who was in charge of the teachers. She gave a wonderful talk. She told personal stories. It was really funny, but the audience was basically white and they sat there straight-faced. I thought, I'm next. The audience didn't respond to anything that woman said. I thought, It was funny and really good, oh boy, do I have to follow that?

So I got up there and did my stories, but they were still straight-faced. I thought, I've bombed, they hate me. My purse was near the door on the side, so when I finish I'll just say, thank you, then I'll go get my purse and go out the side door and they can finish eating and have their coffee. I finished my story, and I said, "Thank you very much," and smiled. I stepped down the step and got my purse, and I was going out the back door. And they ran up to meet me. "You were wonderful. We loved you." I never would have known. They didn't show me anything.

The more I tell stories to different kinds of audiences, I'm learning different cultures respond differently and have different ways of taking things in. And you can't always think that you're failing because of the different ways people respond to stories. So that nightmare turned out to be really good. A man who was there invited me to come to his school in Australia. He knew I was going to New Zealand, and said, "Since you will be so close, can you come to Australia, to my school?" I said, "If you'll get me there." And he did, he flew me from New Zealand to his school. So you never know.

Margaret Read MacDonald: I think one of the worst ones was the very first time I told before a large group of three hundred children. I agreed to tell for a Girl Scout gathering in an elementary school gymnasium. They were to have hot dogs for their dinner and then I would tell them a story. But they ran out of hot dogs at the point when I was to go on the stage and tell a story to these three hundred milling little girls, one-third had eaten so they were happy and sat down to listen; one-third were eating and they were not listening especially; and one-third hadn't eaten and they were standing in line waiting around miserably for their food. That was one of the first times I had told to a large audience, so it was not an especially good situation and one I had no control over at that point. You try to make sure everything is going to be all right for a good performing experience, but sometimes you can get stuck. They run out of hot dogs and you're the pinch hitter to keep them quiet until the hot dogs come.

Jim May: The very expensive preschool Halloween night with children in fancy costumes. Need I say more?

Len Cabral: It was an opening of a health center in Lynn, Massachusetts. It was outdoors, just a vacant lot. They put up a tent. They put up chairs and all around is traffic. It was right downtown in a busy city and there was traffic, and all these distractions. The people came there because free orange juice and popcorn were being given out. People were just sitting in the chairs— young parents, teenage parents and just people, the unhealthiest-looking people in the world. I couldn't wait for the show to be over. It was a short show because they didn't have a mike stand. They had a rinky-dink sound system. Somebody went in and came out with one of those gooseneck lamps, a floor model gooseneck lamp. They got some duct tape and taped the microphone on the lamp. There was this big silver lamp shade and tied just above it was the microphone. It was terrible. I talked about twenty minutes and got out of there. That was it.

Milbre Burch: The one unrelated child's birthday party I ever agreed to do is deeply etched in my memory. I knew I'd made a mistake as soon as the parents said they'd meet my price. But, hey, why not, they'd already forked over for a meeting room at the Marriott and invited innumerable costumed six-year-olds to run amok therein. Bad signs followed bad premonitions. The adults stood on one side of the room drinking wine, and a videotape of "Ghostbus-

ters" played continuously next to the buffet. The birthday boy was on top of one of his guests, pummeling that boy's head into the wall-to-wall carpet in between runs to the TV set to replay the moment in the movie when Sigourney Weaver levitates off the bed. Needless to say, it wasn't one of my finer moments as an artist, but it did teach me to listen to my guts about that kind of gig.

Jay O'Callahan: One of my worst was performing for an annual dentists' dinner. It was in Worcester, Massachusetts, and there were maybe two hundred dentists and all their staffs. So there were five or six hundred people, all their secretaries, and their wives. They're all eating and I'm on this enormous stage, and I was new enough not to realize they just needed short stories. Ideally, they needed somebody up there singing, someone to make them laugh and go home.

I started to tell "Magellan." This is a forty-five-minute story that you have to be silent for. It's a historical story, and you have to concentrate. Some people like history and some people certainly don't, but you probably won't like it at your annual dinner when you're there to have a few drinks and relax. I started in on "Magellan" and I realized within five minutes I was sailing alone. The other six hundred people went on talking and laughing, paying no attention except for the poor head table who were very close to the stage, so they had to crane their necks, and Magellan sailed for forty-five minutes. At the end, a few people from the head table applauded. The others looked up and realized this guy was gone.

Judith Black: Big mistake: Not knowing who your audience is. I got a call from a friend who needed a sub the following night to entertain the Superior Court judges of Massachusetts after a day-long workshop and evening meal. The word was: don't be childish and don't be too risque. I thought to myself, "This will be a group of sophisticated, politically savvy adults. I'll play with political humor, do some 'wise judge' type tales and round the night out with a couple jokes. Piece of cake."

Piece of death. The first joke with a gentle sexual edge was received with silence from the men (their wives chuckled slightly). The second story, a political satire of the right fell like a lead balloon into molten lava. They listened to nothing else. The upshot was that this was a very self-involved, conservative, male-dominated group, that was used to being adulated, not teased. After a hideous sixty minutes I crawled away, knowing I had not served my audience. Now, in hindsight, I would have done the same material (these folks needed some nudging), only the order would have been different. You see, you can't take anyone on a trip unless you pick them up where they live. I should have begun with the heartwarming "wise judge" material, allied with them and gently moved toward the left. Live and learn.

Pleasant DeSpain: I was giving a school program sponsored by a State Arts Commission. I got to the school and the gym was full of fourth, fifth, and sixth graders. About ten minutes into the program, ten buses arrived and in marched another school. The principal had invited his principal-buddy's school to come and listen. Everything stopped and they told me what was happening. The gym was so over-packed, it was unbelievable how many kids they stuffed in. They said, "Well, let's get started again." I had to pick it up from that point. But fifteen minutes into a great story, the school that arrived late got up *en-mass* and walked out. They had to get back. That took another ten to fifteen minutes. Then the bell rang. The principal said, "I

guess I didn't plan this very well, did I?" I was left with a hollow feeling. I was angry. I had a long talk with the people who run the Arts Commission. That was really the worst.

Joseph Bruchac: I was asked to do a program in Albany, New York, at the state capitol rotunda as part of an outdoor festival. I was supposed to do this program in front of a hot air balloon as it was being launched, and about every five words I spoke, they turned on the burner of the balloon and the roaring sound drowned everything out, and the wind began to blow, and the balloon was moving back and forth behind me. I couldn't see it, but I could see everyone in the crowd swaying first to the right, then to the left, then looking up, then looking down. I don't even remember when I finished what I was doing.

Jon Spelman: I can remember being in a junior high school in an upper middle-class community where everybody, including the teachers, talked so much that I stopped several times in the middle of a story and asked for attention. I'd say something like, "Adults, would you please stop talking because I think it's encouraging the kids." Nothing worked, so I finally said, "I'm going to start this story again, but if you all are still talking, I'm going to leave." I started it again, they kept talking, I said, "I'm going to leave … You see I'm now leaving … I'm picking up my things and I'm leaving." And they didn't notice, so I left. I'm not sure they ever knew I left. For all I know they could still be sitting there talking to each other.

Steve Sanfield: San Francisco Children's Festival! It sounded wonderful to me on the surface. When I got there, the storytelling stage that I was to tell on was sandwiched between a merry-go-round on one side and a man with an organ grinder and a monkey on the other side. No micro-phone! That was absolutely the worst experience I have had. I told one story. It was so perverse to me that I stood there and—you know, hundreds of people milling around—I stood there and mouthed the story without uttering a word. And nobody seemed to notice that I wasn't saying a thing.

Susan Klein: Walking into a junior high and having the principal say to the audience, "You haven't had any kind of assembly for three years because you don't know how to behave, and if you don't behave today, you are not going to get another for the rest of your school lives—please welcome Susan Klein." Then trying to let the audience know that I appreciated each and everyone of them as a human being with thoughts and feelings and the ability for us to create something together was the hardest damn work I have ever done in my life, because this fool only wanted to show that he was an authoritative power, and he didn't care about anything that was going on and it was real hard.

Carol Birch: Superficially, saying, "Grandma, what big EYES you have. The better to EAT you with, my dear." I was telling "Red Riding Hood" and actually said that. I learned as much from the recovery as I did from the mistake. I learned that an audience will help you when they can. "Boys and girls," I said, "Did my tongue get ahead of the story?" Yes, they nodded solemnly. "Would you help me?" I asked. They nodded again. And I began saying, "The line goes: 'Grandma, what big eyes you have' and she says …" I couldn't remember the next line and they could, so they said, "The better to SEE you with, my dear." That must have happened nearly twenty years ago.

David Novak: At a high school in China-town in New York City; I was the wrong teller in the wrong place at the wrong time. I was outside of my cultural loop. I had non-English speakers, many with poor language skills, through no fault of their own. I had a very angry inner-city audience and there was racial tension. I arrived with a collection of stories that I had been commissioned by Lincoln Center to tell. These stories were extremely verbal. I got there and one of the teachers said, "I know your stories are wordy. I wonder if you could make them a little less wordy?" The whole point of my program was working with language. I was really in a bind, because I was commissioned to tell these specific stories and yet I was in an impossible situation to tell them. Halfway through my performance, I was being heckled by a couple of kids in the audience. I stopped and announced to the audience that I was going to go offstage and wait a while until this calms down and come back when they were ready to listen. The teacher confronted the students that were heckling me. Well, there was a fight between the teacher and the students. Finally the student was hauled out of the room and things began again. I cut to the last story and got out of there as quickly as I could. It was an awful experience. The big reason it was so awful was because my prerogative to respond to my audience as a storyteller was denied me.

Elizabeth Ellis: When I was telling at an outdoor event and discovered about midway through my first story that I was standing in an anthill. It was memorable. In Texas, ants bite.

Several years back when gauze shirts were popular for women, my mother sent me a very breezy gauze top which I thought would look great for telling stories. It was quite suitable for Texas weather, but I took it to Wisconsin. The wind was blowing very hard when I got onstage. I ended up spending the entire set trying to fight my shirt down. It kept trying to blow over my head. The audience found it very entertaining—much more so than I did.

Gayle Ross and I once told stories at a library that had an outdoor performance space. They didn't tell us it was between two major thoroughfares. It was like telling stories at the end of an off-ramp. We were trying to tell in tandem. We were standing just a few inches from one another and literally could not hear a word the other was saying. I don't know how the audience could have heard anything we said. It was exactly like telling on the median of a freeway to passing cars.

Barbara McBride-Smith: I was storytelling in a mall. I look back now and think, why in the world did I agree to do that? I was telling between Roger Rabbit—the movie had just come out—on one side and the Easter Bunny on the other side. It was awful. I didn't have candy to give away. I didn't have balloons to give away. All I had were good stories to give away. It was horrible. I have never again told stories in a mall.

Bill Mooney: I was performing the poems and stories of e. e. cummings in a one-man theater piece entitled *Damn Everything But The Circus* at the American Theater in Washington, D.C. The notices had been good, but neither cummings nor I could attract much of a midweek crowd. On this Tuesday night in the second week of a three-week run, we had maybe one hundred and twenty-five paid admissions in a six hundred seat house.

Midway during the first act, a little boy started running up and down the left aisle slapping down the seat cushions and laughing uproariously as they sprang back. I didn't know why anyone would bring a

child to this sophisticated-language program in the first place. But I really couldn't understand why someone—his parents, the ushers, the house manager, *anybody*—didn't quickly get him under control. It finally got so bad, I had to stop the show and ask that something be done about the child. The audience applauded. I thought everything was OK, so I started again. The child started running up the aisle and banging the seats again. I stopped the show once more and begged that the boy be taken away. This time it worked. But cummings' material is fragile, it needs a special atmosphere. I knew there was a big tear in the first act that couldn't be mended.

At intermission, I learned from the house manager that the little boy was the son of foreigners. They had only been in the U.S. a short time. The mother had seen me on television, so she brought her family to the cummings show not knowing what it was about and speaking only a few words of English. She had not understood what I was talking about when I asked that her son be contained. She thought it was part of the performance.

After intermission, I launched with renewed vigor into the second act, the beginning of which is extremely delicate and difficult to perform. After about five minutes, I noticed that a great many people from the center orchestra section were getting up and leaving. I was furious. I kept thinking, damn, they had the entire first act plus the intermission to figure out whether they liked the piece or not. If they were going to leave, why didn't they leave then?

I kept pushing through. After a couple of minutes I saw some people returning to the orchestra section and they had flashlights. By this time I was fit to be tied. I thought, damn! Not only have they decided to leave in the middle of my piece, but they forgot their purses and now they've come back with flashlights to find them! More people got up and left. I watched the flashlights flicker and flit around for what seemed like a century before these folks finally found what they were looking for and left. I managed to wallow through to the end of the show, but I was rattled beyond belief. I kept wondering when the next bomb was going to drop.

At the curtain call I apologized to the audience and offered them free tickets for any of my remaining shows. "Come back and see a real performance," I said, "not this fiasco we've just gone through."

The house manager informed me later that two women in the center section had become sick to their stomachs and one of them had actually thrown up (not due to my performance, surely!). The crowd around them had moved to get away from the smell. But the women felt bad about the mess they'd caused, went someplace, armed themselves with flashlights, buckets and mops, and came back into the auditorium to clean it up while cummings and I slogged away on stage.

It took me several weeks to find any humor in this story. It took me several months before I could tell it to anyone without breaking out in a cold sweat. I've been through some rough times on stage, but this one sticks in my memory as the worst.

HOW CAN A TEACHER USE
STORYTELLING IN THE CLASSROOM?

◆ ◆ ◆ ◆

Every person interviewed for this chapter is or has been a public school teacher. They all have had extensive experience telling stories in the classroom. They all have seen how stories can be at the core of the curriculum, regardless of the subject matter. Each one of them stresses that no special skills are needed in order to tell stories. Our experts agree that you can start telling stories tomorrow and be effective.

We know that teachers are busy people. We know that school schedules, over-crowded classrooms, administrative responsibilities, and a hundred other duties and obligations leave little time for absorbing different methods of teaching.

The use of stories in the classroom is arguably the most effective teaching tool we have. Stories not only capture our attention and entertain us, but they teach us. Stories teach on many different levels. They also help us, through association, to remember important facts. Stories help us to understand ourselves and the people around us. Both the listener and the storyteller see themselves reflected in the stories that are told. Stories teach us about other cultures, both modern and ancient. Stories are a terrific way to convey factual information, from how plants develop to how numbers work.

When stories are told in the classroom, students get to hear new language patterns. We all learn by modeling ourselves after people we admire. When teachers tell stories from their own lives, it helps the student grapple with immediate questions of ethics, morality, and civics.

We anticipate your cries of "I'm not a storyteller! I can't tell stories!" or "Tell stories! I can barely get through the lesson plan as it is!" Each person interviewed speaks directly to these concerns. We are convinced that stories can be used as the core of a curriculum.

Roberta Simpson Brown: I've never seen a classroom where storytelling couldn't be used easily and effectively to teach any subject. I've taught for twenty-nine years, seven years in high school and twenty-two years in the same middle school. I've used storytelling the whole time. I really do believe that storytelling is the best device a teacher can use in a classroom. It's saved me in a lot of situations.

Kentucky has the Kentucky Education Reform Act (KERA). This act mandates that students have to have portfolios filled with specific pieces of writing from different classes. One piece that is required is a personal narrative. To get my students started, I do a unit on short stories at the be-

ginning of the year. I use some of my scary stories to get them started on their personal narrative. I tell them I want their first personal narrative to be a scary story. It doesn't have to be a ghost story like one of mine. It can be something funny that scared them. They work with that idea because the stories in class have given them ideas for their own experience.

Our faculty works hard to get parents and members of the neighborhood involved in our school. Each year, I have students do an interview with their parents or some older person in the neighborhood to get a story to share in class. I invite parents and neighbors to come in and tell their own stories. Three or four each year actually take me up on it and come into the classroom and tell their stories. Students take more pride in their roots and their community when they hear these stories shared in class. These stories that they haven't paid much attention to at home take on a new importance when they hear them in school. Of course, in the process of interviewing, writing, telling, and listening, they are also learning basic communication skills to use in every class or real situations.

[Do you have them tell their stories, or just write them?]

I have them do both. They write them first, but then they must tell them to the class. They may tell up front or we may sit in a circle, but they can't just read the story. Most of them actually come through. Only a few want just to read. If I am doing workshops with students too young to write, I will allow them to draw a picture and tell about it. I say, "Give your fear a face and give it a name." We talk about how, if you have a fear, you really have to identify it before you can deal with it. Then they tell a story about what they have drawn. It's very interesting.

[You teach in an inner-city school, right?]

Yes. It's nicely called "a troubled area." It's an area that includes families with their own homes, but also many low-income housing projects, single-parent homes, or broken homes. More than eighty percent of our students are on free or reduced-price lunches, and some are into drugs and alcohol and bring weapons to school. One or two gangs tried to get started, but we were lucky to keep them out. It is an extremely difficult group of kids to reach.

[How do they respond to your stories?]

It's amazing. Behavior and interest improve dramatically. If I'm just "teacher," they don't respond nearly as well. But if I tell stories, they are really hooked on them.

[Has listening to stories helped elongate their attention spans?]

Absolutely. They hardly move while a story is being told. I think it's the human connection that hooks them. We have a closed-circuit TV system in the school and the news is broadcast over it every morning. It's a battle to get the kids to pay attention all the way through. I was asked to come and tell a story on the news in celebration of Black History Month, so I told a short ghost story about a group of slaves who died for their freedom. Later, many teachers said to me, "I can't believe how they actually listened." Several students said to me, "I wish you would tell us a story every day."

[Have other teachers picked up your cue and started telling stories?]

Some have, but I think most are hesitant to tell stories themselves. Some invite me to tell in their classrooms. Too many teachers—and even librarians—think you've got to be a professional storyteller to tell stories. That's simply not true. More than any other point, I hope this point gets across to regular classroom teachers. I told stories before I was a professional. Just be yourself and tell your stories! It really gets the students going.

There's a Jack tale that I use when I'm teaching sentence expansion and the use of clauses and phrases. I'm not really into Jack tales but I heard a great storyteller and friend, Mary Hamilton, tell a Jack tale in which Jack gets only one wish and he is not allowed to wish for other wishes. He has twenty-four hours to think it over, so he goes home and tells his wife and blind mother-in-law, who lives with them. His wife wants a child. His mother-in-law wants to see, and Jack wants gold, so he won't have to work. Finally, he figures out how to have it all. He says to the wishgiver, "I wish that my mother-in-law could see my child eat off gold plates for the rest of our lives." Then someone will say, "Well, Jack didn't say anything about his wife." So someone else will say that Jack could wish for his mother-in-law to see his wife and child eat off the gold plates. Another will say, "Why doesn't he add *long, healthy* lives, instead of just saying lives?" They keep expanding the sentence. It works much better than opening a grammar book and saying, "I want you to combine this list of short, choppy sentences for me."

[Do you tell them stories that relate to them?]

Yes, I try to. Since I specialize in scary stories, I want to tell things that relate to them, because it's the familiar things that scare us most of all. My tape *The Scariest Stories Ever* has my story "Lockers" that I wrote about our school. The kids ask for it over and over. It's set in a school where an intruder stealing money is discovered by a little girl in the locker room. The man cuts out her tongue so she can't tell about him, and she dies. He thinks some students who happen in and run for help can identify him, so every year this crazy man comes back to school looking for anyone out in the hall after the final bell. When the killer is near, the ghost of the little girl bangs on the lockers to warn the other students. You're probably not warped enough to tell my stories, but, believe me, this story makes students aware of the national problem of intruders in the school.

If I really want to be mean and stress the point even more, I go down the hall behind them and bang on a locker. Lockers are familiar. They see rows of them everyday. The story makes them think about the fact that even familiar things are not safe.

I don't always tell scary stories to frighten them. These stories are exciting and they hook the students on reading! They also serve as excellent springboards to help students discuss fears, consequences of violence, and ways to deal with

these things. Urban legends are often helpful in teaching because they touch on subjects that relate to the lives of our students. Our students' lives are often filled with scary things. Once we deal with that, we can move them on to things more sensitive and beautiful.

When I teach character development, I use "The Crack of Dawn" by Donald Davis. It's a beautiful, sensitive story about Donald's Aunt Laura who was a "floater." A floater is a person who lives with one set of relatives for three months or so, and then moves on to another and another. I had a wonderful Uncle Charlie like that. I didn't know that the stories about the floaters would relate so well to my students when I started using them, but because of the homeless problem, a lot of my students have relatives who have had to move in with them. I got a flood of stories and character sketches because of my Uncle Charlie story and Donald's story of his Aunt Laura.

Stories make students more sensitive to the needs of others. We had a tornado warning at our school last spring and we had to stay in the hall for some time waiting for the signal that the storm front had passed. Many students (and even a few adults) called down the hall to ask if I thought my story "The Storm Walker" would help us. The story was as real in the spring as when I introduced it in the fall. Two sixth-grade boys invited me to kneel by them because they knew that I'm terrified of storms. "We're praying," they said. It was a shock to me to hear these boys admit they were frightened and praying in front of their friends. Almost everyone told me in some way that they had found comfort in my "Storm Walker" that day.

[I don't know of anything that leads kids to reading and writing faster than stories.]

I don't, either. They keep my books checked out all the time, and when I tell someone else's stories, they look for the book with that story in the library. I use "Owl" from Diane Wolkstein's book *The Magic Orange Tree* when I'm talking about self-esteem, because most of our students have low self-esteem. In this story, Owl thinks he's ugly and tries to hide his face from his future bride. Her mother exposes his face, however, and Owl is so horrified that he runs away and never comes back. The girl's heart is broken, because, to her, he had the most handsome face she'd ever seen. They read the book because of that story.

Since my own books have been published, students from my classes and from other classes that I don't teach bring me at least half a dozen stories each week and ask me to read them. It is very exciting to me when a student writes something for the satisfaction of writing it and not just because it is an assignment. The stories definitely lead to that.

[You think teachers can use stories no matter what they're teaching?]

Definitely. My health teacher in the eighth grade was a wonderful storyteller who told about health problems in books like *Forever Amber*, without the steamy stuff. My history teacher made history come alive through stories. There are endless possibilities in science for exciting stories. You don't have to polish stories up into an act and take it on the road. Just put the stories in your own words. Teaching is a tough job. Storytelling can make it a lot easier.

Syd Lieberman: When I taught high school, I told stories in the classroom. Kids need to hear stories from their teachers. They really want to know who you are and what you stand for. I don't think they hear enough stories from the adults around them. Kids are in the identity business at that age. They are trying to discover who they are. They are thirsty to find out what

adults really stand for and what they believe, so they can identify with them or reject them. They need to know who the adults are.

I don't think we let them know enough about who we are. We tell them what to do, but we don't actually live with them and reveal who we are to them. I think that's important for kids to hear so they can discover who they are.

I'm color-blind, so when I get dressed in the morning I always get advice on what to wear. I have a funny story about being color-blind that I always tell to the kids, which has to do with not being neurotic about things. I'm always telling that story, because I'm always making this point about being neurotic. I'm a little neurotic when it comes to art. The other day a kid comes up to me and says, "Mr. Leiberman, you be dressed well." That's OK. He's identifying with that somehow.

I also use stories in a particular way. If I want to make a point, a real point, I always make it by telling them a story. When kids think you are getting off the subject, they suddenly wake up. I use that to my advantage. When I really want to teach them something, I always drop a little story in there to get their attention. It's like watching fish come out of the sea. Kids pick their heads up.

The other way to use storytelling in the classroom is to get the kids telling stories. When you get a kid telling a story out of his own life and it's good, you're validating the kid. You're saying to the kid, "What a thing you did!" The more that happens in public, the more validation the kid gets. Even if the kid doesn't tell the story, but has written a story, I will read it in the class, so that the kid can watch the others in class. I do the reading so that the kid can hear the laughter. I want the kid to actually see the people as I'm reading. I think it's important to get kids telling stories out of their own lives.

A lot of times a kid will leave the story in his head and not get it down on paper. One way to get it out of his head is to have him tell the story. Usually I have the class ask questions about things they want to know more about. That's how we get the story. Kids will leave things out. They are unsure. Either they don't know what's important, or a lot of times they think they're going to bore you with the details. A lot of times they leave the *golden* story out. They're not good with stories yet. They don't know why they're writing it or what's important. I get kids up telling stories a lot to help flesh out the writing. I don't try to make them storytellers. I think they have too much to do to make them do that.

Elizabeth Ellis: Storytelling is one of the most useful tools that a teacher can have in her bag of tricks. There are loads of reasons for using storytelling: to use as an attention-getter, to focus the class, to introduce a concept, to provide a transition from one activity to another, to change a mood when something unpleasant has happened in the classroom, to stimulate discussion, to build community, to offer a reward, and to provide closure.

Storytelling is a classroom management technique. When I taught, storytelling was extremely useful to me as a way of managing my class. I don't hear people talk much about that, but I think it can be a very valuable way to tell people things you want them to know without preaching to them. Stories help people see other people's points of view. I have been involved in several situations where unpleasant things happened and the telling of stories seemed to be the very best way to change the mood in the room and move on from the unpleasantness.

[Syd Lieberman says that if you want to get the class's attention, tell them a story because they think you're deviating from the lesson plan.]

Right. And it may be a long time before they realize that the story was a part of the lesson plan or the story *was* the lesson.

[How would you respond to teachers who say, "I have so little time to cover what is in the lesson plan, I don't have time to tell stories?"]

I'd say you don't have time *not* to. Since you have such a short time with the children, you have to use the most effective method possible of reaching them. That means telling them stories.

[So you think stories are a good didactic method as well as being a pure gift.]

Absolutely. They are powerful enough to be both at the same time. All the things I mentioned as classroom management techniques are valid reasons for telling stories. The stories the teacher selects to tell would be decided by her curriculum needs, what academic goals she has. The opportunity for children to learn to care about what you are trying to teach them is in the framework of a story. You cannot teach somebody what they do not want to know. No matter how hard you try. So utilizing the story gives me the opportunity to help the children care about what they need to know, whether it be a scientist who made a discovery or a historical period that we're learning about or a composer. Nearly anything that you want children to know can be presented to them in a story format. And much more powerfully than giving them the material in some flat lifeless form. I can't imagine children in middle school hearing the story of Galileo and not being on fire to learn about science.

Margaret Read MacDonald: There are so many ways that stories can tie right into the curriculum. Stories strengthen the kids' listening skills. They strengthen speaking skills. They can stretch kids' imaginations. You can always pick classroom themes to develop stories around. All of these are important ways that story can be taken into the classroom and justified.

It's probably worth mentioning that storytelling has been used by cultures as a teaching device for centuries. Stories have always been used in just about every culture as a way to teach. When you wrap an idea in a story, you sneak it in very quietly. People get the point without being hit over the head with it. So you can use stories to teach concepts and ideas and morals.

[Isn't it Johnny Moses—a Native American storyteller from Washington—who says that he never heard his grandmother refer to them as stories—she always called them simply "the lessons"?]

The idea of using story as a teaching device is as old as mankind. It's important to keep using it. But beyond the actual teaching-value of story I feel it's important for teachers to use storytelling as a way to connect to children. When you tell them a story, it's a one-to-one relationship. It's a gift that you're giving from your inner self, and they really sense that.

When the book is put away and it's just you and them and the story, there's a closeness that comes from that kind of relationship that is very enduring. It's something the students remember long after they've forgotten the lessons and everything else. They remember that moment of closeness with this other adult individual who was sharing stories with them.

I think that closeness is very important. It is more important than any other reason for telling a story. It's so important that I think it is the most important reason why stories must be told by teachers. They absolutely must take the time to sit down and share stories with children.

Teachers tend to think that storytelling is a big event, that they have to take time and plan it way ahead. Then they have to somehow work it into the curriculum and make it fit. Teachers don't stop to realize that a story takes—what?—seven minutes

to tell? They can find seven minutes in a day. They really can. They can sit the kids down for seven minutes and tell them a story. It will make such a big difference in the lives of those children, and the way the teachers relate to them.

So teachers have to be encouraged to make the time to tell stories and not worry about whether it's in the curriculum, not worry whether it's going to be something that teaches a great lesson. They just need to share the story for the joy of the story itself. They need to make story spots in their classroom life where they can just sit down and share a story.

I should mention how useful storytelling is for substitute teachers. They find having a story or two or three a useful tool when they are subbing. They take the story out of their pocket—it's a fun thing—and it helps relax a class and draw them toward you. It also makes them feel more open toward you. So substitute teachers seem to like to use story quite a bit. That's the great thing about storytelling. Once you're hooked, you're hooked!

Mark Wagler: Many people have the unfortunate image of storytelling that somebody else can do it better. These feelings of inadequacy get in the way when people think consciously about telling stories. Teachers are some of our most fluent speakers. They listen well. They notice things. They know their audience. They're theatrically precise in the classroom. But the minute someone from the outside comes in and watches them, or the minute we name it "storytelling," they suddenly freeze and say, "I can't tell stories!"

When I was teaching storytelling workshops, I'd say, "Listen, you teachers can impress people with the beauty and power of your storytelling better than any professional group I've ever encountered. Just think. Who else gets to speak and listen as constantly as you do? A minister? A half-hour to forty-five minutes a week. You teachers talk and improvise all day long. You are masters of storytelling!"

It's so important for teachers to use stories constantly, because kids learn the power of language by listening, by using the whole process of oral-to-written language. Storytelling is our native language.

When the talking professionals (teachers, therapists, the clergy, et cetera) hear a professional storyteller, they usually don't realize they're listening to polished pieces. I hardly ever tell my polished stories to the students. Why should I? If you and I were sitting around a dinner table, would we bore each other with our polished stories? No. They're what you do for strangers. The really good stuff is stories about who we are.

It's sad when people hear the eloquent trained voice and exquisitely presented language of the professional storyteller and then think, I wish I could tell stories that way. But because I can't, I won't tell stories. They think that everything else that is truly story isn't really storytelling. But most stories told around our dinner tables, at barbershops, in courts of law, are not long historical legends or biographies. Most of them are not folktales or epics. Most are personal stories that incorporate bits and pieces of folktales and epics. The predominant shape of storytelling in our culture is the stuff that pops up everywhere.

I'd been a professional storyteller for seven years, but I kept coming back to teaching. I'd previously taught in an Amish-Mennonite school, an alternative elementary school, in a community college, and a state university. Teaching and stories were central to my life, obviously. In every workshop and residency I did, I kept being challenged by the question, "How is story a part of curriculum?" I had lots of lovely ideas. I would offer them in hundreds of workshops for teachers.

It was around this time that I made a decision not to spend my life on the road as a professional storyteller, but to be at home with my family and my community. So I returned to teaching. I immediately tried to see whether all those things I'd been saying about the use of stories would really work. Wherever I went, people were asking, "Could you do this? Can you do that?" I was constantly improvising curriculum. I believed I could teach anything using stories. So when I got into the classroom, it didn't take long before I saw that I was not able to teach in the standard way.

I would come in the morning and write out a schedule like the other teachers. But I couldn't keep to it. Things always surprised me and we'd go off in another direction. After a year or so of this, I finally asked, "Can I just combine all of this curriculum in a carefully thought-out coherent sequence of units?"

A narrative classroom has to be far more deeply connected. A narrative structure in the classroom means there is so much present that we actually can't control the whole thing. Everything is present. The past several days in my classroom we've been moving from event to event. There is no way I can plan and foresee and understand the whole thing. It's like a prairie.

Traditional classrooms are like corn fields. The farmer plows the whole field at one time. One type of corn is planted with a standard distance between the rows. Every row receives the same amount of fertilizer. Each plant should look about the same and will be harvested at the same time. A very simple structure.

My classroom is more like a prairie. The grasses, insects, mice, and hawks co-evolve. Each species is dependent on countless others and also on soil and climate. A prairie is difficult to establish, but in place it endures—a very complex structure. We can be like Thoreau and study it forever. It's not a curriculum that can be mastered.

It has endless depth to it. There are infinite surprises. Every possibility in the world is potentially there, until we make a choice and limit it for that moment.

[How would you describe your school day?]

I think of my days in the classroom as rituals, but not rituals as in "repeated." I think of them as certain ritual structures that have a *shape* that is repeated, but the content changes constantly. Then we have the projects we do. Finally, there are the surprises.

First thing the kids do in the morning is sit down and write. When the fourth-graders first enter my classroom, they often write about three sentences and think, "We're about done now." They look around at all the fifth-graders still writing. "They've finished a page already! My gosh, what's going on in this classroom?!"

The first few days, I'll say, "Who still needs more time to write?" The fourth-graders see most of the hands going up. For a kid who doesn't write very much, he's thinking, "What's going on here?" You see, I have continuity. I have half my kids coming back. Most times they have total freedom of what to write. That's frightening at the beginning. But the first thing in the morning, the students write. I make it sound like we don't have quite enough time for writing and reading. So it's like, "Oh boy, we're going to have to really get to it!"

[How do you have a mixed class of fourth and fifth graders?]

I asked for it.

Because of the way in which I teach, there is nothing I do different for fourth and fifth graders except deal with the public. So for two years we are a community. You enter as a beginner and you leave as a kind of master.

After they write, the kids come up front. My room, as my kids describe it, is a little more like home. There are three couches in a "U" shape against a long wall. That's where we meet for large group events. There are tables scattered around the room, along with various dividing objects like bookshelves and sandboxes. There's a computer and a modem. There's lots of lab stuff, animals, and plants. There are chess sets everywhere. When you walk in, it doesn't look like a classroom. So the kids operate in that space.

The kids come up front and it's time to read. Sometimes I struggle because more kids wanted to read than they have time to. They love to read from their journals. Mostly they write stories. They write stories about their lives. They also make up stories. Currently the rage is making up pretend stories about our classroom.

They write, they edit, and then they come up to read. It's always the same. It's as comfortable as getting up and having breakfast. I am very fierce in that time frame. There is absolutely no talking during writing. Nobody speaks except the person who is reading. Nobody comments. Nobody makes judgments. Nobody asks questions. I'm the only one who comments during the reading time. I reflect on structure. I ask questions, tell things I delight in, but essentially I teach writing by highlighting the things that are happening.

Everything the kids need to know about writing appears. I'll make some comment, have some interaction, but it's always brief. I might just say, "Mmmmm," and then go to the next person. They never know how I'm going to respond. That's part of just being there with our stories.

I don't want to make this sound like it's nothing but heaven. Many kids come in with a lot of pain. There are kids who have been failures many times in their lives. They struggle. We get angry at each other. There are a lot of things that happen. I love the class, and I think my kids take delight in being there. But there are times when it is too much, like any other area of school. Because my kids are writers, they're able to do independent science and math. If they weren't writers and they watched a snake for a few minutes, there would be nothing to do. They would just be seeing the snake. But because they are writers and they can write endlessly detailed descriptions, they can describe every movement of the snake, every little pattern, every shape, every question that comes to their mind. They can sit there for a half an hour looking at a snake. If they weren't writers, we couldn't do independent science. They couldn't do their independent math explorations.

Today we were working on prime numbers. The kinds of things we do depend on the kids loving to write. Even with the kids' writing that you can barely read—some of the fourth graders' grammar is quite poor—they're fluent. They write a tremendous amount.

I changed my idea about what it is to be a teacher. I decided a teacher should be someone who is also involved in the inquiry, someone who is both developing mastery and is involved in inquiry. When I worked in a lab, no one sat around giving lectures all day about what was already known. You're always working what you don't know.

The math we teach in schools is usually teaching people how to be clerks. But mathematicians don't spend their time talking about what they know. They spend their time taking what they don't know and exploring it, using what they know as tools. The only thing a mathematician is interested in is what he doesn't know. Isn't it lovely to be in a classroom where you get to do that all day long? So I'm constantly nurtured by what I don't know. That's the place where my delight lies.

Their assignment sometimes is to write their autobiography. They have to interview people. They have to look at documents from their family. Every night they have homework to write about culture.

About three years ago, I told my kids, "The entire curriculum this year is about *paying attention*." Then the next year (I had a lot of my fourth graders returning for their fifth year), I said, "The curriculum this year is about imagining the world we want to live in, and then creating it. That's the entire curriculum." The new kids just stared at me. The older ones who had been with me for a year said, "Ye-e-e-a-a-ah, that's Mr. Wagler."

Flora Joy: Walk into practically any classroom and say, "Students, get out your textbooks," and hear their moans and groans. Walk into the same classroom and say, "I have a story for you," and you will hear a completely different reaction. Teachers and storytellers need to empower themselves with stories to help them with practically every aspect of the curriculum. Teachers can create "teachable moments" for building any or all academic skills. And when they do, they'll watch their students' motivational levels soar.

"I would love to have storytelling sessions in my classroom," I heard a bright young teacher say, "but I don't have time. I have to teach the *skills*." How unfortunate, but her statement reflects the attitude of many teachers. They seem to think that storytelling in the classroom either wastes time or fails to build academic skills, but just the opposite is true. Storytelling can be used to enhance all language and/or communication skills as well as the skills in every other subject in the curriculum. It builds a positive attitude toward learning.

Let me show you how an old folktale, "The Turnip," can be used to play a vital part in the classroom curriculum. It's a simple story about an old man's attempt to pull an enormous turnip out of the ground. He can't pull it out by himself, so he calls his wife to help him. The two of them can't do it either, so they get additional help from, first, their farm animals, then their house pets. Finally, it's a tiny mouse that makes the difference, and the turnip gets pulled up.

This story has many possibilities for educational enhancement. When I tell it, I gather the children close in front of me. I ask them if they know what turnips are, where they grow, what they taste like, etc. Then I place cut-out felt letters—T H E T U R N I P—on a flannelboard or on the floor and announce that I'm going to tell them a story about an *enormous* turnip. The story has lines that are said over and over, so I encourage the kids to say them with me if they wish. Then I tell the story, giving them a chance to *hear* the melodic, the rhythmic, the repetitive flow of language. Soon they join me saying,

"… The old man tugged at the turnip,
The old woman tugged at the old man,
The dog tugged at the old woman,
They pulled and they tugged
They tugged and they pulled
But the turnip would not come out of the ground …"

These lines are repeated each time there's a new tugger. The children soon begin to join in. Thus the communication skills of enunciation, phrasing, fluency, et cetera, are being reinforced and practiced. Also, they are verbalizing appropriate sentence structure, appropriate grammatical language subtleties, et cetera, all of which are vital to thought preparation in both oral and written language.

After I finish telling the story, I give them a copy of it along with some flannel-board characters I've made. I put the story in a "Story Box" and encourage the children to tell it to another classmate. Those who do so are now involved with *all* word recognition and comprehension skills.

After several of the children have retold the story, I introduce a "Word Fun Session." This can be anything appropriate to the development of language skills. With this story, I ask questions like: "What other words than 'enormous' can we use to describe the turnip?" The kids then tell me as many synonyms as they can for *big*. After that, I say, "Here are the letters I used earlier for the title of the story. Who can place them in the right order?"

Next I ask for volunteers to re-enact the story. The actors will play Turnip, Old Man, Old Woman, Dog, Pig, Cat, Mouse, and Narrator (the storyteller). The students plan how they will tell the story—thus they become involved in plot analysis and co-ordinate physical movement. We later extend the activity into a playground "turnip tug-of-war," which moves the story into physical education.

I take a real turnip into class, one with the greens still on it. There are always some students who have never seen a turnip, much less eaten one. I suggest that they could grow turnips from seed in the classroom (or at least, discuss how they are grown, the type of soil, how much water and sun they need, where they were eaten, who ate them, who still eats them, et cetera). Sometimes we discuss the difficulty of pulling them out of the ground, which then poses the question of how large would a turnip have to be to need this many tuggers? All of the questions develop higher-level comprehension skills of fact, opinion, reality, fantasy, making comparisons, et cetera. I end the session with an actual taste of the raw turnip.

As I leave the classroom, I tell them, "This story is now *yours*. Take it home with you and tell it to a family member."

The example I've given is, of course, suited for younger children, but you can use stories for whatever age level you're teaching.

It is my hope that teachers who are not now using stories will start using them. I get excellent results in middle school with a story called "Phobia" by J. B. Stamper in *Tales for the Midnight Hour*.

I start off rambling mindlessly about a very uninteresting topic. Suddenly a (preplanned) wild and crazy person comes barging into the classroom screaming at the top of his lungs: "Get it away from me! Get it away from me! Y-I-I-II-!!!?! I can't stand it! Get it away from me!" My screaming intruder runs all around the classroom in wild hysteria. Finally, I walk over and slap my hands right above his head as if I've just killed a bee. The intruder sits down and pants heavily. I turn to the class and calmly say, "You have just witnessed a reaction of a *melissophobiac*. Who can explain what that means?" I then explain that the intruder was preplanned and that he has a phobia: Melissophobia, the intense fear of bees. I say, "Everyone in the universe is afraid of something. Not everyone has a phobia, however, or an intense fear. Think for a minute about what you are afraid of. Now I'll tell you a story about Ellen, who has a deep-seated fear. As you listen, think about whether you would have reacted the same way Ellen did."

I tell them the story. Then, afterwards, we discuss it. The story lends itself to three major areas of academic involvement. One is a discussion of the psychology of fear itself—with special regard to the content of the story "Phobia." The second is a rather detailed vocabulary study of words with the root —*phob*— in them. The third is a series of little improvised plays to help them begin to understand, cope with, and control their own personal fears.

It is my hope that teachers already using stories will continue to use them more and more. Storytelling is such an invaluable tool for learning. And you know what? It's fun!

Fran Stallings: Sharon Gibson, who teaches a sixth grade class in Bartlesville, Oklahoma, is a real inspiration in terms of what she does with storytelling in building a classroom culture. She started with storytelling for curriculum enrichment, picking up from when I visited her classroom where my daughter was in the sixth-grade. I came in to do some folktales that connected with the studies they were doing of ancient Egypt as part of their world history. Sharon said she listened to me and she thought, aw, I can do that! She took over telling some of those stories and then she began calling me periodically saying, "Fran, I need a lizard story!" She saw a curriculum connection.

Sharon noticed that when she began a class session with a story, the students would settle down and focus. They would get into a quietly intense mood that would last throughout the class. Not only if they did seat-work the rest of the period, but even if they were getting up and building castles out of sugar cubes or whatever, this listening-set or learning-set would last through the period. That motivated her to learn stories even if they didn't relate directly to curriculum content. That's when she began telling stories that just plain appealed to her. Those stories tended to be teaching tales from many traditional cultures that had something to say about how you treat other people or what expectations you have of yourself.

The kids enjoyed the stories and asked to hear them over and over. What Sharon then discovered was that the students were *referring* to the stories. And she could refer to the stories in order to make a point, in the way that we might say, "He's just crying wolf." Everyone knows that story, so just a reference to it brings up a whole concept. She found that these stories had created a unique sub-culture among the students. She could use the references to the stories in the traditional way that teaching tales were used—almost like proverbs.

She became a true believer. She found stories on her own. She still calls me for stories. It happened that the same year my daughter was in the sixth grade, another teacher, Terry Hughes, was in Sharon's classroom as a student teacher. He also thought, I can do that! So when Terry began teaching social studies, math, science, and all kinds of subjects, he began using storytelling. They are both true believers.

[What do you do to try to convince teachers that they have the time and the ability to tell their students stories?]

I start by relating anecdotes from the experiences of other full-time teachers. There's no reason why teachers should take the word of a visiting circuit rider. So I use anecdotes from teachers' experiences. A way to get a toe in the door is to make points about the curriculum applications of the stories to introduce a subject area to planned information that you're going to use later.

[Like what, for example?]

Well, I'm a biologist by training. I do stories and songs for a green earth. They are stories that contain concepts of ecology—like species—diversity, population balance, the importance of the different species sharing the same environment and not pushing each other out, what happens if things get out of balance—not environmentalism. Our ancestors recognized these things long before the word "ecology" was ever coined. I use traditional stories that plant a concept in the listener's mind in the guise of delightful entertainment, along with valuable teaching about human nature, although the story may be one that purports to tell something like how a certain kind of animal got its stripes.

The reason traditional people told the story was that it had something to teach about braggarts or excessive pride or underestimating an opponent. It still teaches that point about human nature, which makes it an appealing story. But the initial premise of the story is that all of the members of the species were identical to begin with, and at the end of the story they got the new colors, new markings, new patterns as the result of this story. The emotional content of the story fixes that idea in listeners' memory. You can then go on to talk about the many species there are now, the functions of the different patterns of camouflage and warning signals and species recognition and mate selection.

In other words, the story provides information that is a hook on which you can then hang the scientists' response to the same question. The story pretends to ask the question, "Why did they get those colors?" Scientists, strictly speaking, don't ask, "Why?" They ask, "How?" They have approaches that have to do with selection in the environment and functions of camouflage, things like that.

I have done workshops all around the country about whole language integration, where you can take the same story and you can go with the colors into visual art work. You can take the plot and go into skits. You can take the action and go into physical education. You can measure the action and go into math. Because teachers have been asking me, "Hey, you know, this is fun, but what's it good for?" I have been forced to come up with these answers of curriculum application.

The first step to convince teachers to try using stories in the classroom is to show them that it does have value. Therefore, it's not taking time out to do something different. It actually is an alternative route for doing what they have to do anyway. It has advantages in terms of appeal, holding people's attention so they'll listen, being memorable, really having an impact that even reading aloud does not have. Thank goodness a lot of teachers do read aloud, bless their hearts, but stories have a very different impact when they are told face-to-face and in your own words.

I feel that—even if the teachers have been given an argument about why it's good and why it's useful and why they should be doing it—if that's all you cover in a workshop or a class, they'll walk out just feeling guilty for not doing it. I feel that when an outsider is doing teacher in-service, it is absolutely essential to get the teachers actively involved in retelling the stories themselves in their own words. Having a ball doing it. Seeing the delight in their colleagues' faces. Discovering what wonderful creative frills they're adding to the stories. They must find out that they *can* do it, *have just done it*, and can try it with *confidence* in school on Monday.

Randy Weiss: All of my middle school students are classified as being at-risk. Basically they come into my classroom because they aren't able to succeed in the main-stream, usually for behavioral reasons.

I don't teach anything that isn't steeped in human passion and problem resolution. My class is interactive and therapeutic, and emphasizes community building among all program participants. My goal is to demonstrate to my students that problems are a part of the human experience and the challenge in life is to learn to deal with them effectively. To illustrate this point, I teach passionate history and literature and together we draw comparisons to our own lives.

Storytelling fits perfectly into my curriculum. For example, I teach a unit on archetypes at the beginning of the school year. For that, I use the Hercules segment from my husband's *Greek Myths* tape. Hercules misuses his strength which results in violent tragedy and he has to pay the consequences via his famous labors. This dynamic story is a powerful way to start children thinking about their own strength and how to control it.

Everything in today's world seems very visual and interactive, perhaps at the expense of auditory perception. In the classroom, this is evident when so many students have a hard time listening to verbal instruction. Storytelling tapes provide a wonderful vehicle for developing and practicing listening skills.

The kids I work with have previously spent a lot of time out of classes due to their behavior. By the time they finally get to my class, I find they've missed tremendous chunks of their early education. I spend a lot of time providing experiences for them that recapture some of what they missed. It never ceases to amaze me when I watch these seventh- and eighth-grade adolescents who have such tough personas lie down on the floor with the lights out and become mesmerized by recorded stories. The middle school environment becomes transformed to the respective meditative states of each individual listener. This is a very personal experience.

I teach a six-week course on the Holocaust. I also teach a six-week course on African-American studies from slavery to contemporary issues. For both units, I use a lot of first-person narratives, both in book and audio formats.

I spend a tremendous amount of my classroom time reading to my students. I never like to hear tellers say for any reason that telling is *better* than reading aloud. There are infinite good reasons to tell a story, but they don't have to be mutually exclusive to reading aloud. I think there's a place for both. Jim and I both feel that there's nothing better than to encourage a child to read a book, and there's no better way to do that than to read to a child. But reading is not in competition with storytelling, not in the classroom and not at home. A storyteller's version of a story, besides being a source of lively entertainment in its own right, is also a great way to introduce a literary or historical genre. I think that reading and telling are intricately interwoven. It's necessary to have both.

Jay Stailey: Let's start with the fact that sharing stories, especially the teacher's own stories about her foibles and tribulations, allows children to see that making mistakes is OK, that everyone is human and the teacher is too. Then you don't end up with the shock children have when they see their teacher at the grocery store. They can't imagine that she could shop too.

Another way that teachers can use stories in the classroom is to focus kids on whatever particular lesson is being taught that day. Obviously, if any kind of cultural or historical subject is being taught, the teachers can include stories from that culture or those historical events. Black History Month is a good time for lots of storytelling.

The other day, one of my fifth-grade language arts teachers was teaching *The Sign of the Beaver*, which is a story of a family homesteading up in Maine. The father goes back to take care of the sick mother and leaves his son in charge of the cabin. The boy ends up meeting and trying to communicate with a young Penobscot Indian.

The teacher came to me and said, "Do you have any Native American stories you could come in and tell the kids?" I looked through some of Joseph Bruchac's collections and found a couple of real simple Oneida and Tuscarora folktales. I went into her class and told those stories. So you can connect stories in lots of ways to whatever you are working on in the curriculum.

Lots of times when I get kids together, I tell a story. Every six weeks we have an awards ceremony. At one of these, I told the folktale about the king and his servant who are sitting at the window. I tell them the king has a peanut butter and honey sandwich just like my mother used to put in my lunchbox. The king takes a bite and a drop of honey rolls out and falls onto the sidewalk. The servant says, "Maybe I should go down and clean that up." The king says, "Aw, not our problem." The

ants come down the wall and start to eat the honey, then the lizard comes to eat the ants, and then the cat to eat the lizard, and then the dog, and then the owners and then the Civil War. All this happened because they didn't pay attention to the little things.

I then talk to the kids about the little things we can do around school. When kids come to my office because there has been a fight, it is never the fight that's the problem, it's the little things kids could have done to stop the problem before it got big. So there are teaching tales that can be used to let kids know.

I also tell a story in my class at the university about "palm wine." It's a story about a village in Africa where one man decides he's not going to put palm wine in his bowl at the ceremony. He'll just fill it with water. No one would know the difference. In the end, everybody brings water instead of palm wine and there's no celebration.

I then let the students know that I realize their lives are busy. I know they have lots of choices to make, but when they come to my class they need to bring wine. Don't bring water. I talk to them all through the semester about the same thing. When people begin to let down a little bit, I tell them they need to go to a different store to buy their wine. Annie Greensprings won't work, can't get you an A. So there are ways you can carry those themes on through for the teaching tale.

A lot of my students at the university are also substitute teaching. I tell them that if they learn just two good stories, they can start their day of substitute teaching with a story. Then they can tell the kids that, if they are really good all day long, they can hear another story at the end of the day. It's a way to help entertain and control, if the kids like the story enough. I've had my students come back and tell me how amazed they were at the attention they got from the kids, how well the kids were willing to behave in order to hear stories.

One of the things we run into these days in this generation of "television kids" is children are not used to making images for themselves. We really need to tell stories from the very beginning with children in order to help them develop their mind's eye. One of the things that makes a good reader is the ability to imagine, to make images of the characters and of the scenes. Storytelling is a good vehicle for that.

Robert Slavin of Johns Hopkins University in Baltimore has a Success-For-All program that's being touted around the county as a great program, particularly for children from low socio-economic backgrounds. One of the key components, especially in the early grades, is a program Slavin calls "Story Telling and Retelling." It basically helps children build frameworks for thinking.

The teacher tells a story to the kids, and the kids re-tell the story to the teacher. The idea being that these kids will recognize in stories those frameworks that allow them to understand what is going on. They need to build those frameworks in their heads.

Many middle-class children come to school having had stories read to them from the time they were born. They come with the idea of what a story and what its framework look like. That creates a foundation for success in those children, because school is very much a middle-class institution. When you get children of poverty who come to school and they've not had stories read to them and not had these frameworks built, something has to be done to jump-start that and get the frameworks built. That's Slavin's theory in his "StoryTelling and Retelling." A lot of people are doing this.

The February 1995 issue of *Inside Story*, the newsletter of the National Storytelling Association, has an article about Deborah Gordon-Zaslow from Ashland, Oregon.

She has created a storytelling troupe of children who learn stories, then go around and tell them. Remember, school is an institution that promotes visual learners, particularly children who express themselves through writing and not through voice. It's the nature of a classroom that, when you have twenty-two kids in it, you just can't let them express themselves all at once. And when they do, they get chastised for it. So children who write well end up becoming successful and children who talk well end up in the office.

One of the things Ms. Gordon-Zaslow has found is that a lot of these kids, particularly kids with learning disabilities, may have trouble spelling and writing, but have wonderful ideas that they can express orally. They find a great outlet in storytelling that they wouldn't normally have in the classroom. She talks about the success of these kids and the surprise of some teachers who didn't realize that they have this kind of talent, because the classroom isn't a place where their talents can be allowed to grow.

[How do you encourage your teachers to use stories in the classroom?]

There have been several ways. One is to use stories myself so the teachers can see what it's like for the kids. Another way is to bring other storytellers into the classroom to try to make connections between the role of the storyteller and the teaching that has to be done.

I had a group of fourth-grade teachers that took a six-week period with storytelling as the theme. We used Martha Hamilton's and Mitch Weiss's book, *Children Tell Stories*, as our guide. We assembled a lot of folktales and had them in files. The kids looked at three or four of them and finally picked the one they wanted to learn. They did story-mapping and eventually heard other storytellers. They worked on those things that make good storytelling or make storytelling compelling: eye contact, gesture, voice. Eventually, they performed their stories in front of small groups in their classrooms, and ultimately, performed the stories in front of other classes, going from fourth grade down to kindergarten and first grade.

[Have you noticed a change in the kids as a result of this?]

In the beginning there should be a general understanding that stories are exciting and fun. I rarely go into the classroom that I don't have some child say, "Will you tell us such-and-such a story?" or "Are you here to tell us a story today?" There's been a general rise in awareness of this connection with stories being exciting and with it being an exciting aspect of school. Some of the children who are particularly skilled at storytelling (they might not be skilled in other areas in the classroom) suddenly become stars.

That's another thing I told my students at the university. I introduced them to William Glasser's studies about the major drives that human beings have. Glasser has done a lot of work with quality studies and has written a book on quality schools. He says that human beings, beyond the drive of survival, have four basic needs—fun, power, belonging and freedom. These theories are in his book, *Control Theory*.

We discuss how those needs of fun, power, belonging, and freedom are met in a regular school setting. There are certain areas where the kids end up meeting their needs by taking over the classroom: disturbing, disrupting, bullying, things like that. They have to have their needs met. When they are not met, they express disruptive behavior. Glasser's idea is that you create an environment where those needs get met, then kids don't have to be disruptive. They will actually buy into your idea of what school is all about. Glasser talks about a child putting school in his or her

quality world. Then you don't have to deal with all the management issues. You can deal with the learning issues.

What we've seen with storytelling, when the child gets up in front of a classroom and all the eyes are on him and everybody wants to hear his story, there's this sense of his being in charge that a child doesn't normally get when he goes to school. The idea that a child can choose his own story and tell the story the way he wants to, adapt it the way he feels is appropriate, allows for a lot of freedom within the curriculum that children don't normally get when they go to school. The idea of doing something that is not a worksheet or a report is fun, and fun is something kids don't normally have when they go to school.

Just about all those areas of how we can meet children's needs and still hook them into school are addressed in the idea of letting children become storytellers. I can see that going on in the classroom and in the school building because of the opportunity for kids to tell stories.

[Since you place an emphasis on stories in your school, have you found that this association with stories has improved your students' ability to read and write?]

I think it has helped them in their writing. I'll tell you about the latest thing we're working on. It's been very difficult. Because schools are middle-class institutions, and because there are different story structures based on class (I've just discovered this), it is a very big jump for kids who come from situations of poverty to understand and work in the school successfully. It shouldn't be a surprise to anyone who thinks about it, because public schools in American have a history of not having a good track record with poor kids. What I'm finding now with the story framework (and what Slavin talks about with story telling and retelling) is basically a framework that poor kids are not familiar with. The storytelling frame they are familiar with from their structure looks very different from the storytelling framework that is the basis for our movies and our literature and our art.

I've just begun to do some work with Dr. Ruby Payne, who is the head of staff development in Baytown, Texas. She's done extensive research on the difference between the culture of poverty and the culture of school. There's not much information on the subject, yet it's an important factor in school success.

From what we've been able to gather, plot is the most important aspect in the framework of a middle-class story. You establish the basic characters and setting early in the story. Then you have this long circumstance of plot, where the tension rises and there are three or four different challenges. Then you have the culminating point, and after that, the story winds up pretty quickly. It's the basic folktale framework.

Storytelling is our most human, natural self-expression.
—Marni Gillard

When we tell our stories, or when we go to movies or plays, we want to see that same kind of framework. If we go to a movie and they don't tie up the ends the right way, we walk out of the theater saying, "Well, it was good till it got to the end."

The story framework for the poverty class is quite different. In the culture of poverty, it's not plot that is important, it's personalities. Their stories may be nothing but anecdotes about somebody's character. They usually don't go anywhere.

Another interesting part of it is that the poverty class usually starts with the ending of a story. Instead of Jack winning the princess or Jack going to jail at the end of the story, that's how it begins. So there are people who might be sitting around saying, "Well, y'know, so-and-so's back in jail," or "Y'know, so-and-so burned down the school," or "Y'know, so-and-so's got their kid on Ritalin." They start with what in middle class frameworks would be the end of the story.

Then there's a lot of interactive commenting throughout the story. They go back and discuss all the things about this character that culminated in the final event they started off with. So it's a different way of dealing with story.

It is important when we sit down with parents at a conference that we let them tell their story all the way through and not cut them off. Because they might start with a comment like, "Well, I know my son is a little brat (or worse)." Our first response would usually be, "Aw, don't talk about your kid that way." But if you back off and let them tell their story, you might find out that they actually have a lot of respect for their child, and there are certain things that worry them about what's going on. If you listen, you might be able to find out those things. But because the framework is so different, we're not tuned in to listening to that kind of story.

[When you use the term "middle class," is this another way of saying "white?"]

No, not necessarily. What we are finding in our schools is that it doesn't make any difference if the kids are black or Hispanic or white or Asian. If they come from a middle-class setting where they have lots of resources at their bidding, they function better within the school setting. Certainly one of the resources is how much money is available, but there are other resources like spiritual and emotional resources, the type of people that are in their support system, role models they have available to see, and educational resources.

There are about six or eight different resources that are important if a child is going to grow up in the best of situations with the kind of support resources that allows him to be successful without much problem. Race, however, is not one of those. Although what we're looking at in America are underclasses of races that have a tendency to be more prevalent in some races than others.

[Do you have a large Hispanic population in your school?]

We're about fifty-two percent Hispanic and thirty-eight percent African-American. There are less than ten percent Anglo in my building.

[Do you find the attention span is shorter for kids from the poverty class?]

Yes, for several reasons. Poor kids are left with television too much. The way our world works, kids want to be entertained. Entertainment is a very big thing in the poverty class. That's what is most important. They don't have a lot of hope for the future, so they want to make *now* as good as possible.

For the poverty class, there is not much reason to sacrifice for something down the road, which is so much a part of our middle-class mindset. We work hard today so that we can accomplish something three or five years from now. Our banking system is set up that way and so is our educational system. But in places where kids haven't had that introduced to them, haven't had the opportunity to think that way (some kids in my school don't even know if they're going to living in the same house at the end of the month), "today" becomes very important.

So they like entertainment, and they want it quickly. They don't have a lot of patience. I think that's part of the reason the attention spans are short.

[Do you find that the use of stories in your school helps the kids with role modeling or to establish their own values?]

I haven't been able to chart that, but it makes sense if kids are going to be able to deal in this framework. My goal with these kids is not necessarily to make them become middle-class, but to give them the tools so that they'll be able to function within a middle-class setting if they choose. I think one of those tools is the understanding of how the world works. There are a lot of hidden cues about a class held within stories. Stories pass on the values of people. If children can be exposed to enough stories to see these patterns of cues about how to interact, then it certainly makes their ability to function within that culture much easier.

It's an exciting time for storytelling. I think that as more people recognize story's importance, it will be put into a larger spotlight. And that's very good.

Ellin Greene: The use of storytelling is only limited by the teacher's imagination.

I think the whole language movement has encouraged teachers to use literature, and I think that literature and storytelling go hand in hand.

I'm most familiar with working with language arts teachers, but I know teachers who have used Carl Sandburg's "Arithmetic" and the wonderful books of Mitsumasa Anno in their math classes. Many Native American legends are perfect for nature classes.

After telling a story, a teacher might have the children draw or paint images—creative dramatics—they saw as they listened or act out the story. Storytelling is a natural lead into writing. Ask the children to give the story a different ending, tell what happened before or after the story took place, or tell the story from the viewpoint of another character. Children already familiar with traditional tellings love fractured fairy tales.

Teachers should avoid using storytelling in a didactic way. I think it's great to use storytelling throughout the curriculum, but a story is there to be enjoyed, to be shared. If you start making it a lesson or asking the children test questions about it, you've taken away the joy of storytelling. It's important to remember that the primary purpose of storytelling is to share, to give joy. Stories nurture the human spirit.

When you tell stories for the pure pleasure of it, children relax and feel comfortable with you. Even though an adult and a child listening to the same story will probably take something different from it, enjoying a story together levels the playing field. It brings adults and children closer. It makes for a genuinely warm relationship between teacher and student in the classroom. I would like to see teachers do a lot more storytelling.

When I ask teachers if they are telling stories in the classroom, most of them tell me "no." Some of them tell me they are reading aloud to their classes. That's fine, but reading aloud is not quite as intimate as storytelling. I tell teachers, "If you don't have time to devote to learning how to tell stories, then at least read aloud." Although storytelling and reading aloud are different, the reading aloud does give the children some connection to good stories.

Several years ago, I worked as the children's literature specialist at National College of Education in Evanston, Illinois. Part of my job was to introduce story materials to the teachers. There was a lab school attached to the college and those teachers really did read to the children every single day. There was such a difference in those children. They knew the literature, they were excited about reading, excited about books. You don't get that in schools where children aren't read to.

If you can't spend the time to learn stories, then read aloud. But it's not the same. I think there is a great hunger for stories. The students come alive when the teacher starts telling stories.

Unfortunately, most teachers have never had a course in storytelling during their training. Teachers need to know children's literature and how to introduce it through storytelling and reading aloud.

Some students come back and take a storytelling course after they've been in the field. But if they take the course during their training, they get hooked. Once they know how children respond to hearing stories, they're going to make time for storytelling. You always make time for what is important to you. But if they haven't experienced that pleasure, they often feel so overwhelmed with all the pressures on them that they are not likely to use storytelling in their classrooms.

Gay Ducey: I would like to make a case for the first way stories are used in the classroom and in the library. It's as a gift, unattached to any curriculum approaches, and that doesn't mean always, but on occasion, stories should be given to students. That telling of the story is a gift to the kids. No payment is exacted from the student or the attendee in the library. Kids get to hear the story and do not have to think what the right answer will be afterward or if they are going to remember all the stuff to tell the teacher. None of those things. The kids hear the story and enjoy it and are not asked to give anything back. That's the first and perhaps the most important use of storytelling in any classroom. If we really believe that stories can teach and that they are important for our cultural and intellectual and emotional life, then we have to give kids a chance to hear them, really hear them.

It can also bring the kids very closely into story-making themselves, of course, in both the library and the classroom. Kids can go out and collect stories from their own communities and their own family members both as a way of encouraging us to appreciate and respect others and the ways in which they live and the backgrounds that they have. This can also give kids a chance to test out storytelling on material that closely resembles their own patterns at home.

Teachers can always use stories as a part of social studies. In some of the new textbooks, that's reflected when we see stories from the oral tradition included in the survey of a culture or a country. I think that should be part of the teaching of that culture or that country. That part of that culture we need to learn about is the way in which stories are told, what kinds of stories are told and what values they represent.

Perhaps one of the most under-utilized areas for storytelling in the classroom is in science. Kids spend hours and hours and hours doing their own science experiments. The same kind of creativity which they employ in doing experiments can also be employed in hearing stories about the way cultures solved problems of science. Sometimes these can be true stories. They can be stories of discovery or invention, they can be stories of the Curies or Pasteur. They can also be *pourquoi* stories about how myth and legend and folktale and fairy tale explain or use science. In Native American stories there are very often scientific lessons to be gleaned and learned.

It's good for kids to know that this is the way people learn. Before there was a written language, it was essential to be able to know a good story in order to understand scientifically your relationship with the world around you.

We often think that stories belong in literature, and of course they do. But they can be used in literature in numbers of ways. One of which is to use a comparative and contrasting technique with the variety of different versions of the same tale. They can also be used simply as good literature, as ways for kids to be exposed to good literature. I think it is good for teachers to remember that kids learn differently (as we know) and they receive information differently. Employing a different series of techniques in exposing kids to literature makes good pedagogical sense. Some young people, like my son, learn much more easily orally—through their ears—than they do through print. For my son to hear a story was a great gift, and one he could utilize quickly as opposed to having to read that story.

[Do you have an answer for those teachers who say, "Stories?! I'm so busy right now, I don't even have time to teach all that's in my lesson plan! What do you mean I should add stories?!"]

That's a fair complaint. It speaks in the larger sense to the way in which the national priorities are obviously reflected in the way we teach our kids. It's actually a bigger question than it is a complaint.

What I say in my own workshops is "You have the time if you take the time." Now no one is asking teachers to learn twelve stories. But perhaps, if you set a modest professional goal for yourself, very modest—like maybe one story this year. That's all, just one. Make it one you really like. That means you may not want to learn a story about froggies for the froggie unit.

Maybe you need to learn a story about weaving, because weaving is something you're interested in. We all tend to learn things that we're interested in. So I would first tell teachers to take the time. Whether they have it or not, they need to take that time. Then make it the smallest investment of time that they can afford. For me, that would mean probably one story for the classroom teacher—a story that I liked, that was worth learning. They should spend only one week learning it and then tell it the next Monday.

When I teach teachers—which I do very often—that's my advice. I have them choose one story, learn it and tell it instantly. Teachers need to understand how quickly they can acquire a story and understand that it doesn't have to be perfect. If we wait until something is perfect, there will never be an opportunity to tell it. Then I think we have a better chance of showing teachers that it isn't the burdensome addition to their complex duties that they believe it is.

I acknowledge that it's going to take some time. Teachers have to first be convinced of its efficacy before they can be convinced to devote the time.

Gwendolyn Jones: Suppose that a science teacher is going to teach her students something about volcanoes. Instead of giving a dry, factual delivery on volcanoes, if she takes the narrative voice—the storytelling mode—and walks into the classroom and says, "I well remember the story I heard about 'Marra and Remo.' They woke up one morning, an ordinary morning, but suddenly there was a graying of the sky, then a sound came to their ears …"

Sometimes, when my teacher-candidate students are teaching units on, say, Japan or China, and their assignment is to bring information about the education, I would suggest to them, "Why don't you pretend that you have a friend in that country. They have written to you to tell you about a day in school." Then having written the letter, my students present it in a conversational, storytelling way, which would be personal history.

When I used stories to teach math, I made up a story about my non-existent younger brother who had a great many newspapers to deliver. Of course, he had to know his multiplication tables to work out his wage. He didn't know them. He was being underpaid because of his inability to do the mathematical process. I would weave these "teaching anecdotes" into a story.

What I've generally experienced is a dearth of storytelling in the classroom, even at the lower levels, grades one and two. Teachers say to me, "Ah, we just don't have the time. We have to cover this. We have to cover that." I say, "But surely, five minutes in the morning …!"

Carol Birch: Doesn't everybody know at this point that children's listening skills need to be developed?

We all have a muscle inside us that helps us see what is not in front of our eyes. That muscle is imagination. One of the wonderful things about storytelling is that it reaches beyond its immediate entertainment value and makes us deeper in ways that we don't know. Storytelling strengthens the muscle inside of our heads that lets us see what is not readily apparent. Strengthening that muscle is the basis of all creativity and all empathy. So when I look around at this sorry world, what I see is that we need more empathic people. We need creative solutions to problems that everybody has right in front of them. That's my rationale for why schools need to ake time for stories. It is so important for the development of whole human beings.

You know how when you travel on airplanes, there's that puzzle in the in-flight magazine that has nine dots. You're supposed to connect the nine dots in the shape of a square without retracing your pencil line. Usually, when you do it, you try to stay within what your eye perceives as a boundary. But the only way you can connect the nine dots, doing what you're supposed to do, is to go outside of the line. One of your lines has to go way up past that perceived boundary, and then come down and go around.

What I say to people is, when you're talking to your administrators, justifying storytelling units in your classroom or justifying more storytelling rather than library skills when kids come to the library, then storytelling is like going outside of the dots. There's a perceptual boundary called the curriculum, and storytelling bursts through those boundaries. I like that image.

The reason I love folktales is that they do two things simultaneously. They celebrate what is universal in the human spirit. At the exact same time, they celebrate what is distinctive and unique about specific cultures.

If you would think of what is universal in a story as being the broth of a stew or a soup, then every culture, every human being, can go to what is universal in stories and, depending on what appeals to them, they can scoop out a ladleful of this wonderful rich dark brown broth. When people of the world make their stews, they add their own seasonings. That's what makes some stews taste of curry and jalepenos, and other stews taste like whale meat. It is the same with stories and that's what I love about them. They celebrate what is distinctive and at the same time they celebrate what is universal.

You, however, have to be careful that you don't inappropriately season a stew that has nourished people for a long time. Because you are outside the culture that created the stew, you might season it in such a way that it suddenly becomes putrid to the very people it used to feed. By the same token, when we're attracted to a story because of what is universal in it, we sometimes try to season it to our own taste. But we have to be careful what we do to stories when we're outside the culture they come from.

That's what I love about stories, and that's what is so appealing about them. They go outside the perceptual boundaries of the curriculum. They celebrate what is universal while celebrating what is distinctive about people.

Marni Gillard: One of the great things I have learned from working with kids and now with adults is the power that stories have. But every time I talk with a bunch of teachers about using stories in the classroom, I come up against their fear of performing. Teachers love to listen to stories, but there is always this fear. They say to me, "Well, you're a storyteller. You have a talent, a gift. But *I* can't do that."

When I was giving workshops, trying to get teachers to come-on-in-the-water's-fine, I realized right away that I needed to stop looking so polished, stop telling stories that were so well-honed. If teachers are going to use storytelling, they have to see it as something possible for them. So I started looking at storytelling as a continuum. One part of the continuum encompasses the well-rehearsed performances of the professional tellers. But there's another big part. It's the storytelling we all do every day.

Storytelling is our most human, natural self-expression. We talk to strangers in grocery stores, buses, trains. We tell incredible stories, sometimes entertainingly and artfully. But we never admit that's what we're doing because we haven't rehearsed them. But there are times when we tell the same story over and over. So in a sense, we *have* rehearsed it, and it moves down the continuum toward a "performance."

When I conduct a workshop or in-service, I give the teachers the idea of this continuum. I get them talking, get them thinking about the stories they already tell—stories about themselves or their kids or some moment in their past that taught them a lesson—stories that are thrown into conversations every day. "Oh, yeah! That happened to me! Let me tell you about the time that I …" I hope the teachers will understand that these are stories too, that they are already telling stories. Storytelling is not only possible for them; it's something they do every day.

I also encourage teachers to tell personal stories to their students in school as a way to get storytelling rolling. Once teachers start thinking about storytelling in that way—that they're already doing it and have been doing it all their lives—it's a lot easier for them to see themselves and their students as storytellers.

[How did you start using stories in the classroom?]

I came at it through teaching writing. I was doing a lot with personal narrative. I wasn't telling those stories. I was writing them and then reading them aloud, acting as a model for my middle school students.

Then I asked to hear my students' writing. I came in through personal stories, but my students and I weren't telling them at first, we were just reading them. I also did an oral interpretation unit each year where the kids and I performed rehearsed, dramatic readings. Basically my students and I learned together what storytelling is.

Another way to come into storytelling, and I did this too, is to think about the stories you loved as a child, whether they were fairy tales or fables or family tales—whatever. My parents didn't read to me a lot, but I did have one fairy tale book. There were five or six fairy tales in it that my mother had to read to me again and again. Those stories became planted in me. I hadn't thought about those stories at all until my mother retired from teaching and brought the book home. I said, "Oh, I know these stories already! I don't have to learn them!"

You see, that's the other big fear teachers have besides performing: learning a story. They feel like they need to memorize it. But all teachers really need to do is just to let go of the written words and make the story their own. That's hard and scary for a lot of people. I feel that my job with teachers is to diffuse that fear. If they come in with fear, it's unnecessary baggage. They carry that fear baggage with them and they pass it on to the kids. The kids then become fearful. We already have a lot of fear in school about performing. You get up to give a report—you get criticized, you get a grade. My whole purpose is to toss that

fear right out the window. The stories will teach us so much if we aren't afraid to step into them.

When I conduct a teacher workshop, we sit in a circle and start listing the stories we already know. The memory of one story will jog someone else's memory. You start hearing, "Oh, yeah! That one about the princess! I remember that. Now what happened in that?" Sometimes they have only a piece of the story, but at least it's a road in. They're willing to go back and pick up the other pieces, not only the images and emotions they remember but what drew them to the story originally.

For me, getting the teachers interested in storytelling means getting them directly involved. Once they jump in—and if they can go even farther and turn it over to the kids—these incredible language things start happening with the kids.

When I taught full time, I would bring in lots of books. I'd get the kids to do the same kind of listing of stories they liked that I did with the teachers. Then they'd go home and raid the attic or basement for the books they liked when they were young. At first, we just conversationally told some of those old stories to each other to recall the feeling of what it's like to tell a story. Sometimes I would give them a well-known traditional story like "The Boy Who Cried Wolf." I'd put them into small groups and they would make up a telling of that story. So as each group got up and told the tale, the others saw right away how you can tell the same story in many different ways. Then you start hearing, "Oh. OH! You mean you can do that? That's storytelling?" Some groups approached it more like a play with a narrator. Others would look like a story being told by a trio. But the important thing was that they got the feeling of stepping into the story.

[What's the payoff?]

The payoff is incredible. I was a language arts teacher. Once the kids realized how stories worked, they wrote more fluently. They no longer had trouble getting a story to work for them. Usually kids in junior high want to write novels because that's what they're reading. It gets way out of control. But by telling stories or folktales that have a main character who goes on a journey or who is involved in a conflict that gets resolved, and hearing other similar stories, they begin to be able to write their stories better. The kids stepped inside those stories and walked around in them—which is what you do, of course, when you're in a story and you're telling it—you experience and internalize it. It was better than any lesson I ever did on rising-action and suspense-building, turning-point and denouement. They figured out what makes a story work. They got it, because they stood inside a piece of literature and lived it.

They also learned how to use repetition and how effective it can be, how the end of the story can somehow circle back to a phrase or image in the beginning. They learned how to use dialogue and how not to overuse it and how dialogue can give you a lot of mileage in a story. They learned a lot of vocabulary. They also learned the different uses of grammar and different literary phrasing.

I was very much a "process" kind of teacher. I would get kids to talk about what they figured out in their stories when they were rehearsing them, or how this telling compared to the telling they did down in the third grade. It was amazing what they were learning about the way stories, language, and audiences work.

One other interesting thing they learned was that when you tell a story, you have to manipulate the text. If you're given a paragraph-long fable and you want to make it a decent storytelling, you have to expand it. You have to fill out the bones of the story,

because really all you have are the bones. If you have a long ten-page story that you adore and want to use, you have to figure out where the bones of that story are, so you can shrink it down to something tellable. The kids would find that if a story went more than about eight minutes, they had trouble holding their audience. It couldn't be a one-minute story either, since they needed more time to hook their audience into the story. So they learned a lot about shrinking and expanding stories.

When I was teaching, storytelling was an amazing way for me to see my kids with new eyes. They told me so much about who they are through the stories they picked. Once they started telling stories, they took their masks off. Of course, there are always going to be some who will balk at doing this. It's always cool in middle school to resist, but everyone became a storyteller. The joy was catching, or at least they saw the power it gave to their friends, and they wanted in on that power.

Another big payoff is the kids finding themselves through stories and honoring themselves, honoring who they are. Often they don't realize they're doing it. Nat was a boy who was really heavy. He got up and told us this hysterical story, "Goldiblob and the Three Blobs," about these enormously fat people. I couldn't believe he was doing it, almost calling attention to his being overweight, but the kids enjoyed the story immensely. He was the first to do a take-off. Nat felt great. I thought, well, he's saying, "This is who I am, I'm fat, and I'm going to enjoy it for what it's worth." It was wonderful. But storytelling is a way to help kids be comedic in school and have it be OK. So often, kids' comedic sides are put down in the classroom.

Besides oral language development, storytelling in the classroom affects the way kids read and interpret text. They learn what it means to dig into a story when they tell it over and over. They get practice in concentration when they tell, and that practice pays off when they read silently. I also think they learn that stories have more than one meaning or theme. That understanding makes them more sophisticated readers and writers.

There is another big payoff for teachers. It helps the kids become better listeners and imagers. I don't know if it improves their ability to listen when someone is lecturing, but it does improve their ability to listen when someone is storying.

I love it when a little underdog kid finds a character like Br'er Rabbit and discovers how wonderful it is. Even though Br'er Rabbit may be the underdog, he's also the trickster. The kids find so much power in that. I've had a lot of hurt kids—kids from abusive homes or kids put down by the other kids—find stories where they have a chance to mourn their lost joy. Usually the stories have hope at the end and you can see the kids reaching for that hope.

Building community is so important in middle school. We build community through storytelling. Sometimes when my kids began telling personal stories, someone would tell about a time when he failed. The other kids would say, "I can't believe he's telling that! … but I've got a story about that too!" We also told stories about successes. Even the most sadsack kid would have a success story about winning the pie-eating contest or whatever. It was always something we didn't know the kid was successful at. So it was a chance for him to say, "See? I'm strong too!" It did so much for building community. That's another tremendous payoff for teachers. When a sense of community is established in the classroom, it allows so many other things to fly.

Sherry DesEnfants Norfolk: I always look for ways to tie stories and the curriculum together. When I was substitute teaching, I found storytelling was a wonderful way to walk in and make friends with those kids right away and get them on my side. It's a great bonding experience. Teachers are always wondering how they can get that kind of bond with their students, particularly with those kids that seem to stay alienated all year long. Storytelling is powerful: it breaks down barriers and gives you a chance to form those bonds.

I tell teachers to start out with, and continue with, storytelling. It makes that connection. It gives the students that shared human experience, and once they've had that, they don't move too far away from it. They have the experience of knowing you because you shared a story with them. Since storytelling is an intense personal experience for every child in that classroom, each child will feel that he or she is special because you are telling your story just to them. The rest of your classroom work will be a breeze.

Start out not by learning the stories but by reading the stories aloud. You read them a couple of times, and you will find that you can put the book down for pages at a time. After the third or fourth time you read that story aloud, you'll be able to put the book down and *tell* the story. If you have time to give it a few extra minutes at home or in the staff room, you can do your readings before you get into the classroom so you're actually ready to tell the story.

Keep the book in your lap if you want to. Nobody is grading you on your telling of the story. You're not performing on stage; you're sharing a story with the kids. So keep your notes there. But, as much as possible, tell the story with your eyes meeting the eyes of the children. I don't think it's fair to tell teachers, "You have to learn a story a day, or a story a week." That's not going to be a good experience for them, probably not for the kids either, because the teacher won't feel very good about it.

In storytelling, you are always sharing your emotions about a story or the experience of telling that story with your audience whether you mean to or not. So when you are telling a story that you feel uncomfortable with or you've decided that you hate because you had to learn it the night before, you're going to be sharing that discomfort with the students. That's not at all what you want to share. You want to share the joy of the story.

A lot of teachers feel like they're doing their job if they're just reading aloud to the children (which is a very valuable thing and they should do it—I would never ever say, "Don't read aloud to the children"), but they lose that strong one-on-one personal relationship with the children when they keep that book as a barrier between themselves and the child. They can't make eye contact. They can't see the kind of response they're getting. Sure, they can glance up from time to time, but it's not the same as getting that constant feedback from the audience, and giving that constant feedback to the audience. They are also losing a good chance for maintaining discipline. If you are making eye contact, those kids stay still. When you look away … "the mice will play."

A lot of times I come into a classroom and the teacher says, "Well, these kids are not going to listen. They never listen to a word I say." What do you want to bet the teacher is out there with her back to them, writing on the chalkboard, or reading to them from a textbook? Never looking at the children and making them real human beings. Storytelling, eye contact, and personal interaction acknowledge children as human beings.

At DeKalb County Public Library, we do a lot of work in homeless shelters on the premise that if we don't tell stories and if we don't share the language with these children, then they are doomed to failure. A lot of people in our society would like to sweep these particular children under the rug and say they don't exist, but they do.

They are the future. If we don't prepare them to meet the future with success, then they will naturally fail.

There are so many children in homeless shelters—and in regular homes—today who are being prepared for failure. We know it is a very simple, natural, and loving thing to prepare them for success. All it takes is talking to the child, listening to the child, and setting a good example. I'm not talking about morals. I'm talking about modeling reading behavior, letting them see you enjoy a magazine or newspaper, keeping books around. They don't even have to be books a child can read, but they have to be an example that language and reading are important. Telling children stories is one of the best ways to demonstrate that reading and books have important and valuable things to offer.

Bobby Norfolk: Back during the 1980s, the moral/ethical issue was at one of its lowest points in America. *Time, Newsweek, U.S. News and World Report* were all asking, "Where have our morals and ethics gone?" This was during the time that Ivan Boesky was indicted, we were experiencing the Iran-Contra hearings, and we were in the midst of the Savings and & Loan rumblings. So Sandy MacDonnell, Chief Executive Officer of McDonnell Douglas Corporation in St. Louis, got together with the CEO of Emerson Electric and the CEO of Ralston Purina Company to explore how we could teach moral and ethical lessons without being preachy. The eleven-year-old daughter of the general manager of Channel Four (KMOV) in St. Louis came up with the answer. She said, "Daddy, we had a storyteller in our school who got everyone excited about reading and learning." They auditioned six storytellers for a pilot program, and I won the audition.

I started working with a puppet operated by my colleague, Doug Kincaid. The puppet's name was Grouchy Gator. The name of the weekly television show was *Gator Tales*. Every Saturday morning we presented a problem, a problem that Grouchy Gator couldn't solve. The problem was presented not only to the camera but to the seventy-five kids in the studio. So when I walked on camera, I listened to an overview of the problem. Then I would think of a solution through story. The ratings went sky-high, and we won three Emmys.

Now how this relates to education and stories in the classroom is that the Personal Responsibility Education Program (PREP) committee created questionnaires. These questionnaires were sent to a pilot group of schools. The teachers took the questionnaire and gave it to the kids on Monday morning. You see, the kids had watched *Gator Tales* on Saturday morning and the teachers would go through the questionnaire with them on Monday morning. The results were sent back to the PREP office. From that, they found out that not only were the kids learning great social skills but their reading skills were increasing as well. At the end of each show, I would send them to the libraries and bookstores to find the books that contained the stories I told. Many teachers called and told me how the reading levels of their kids had gone up. So we brought storytelling right in your face, right into your home every Saturday morning, and this was against a heavy cartoon lineup.

After that, whenever I went into schools to tell stories, I would always explore five character traits, building my stories around self-esteem, responsibility, teamwork and cooperation, respect, and humanity. Within each story, those character traits would emerge. I'd usually do three stories in the forty-five minutes, telling them

where I found them, the authors' names, and how the kids could find them and others like them. Invariably, the librarians and media specialists would call me later and tell me about the huge run they'd had on those books. It happened every time. These kids would go to the library the first chance they got. I found that to be a powerful marriage between story and education.

Teachers can use that same technique. They may be fearful of dancing around like I do and cackling like a hen or laughing like a witch. I always tell them, though, it's easy to do if you get lost within yourself. You have to become the persona of the character. A lot of teachers ask, "How can we keep our 'respect' if we do that?" I tell them that it's a matter of style. You don't have to do what I do. You can simply read the story to your kids if you don't want to tell it.

I was at the University of Chicago a few weeks ago. There was a group of middle schoolers sitting around a woman in a rocking chair who was reading to them. Nothing but rapt attention!

It can be done exactly that way in the classroom. Specific times can be set aside, just as is done for recess or gym. Bring the kids to a storytelling space, sit them down, and immerse them in the plot of a story. It needs to be done. Just like saying the Pledge of Allegiance to the flag each morning. It may mean spending less time in the computer room to do that. Some people are convinced that the computer is going to take over conventional book reading and storytelling. Don't you believe it. Story lives and will continue to live. Nothing humans can contrive in a laboratory can outdo the biological computer—the human brain.

HOW CAN A MEDIA SPECIALIST IMPROVE AND EXPAND STORYTELLING IN THE LIBRARY?

◆ ◆ ◆ ◆

Librarians have been instrumental in keeping public storytelling over the years. There is not a librarian or media specialist who does not want storytelling to expand. But how to do it given the time frames? There are only so many hours in a day and librarians have more work than they can reasonably keep up with.

We interviewed a number of storytellers—some are currently librarians, some retired librarians, some are teachers and principals—who offer ideas that you will find interesting and useful for expanding storytelling in the library.

Barbara McBride-Smith tells how she employs her students to winnow out every version and variant of a Greek myth, helping her by suggesting what works and doesn't work in her unique telling of these ancient tales. Barbara sees this activity not only helping the students to become better readers but to become good decision makers as well.

Margaret Read MacDonald, Gay Ducey, and Ellin Greene propose that media specialists expand storytelling by offering short storytelling workshops or in-service training sessions to the teachers in their schools.

School principal Jay Stailey suggests that media specialists should encourage the students to become storytellers.

Sherry DesEnfants-Norfolk closes the chapter by explaining how every area of the curriculum can be enhanced by storytelling if media specialists know their collections well. She gives example after example of how storytelling can be applied to any subject.

Barbara McBride-Smith: Storytelling exposes children to a wealth of experiences outside their own. It stimulates imagination. It stretches attention spans. It nourishes their emotional development. It reshapes negative attitudes to positive ones. It introduces the English language in a way that children cannot hear on television.

All of these things being said, and I believe them to be very important, there are really only two reasons I tell stories to kids in the library.

In the first place, I use storytelling as an advertisement. I want to motivate kids to read. As a librarian, that's my goal: to turn kids into lifelong readers. As far as we

have come in this business of turning children into readers, we're not there yet. I think we're doing a good job. We see statistical evidence that kids are reading more now than they were ten years ago. But I just came across a recent statistic in *The New York Times* that said ninety percent of fifth graders in the United States spend less than one percent of their free time reading. Ninety percent!

I work with fifth graders a lot. They are right at that turning point between being children and being teenagers. I figure if I'm going to make an impression on kids before they leave me, before they go on to the bigger world of junior high and high school, I've got to make every effort to do that with the fifth grade. So when I read a statistic that says ninety percent of kids are spending less than one percent of their free time reading, I'm going to do everything I can to change that before they leave me. Storytelling, to me, does that better than anything I've tried, and I've been doing this for twenty years.

If I tell a story and immediately follow it up by saying, "You know, there are other stories like this." Or "There are other stories from this country." Or, "There are other Greek myths. Did you know you can find them in the library? And here's how you look them up." The kids literally break down the library doors to get those books. I have not found anything else that effective. That's my number one reason. I want to make lifelong readers of these kids, and I believe, through stories, I can do it.

[Is there a difference between reading a story and telling a story?]

Oh, absolutely. That's not to say that reading stories to kids is not terribly important. It took five years for me to be able to say that every single teacher in my school now reads aloud to their kids at least twenty minutes a day. It has made such a difference in kids' love of literature, in their love of books. So if I can get the teachers to do that, I don't need to be the one who reads aloud. Then once the teachers start, the next project is to work on the parents to get them to read aloud to their kids. If we could get every parent doing that twenty minutes a day at home, we'd have a revolution in how kids view reading.

Teachers come to me and say, "Oh, my kids and I cried together over this book!" That's exactly what I want to have happen. With the teachers reading aloud, I can move up to the next rung of the ladder. To me, that's storytelling. Once the teachers are reading aloud, I can start sharing literature with the kids—in another way in a way that I consider a more intimate form.

Stories become more personal when you tell them than when you read them.

Some teachers don't feel comfortable telling stories, and that next brings me to what I urge them to understand. The kind of storytelling I do, day by day with my kids, is not polished performance storytelling. Teachers see me in performance at a concert and they say, "Aw, if that's what you have to do to be a storyteller, I can't do it!"

Well, you don't have to. That's not what I do five days a week. I can't work up polished stories for six different grade levels five days a week. I have stories that are conversational in style and still rough around the edges. I'm not always sure how they're going to end. Sometimes I say to the kids, "You know, I'm working this story, but I'm not real happy about the ending. Let me tell it to you both ways and see what you think."

I am convinced that the stories I do in performance are only as good as they are because I've had so much help from my students along the way. They hear my stories before I ever perform them. I sometimes find that what I think will work doesn't work at all, or the kids will come up with a wonderful idea and I end up slapping my head and saying, "Why didn't I think of that!? That's wonderful! Of course!!"

Another wonderful thing happens. Not only have they helped me create this story, but they are in my library for days and days after this doing research on the story, finding every version and variant of it, trying to find every piece of information they can about the characters. I call down to the public library and say, "I've got some kids who are going to be coming down there. Get ready for them." Sure enough, they go. They read everything they can get their hands on so that they can help me put this story together. They are a part of the creative process. They're exploring folklore and mythology. They're brushing shoulders with great literature, and they're learning that the story doesn't have to be just one way. This is all part of what goes into helping kids become good adults who can make decisions. It helps them realize that when we make decisions, there's not just one right answer. They learn how to get the help they need to make a wise decision. That's what good teaching is all about. Whatever you teach, whatever way you teach it, you're trying to help kids become good creative decision makers. Storytelling is the tool I use to teach that.

Every year, I offer district-wide in-service workshops where teachers can come and learn some techniques. I always say to them, "Don't think you have to have this story absolutely perfect before you tell it to the kids, because if you do, you'll run out of time. You won't have the time to hone it and do all the other things you have to do as a teacher. So make it a process." Once they discover that's OK, they're a lot more comfortable with it.

I've said there are two main reasons I tell stories. First, it encourages kids to become lifelong readers. The second reason I do it is that it simply feels right. It gives me a good feeling. I may say to myself, well, I'm doing this because it's the right thing intellectually. Or I'm doing this because the state mandates that I meet these objectives. All that's important stuff. But if I teach something and I don't feel good about it, if it doesn't feel right, if it doesn't nurture me emotionally, if it doesn't improve the quality of my life as a teacher, then I'm not going to continue doing it. It feels right when I tell a story. It feels good. I come out saying, "I think the kids got something out of that! I think I got something out of it." I feel like I've done a good job as a teacher.

Margaret Read MacDonald: It's much easier for the media specialist to use stories than it is for the classroom teacher. The media specialist has class after class coming in. It's so easy for them to learn a story to tell, or it should be. They have a chance to tell a story over and over again.

They should be bold and tell the same story to kindergarten through sixth grade, because a story is a story and all ages love a good story. They shouldn't be shy about telling to the sixth graders. They should just get a good story, work it, and keep telling it to every grade, share it clear across the board. If they do this, they can get a lot of mileage out of just one story.

My technique is that I don't spend hours and hours learning a story and trying to get it perfect. I find a really good story. I get the gist of it and begin telling it. By telling it over and over again, I perfect it. Then I always suggest that the tellers tape the story at their last telling, after they've been telling it all day, or telling it in several classes. They should make a tape recording of their version and keep that. The next year they can just pull out that recording, listen to it, and they are ready to go again.

I think it can be very easy for school librarians or media specialists to add storytelling into their curriculum. What does it take? Seven minutes. It's something you *can* fit into your program, even though you have to do a class and teach other things. You can take seven minutes to include a story.

Ellin Greene: A lot of school media specialists tell stories when the classes come in. When the teacher is present, the school media specialist is "modeling" how to tell a story or how to read aloud. I think modeling is something the media specialist should be doing, because more of them have had courses in storytelling than teachers.

I know some media specialists who give short storytelling workshops for the teachers—a half-hour after the school day for several weeks. The workshops cover the literature—stories are the most important part of storytelling, techniques of telling and reading aloud, and provide an opportunity for practice.

Teachers need to know that there are different styles of telling, that there is no one right way to tell a tale. The school media specialist presents one model. She can introduce teachers to other styles of telling through the use of videotapes or audio cassettes of storytellers, or, budget permitting, by inviting a professional storyteller to one of the sessions. And, of course, the teachers will see different styles when they tell to each other.

Some media specialists are teaching the kids to be storytellers. Kids need stories. We need to encourage teachers. We need to encourage parents. We need to bring back stories.

Gay Ducey: Here's one more pitch for the story being a real gift, a pure gift that does not interfere with a child's ability to enjoy it. This is hard for teachers, and it's hard for us as parents and educators, because we know there are things we want that kid to take from the story, we want to be sure they get it—*however* ...

People in the library, particularly the media center (I'm going to distinguish here between media centers and the public library) have a golden opportunity to give kids that story gift. They have many goals and objectives in their own teaching of the kids in the library, but they also have, by virtue of their position, pretty much *carte blanche* in giving kids stories and having them be a gift. So that's always my first wish.

If you really want to strengthen storytelling in the media center, or in the public library, you probably have to get some administrative support for that activity. It's fine to sit and tell stories in the media center. It's a good thing to do. In fact, it's the best thing to do. But, sometimes, as a part of our responsibilities as library educators, we need to acquaint both faculty and administration with the importance of this activity.

In some ways, we need to take stories out of the media center and out of the library and bring them to the faculty and bring them to the administrators to make a good case for the need to support this activity administratively. That might translate into a budget for the library staff person to attend in-service training. It might be that person needs some extra time to learn some stories, unencumbered by classes visiting the library. It might mean lots of things once the administrative support is there.

Storytelling is not something to hide under a bushel. It's something to get right out in the open in the library and to say, "This is *so important* to the kids and to their own cultural and emotional life that I want to be sure that I've got the support for this." Maybe, too, that person can act as a trainer, depending on the skill level and the interest. Library media specialists make real good storytelling teachers for other professionals.

One way to use the stories in the media centers, curiously enough, is to take them out into the classrooms, and to give some in-service training to teachers themselves, so that those who are interested but alarmed by acquiring this new skill can use the media center specialist and can gain the skill through that person.

So both are ways to take it into the library and then right out of the library. There are some special activities that help. Kids can come in during the holidays, for instance. There are lots and lots of holidays besides the obvious ones. Each holiday can be considered (and sometimes is in some centers) an automatic storytelling program by the media specialist, not just holidays like Kwanzaa and Chanukah and Christmas, but also less popular events like Arbor Day. There are lots and lots of stories about the importance of trees. Those stories can become the basis of sound ecological practice. Some occasions, particularly holidays, can thread storytelling throughout the seasonal and the celebratory year in ways that kids begin to associate celebration and the thoughtful aspects of that holiday with stories.

The media specialist can also do what the classroom teacher does. And that's not so hard if he or she is presenting a unit or a talk on books that are available about—say, big cats—that's one of my favorites. As you well know, there are ample stories about tigers and lions and cheetahs and mountain lions and panthers and all those wonderful big cats, which can act as counterpoint and centerpieces for the study of that particular unit.

Kids can use the media center to learn their own stories. Depending on the way in which the kids relate to performance, the media center specialist can form her or his own storytelling troupe, as many folks do, taking the older kids into the younger kids' classrooms, and having them hear stories, not just by the big guys but also their own peers a few years older.

It would be good to consider storytelling not just as something that's the responsibility of the media specialist. With some administrative support, the media specialist can do things like create a real solid part of the collection in storytelling. That can include books of stories and a good selection of storytelling cassettes. Most school districts don't have the money to buy sizable numbers of videos, but they do have the money, sometimes, with some administrative support, to put together a nice representative group of audio cassettes.

They can also purchase professional materials related to storytelling, which teachers themselves can use. There are dozens and dozens on the market now. The kids can use the ones in the collection. Teachers and other educators and parents can use the ones for them and everybody can listen to the tapes. That's putting some money behind the idea that storytelling is useful. It really does require some budgeting and some discussion with one's administration.

In a curious way, when you expand the definition of storytelling and see it as a way to enhance any part of the curriculum, you've broadened the way in which stories can be used and threaded and filtered through everything that you do in the library. But you can, at the same time, crystalize the definition of storytelling and simply see it as something that belongs in the library anytime, anyplace, anywhere.

The library media specialist is in a good position to make storytelling important and to make it responsive to the whole curriculum. The media specialist is responsible to support what is going on in the classroom by developing those collections and activities.

If storytelling is seen as the tool we believe it is, then it's not so hard to thread it through anything that's going on in school. So if there's an assembly planned for teachers and parents and kids on, let's say, issues of personal safety, instead of just having Officer Friendly come in to talk about bike safety and such, the media specialist can put together a brief program on *stories* that have to do with safety. Now you see what I mean when I say that it requires some administrative support because we're hoping the media specialist will have purchased the collections necessary so that he or she can nip right in there and get the stories that are needed.

Elizabeth Ellis: The hidden agenda of the media specialist is to encourage people to utilize the library and to read. The most effective way would be to tie storytelling in the library to subjects you want the children to explore—extend the curriculum.

For instance, children will read widely in any area where you have presented them stories. If you tell Native American stories, you're going to increase their interest in and enthusiasm for learning about Native American culture. Those books are going to circulate. If you tell Greek myths, they're going to become interested in mythology and want to read about it. You can utilize storytelling as a bridge between the child and the collection, or between the child and the curriculum.

Jay Stailey: First of all, the media specialist needs to be aware of how important it is for kids to hear stories that are not connected with books. When a librarian reads a story from a book, the children really get the message that the story is of the book, and doesn't exist in and of itself. So I encourage my librarian to *tell* stories. That way the children see that the story exists in and of itself and the vehicle for the story is not the book but the person. The librarian then becomes the vehicle for the story. It's an amazing thing. When any one of my students at the university go into schools and tell stories to kids, they always come back with a sense of wonder that the kids were so interested in their story. I've found that a lot of kids are amazed that stories can come from people's mouths and not from pages in books. We've exposed lots of kids to lots of stories through books but not the other way around.

We need librarians to encourage kids to re-tell stories and become storytellers. We need to pass on that tradition that books are a resource to us if we want to use stories in other ways. They're not the be all and end all.

I encourage librarians to think about the fact that we are very much like television sets if we always connect stories with illustrations. When the kids think of a story, they only think of the picture that the illustrator has drawn. It's that old story of the person who reads the book first and then goes to the movie. There was a big fuss about Tom Cruise playing the vampire (in *Interview with the Vampire*), because nobody could imagine Tom Cruise being that character. They all had a different idea of what the vampire looked like. Tom Cruise didn't fit the picture. If you see the movie before you read the book, then the whole time you're reading, you have this image of somebody—Tom Cruise—in your mind as you read the book. So kids need the opportunity to create images themselves before they see somebody else's creation of the image for the story.

I don't tell my librarian not to read books to kids. You do that too, but the kids need to see both sides of the picture. It's not something that is normally pushed in library school as they are training librarians.

Sherry DesEnfants Norfolk: My first degree was in elementary education. I taught preschool, kindergarten, first and second grades. In each one of these classes, I found that I was teaching all of my subjects through storytelling. I'd find a story to tell about the math lesson or a story to tell about the science project we were going to do. I was always looking for books. Since I found that was what I was doing the most, I realized that I really wanted to bring children and books together. That's when I went back and got a degree in library science and became a children's librarian. I've always used storytelling with children. I didn't call it that when I was a teacher—I just called it "enhancing the lesson."

The most obvious thing to me is that stories do enhance every area of the curriculum. That's the way to bring all areas of the curriculum together. You can tie in everything through stories. You can also enhance the children's interest in what they are learning. You can make them want to learn about science through a story. Where they may not be at all interested in the dry facts or the formula, they'll be very interested in the story behind it. I would do things like tell the mythology behind why there are phases of the moon before we studied the scientific reasons for the phases of the moon. I did this when I was teaching, and I continued doing it when I was a public librarian going to the classroom at the request of the teachers. They would say, "We're studying this or that." I would find stories that would help to introduce the subject. Most of the time, I would be brought in at the beginning of a whole unit. If they were going to be studying the moon, they would have me come in at the beginning and tell stories about the phases of the moon, what the moon is made of, tell them the folklore of the moon. The teachers would then go into the scientific facts. I encouraged them to try to figure out why people came up with the stories they did. What was so interesting about them? Was there any fact? Or was it all fiction?

It's not easy; it takes a lot of time as a media specialist or as a public librarian to be aware enough of your collection and what's in it so that you can tie everything together. It is difficult, but it's very rewarding. I tell teachers, "Let me know what your topic is and the grade level you are working with, and I'll put together twenty-five books on the topic. Some will be fact, some fiction, some mythology. Some will be biography. I'll also show you books you can read aloud as stories, or that you can tell as stories." That was one of the things we offered as a service. It's very time-consuming, but it is what gets the kids and the books and the stories together.

Studies have shown over and over again that the only way children are going to learn language is if they are exposed to language. They also have to be exposed to the kind of language that builds language skills. If all they ever hear is "no" and "don't" and "put it there" (with no definition of "there" as "put it on the table" or "on the bed"), they are going to be behind when they reach school, because they are not developing language skills. Children who are not talked to and not read to will typically enter school about two years behind in readiness to learn. And that is readiness to learn *anything*—math, science, or reading.

Children who are surrounded by language, who are talked to, who are read to, who are surrounded by books and magazines, and by *people* who read books and magazines, enter school ready to learn. They are already versed in emergent literacy skills. They not only know what a book is, but they know how to hold a book and how to turn the pages from right to left. They may not know how to read, but they know that the reading goes from left to right on the page, and they know that the little squiggles on the page are words and that they have meaning. More important than all of that, they know that the meaning is something that is important to them. They've either had a fun experience with it or they've learned they can get basic information they need from those little squiggles. When children get to school they have to have a reason to begin the hard work of learning to decode those squiggles.

Children who enter school without a basic background arrive with no knowledge of how to hold a book, how to turn the page, and no background in what those little squiggles are. They have very little reason to begin the hard work of decoding them.

Children have to be able to imagine and put images with words after they've learned to decode them. If they read the sentence, "The brown cow was eating grass in the meadow," they have to be able to put the image of a cow and the image of a green meadow together and make it real. They have to be able to create the landscape and the characters in their minds. Television does not allow them to do that.

Television creates those things for them, so they don't have to learn how to create images. If they are not able to create images, they can't put meaning behind the words when they're decoded. They never become fluent readers, and they never read for pleasure. If you're not becoming fluent and you're not reading for pleasure, you're not going to do more of it. Nobody does anything if it's not fun and they don't see value in it.

There's a high cost to pay for not becoming a proficient reader. Eighty-five percent of juvenile offenders in this country are disabled readers. In fact, illiteracy is the common denominator of many social problems. These facts make it imperative to motivate children to read and to keep them reading—and succeeding.

[Talk to me about the special problems in storytelling that librarians and media specialists face and how they can overcome them.]

Children's librarians are always doing some sort of programming, and it's often emergency programming. From toddlers to middle school, it is a shotgun approach. The kids walk in, you do the program, and you do it fast. You prepare it quickly; sometimes you just grab some books off the shelf. If you have the time, you grab those books a couple of weeks in advance and try to put it all together around a theme. Nonetheless, you're not going to have time to learn and polish the story.

Often a school will call and say, "We're going to bring over the sixth grade, and we'd like it if you could tell stories from Greek mythology, because that's what we're studying next." Now that librarian may have the skill to tell those stories having read them once or twice, but she's not going to have the time to polish them. Unfortunately, librarians hear a well-known storyteller, like Barbara McBride-Smith, and they say, "Oh, gosh, I'll never be like her. I can't be that good so there's no point

in my doing it at all." Teachers do the same thing. They compare themselves to the person who does it for a living, who has all the time and the background to polish those stories and make them perfect.

[They don't realize how long Barbara McBride-Smith takes to get those stories where they are.]

Right. They have very little concept of how long it takes or the kind of background that Barbara has—all the things that she has put into the telling of her stories. The first time Barbara told a story, it didn't sound like that either. Well, this is the first time this librarian is going to tell a particular story. She may tell it twenty more times, but it may never reach that same degree of perfection that Barbara gets.

Librarians may not have all that amount of time or energy, but what they do have is a deep knowledge of the collection. So where a professional storyteller might be asked to come in and do stories on springtime for the second grade, that storyteller may not have any appropriate stories in his or her repertoire and may not really know how to go about researching and finding the right stories for the right age group. The librarian can. I think that's the greatest thing librarians have at their fingertips—the absolute knowledge of what is in the collection and who it is for. We work with these kids day in and day out at different levels, and get a fine-tuned knowledge of what appeals to children at each age level, what they can tolerate, what they can handle, and what is in the collection that meets their particular needs. This takes the professional storyteller years to develop. Some never do. Librarians get it by osmosis, if nothing else. The better ones have usually had child development classes, or they've learned a lot about child psychology one way or another. I think that's an area where the librarians and the media specialists have a real edge.

[Do you think it is necessary for librarians and media specialists to be as skilled as the professional storytellers?]

No.

[Do you think it makes any difference?]

I really don't. They don't have to be slick about it. They don't have to be polished, because if they're waiting for that, they'll never ever tell a story. But they have to follow the one and only rule that I preach about storytelling: they simply have to love the stories they tell. They have to go through their collections and find the stories that appeal to them. If they do that, they will tell the stories with enough passion (of one type or another) to convey that story to their audience. They may not do it with polish, but if they do it with passion, it will work.

It is absolutely unnecessary for librarians or teachers to strive for the kind of perfection they see onstage at Jonesborough. Time and again, I have heard people say, "I will never tell stories because I'll never be that good." Obviously if you never tell them you won't be any good. But nobody was that good the first time they opened their mouth and told a story. It would be a terrible shame to deprive children of all those language experiences simply because this person is too much of a perfectionist, too unwilling to take chances. So when I teach storytelling classes I tell them, "The story is never going to be perfect until you've told it over and over again. It'll never be perfect if you keep it in your head, or you just tell it to your windshield

as you're driving to work. It's only going to be perfect after you've told it to the children over and over again, and listened to their responses, and seen their faces, and responded to the way they're listening. But don't ever give it up because you don't want to tell it until it is perfect."

When I first started working in Miami, they built a brand-new library in an area where people had traditionally not been library users. The library was a five million dollar building. It had a humongous collection: the children's section alone had 50,000 volumes. We had six children's specialists.

But no kids.

We began reading all the literature about how to bring kids into the library. We started going out to the schools. We did puppet shows. We did storybook time. I got tired of lugging all that stuff around, so I started simply telling the stories—and that's when the kids started coming to the library. It was like magic. It wasn't just me. We all said, "Aw, let's leave the puppets at home. I'll just tell that story. I think I can do it."

We had brought in only a few kids with puppetry and all those other things. But when we started telling stories, the kids came in mobs. After that, literally three hundred kids would come every Saturday for storytelling. We'd get fifty or sixty every day after school who came for storytelling. If we said, "Well, today we're going to have a movie," or, "We're going to have crafts instead," they'd say, "What! No story?! We'll come back when you have stories again."

WHAT SHOULD I KNOW
ABOUT CENSORSHIP?

◆ ◆ ◆ ◆

Censorship is an issue all storytellers will face eventually. It crops up many times when we least expect it. Stories that we have been telling for years suddenly fall under attack by one group or another. If you continue to tell stories it is highly likely that you will be confronted by any number of special interest groups, each with an axe to grind, each wanting to change you and your story.

Today the mass media has become the dominant storyteller in most people's lives. In movies, television, and print, we are constantly told slanted stories and given biased information. Since complaints to the mass media often seem futile, many times the living, breathing storyteller becomes an easy target to vent frustrations. Every audience has a few people who are eager to give the live performer a piece of their minds. You, the storyteller, are accessible and vulnerable. When do you stand your ground? When do you give in and change your story? When do you find a compromise? As a storyteller, it will help you to think about these issues before being confronted.

Everyone we interviewed has faced some surprising forms of censorship. Heather Forest tells about an experience in which she was told not to celebrate the imagination because it was part of new age theology which would take children away from the Bible. Gayle Ross, a Cherokee storyteller, describes running into trouble when sponsors told her to refrain from telling creation tales not found in the Bible. She says, "They insisted that I not tell creation stories, or mention witches or magic—all the things that are an inherent part of the Native American tradition of storytelling." Carol Birch relates an instance when a sexual connotation was perceived in a story deemed appropriate for pre-school through second grade.

This, obviously, is a highly personal issue. All tellers must decide for themselves.

Margaret Read MacDonald: If we stop telling certain tales, then our critics aren't the censors, we are. We have to keep on doing what we feel is important—sharing the stories that we feel are important to hear. One individual in a school can turn the entire school into a censoring agency, and they do it all the time. These folks are very well organized and we have to realize that what sounds like a public outcry against these stories sometimes is an ill-informed outcry.

We had hearings here in the Washington school district a couple of years ago led by a parent and people from a fundamentalist church who were attempting to remove all of Alvin Schwartz's scary storybooks from the library and they got a lot of support from the community. No one had read the books but they had heard what was said about how horrible they were and assumed the books were really horrible. The censors were pretending that their concern was because the books were scary. None of this made a lot of sense to me. Then during the hearing, the censors told the panel to please read certain books before they voted. I got the books from the library. One is called *The Seduction of America's Children* and one is called *Like Lambs to the Slaughter*. These books explained that librarians, teachers, and storytellers are aides of the devil, and that we're leading these children to the devil. These books include rituals and rites to perform with your child each night to get the devil out of them that was put in them at school.

When you realize where these children are coming from, you realize why the Schwartz scary stories are intensely horrifying to them. They really believe the devil is out to get them. It gives you a different insight as to why some of these parents can actually claim that an innocuous story that shouldn't scare anybody would scare the living daylights out of their children.

Again, we have to go back to saying that we cannot let these few people turn us into censors. On the other hand, you have to make a living, so, if the school says up front "Don't do that," then you've got to do what you've got to do to make a living.

But if you start banning, there's nowhere to stop. The same people who want the Alvin Schwartz books out of the schools also do not want their children to do any kind of creative visualization. They don't want you to say, "Close your eyes and imagine." That is just as bad to them as the Alvin Schwartz books.

I think, however, you have to feel comfortable if you're going to use stories that are scary or maybe somewhat gross or violent. If you think they're gross, disgusting and scary and a little bit questionable, you shouldn't try to tell them. Sometimes at Halloween people will tell stories that they don't really feel comfortable with and that's always a mistake.

On a milder stance, I had a class of teachers one year when I was doing in-service in the school district. Everything I told them, they would just say, "Oh, we can't do that. He goes off with the jewels when they aren't his. That's immoral, he shouldn't do that." In "Jack and the Robbers" they take the money from the robbers! "Why, they're robbers themselves. They shouldn't do that." And in "The Whale of a Tale," "That little boy pulls off

the heads of fish. How disgusting. We can't tell that." They wouldn't tell anything that I tried to show them. So based on my experience in that classroom, I began to look for stories that were very gentle and didn't have violence in them.

I came up with a book called *Look Back and See: Twenty Lively Tales for Gentle Tellers*, which is my answer to people who want stories that are moral and aren't violent. Basically they are stories that are gentler and milder.

It was very hard to find these stories. I actually started out thinking I would find stories that had strong morals. I got a nice little collection, but when they had strong morals, someone got their comeuppance but good, and they were really ghastly and gory. So I went back looking for stories that were gentle. It's a lovely collection, but even then, there is some violence because there has to be that conflict.

Next, I brought out my collection of peace tales, but there's still a lot of violence in those stories because they're about avoiding war. It still comes up. It comes up constantly. We just have to keep telling the stories that we think are good stories.

David Holt: When I am performing for children, I ask the sponsor if there is anything they particularly want or don't want to hear. This gives them a chance to request any favorites or to tell me if there is a story they have heard too often or if they have a particular issue they want me to avoid. The subject of witches seems to be the big issue today. I have a number of stories about witches or warlocks, but I have plenty of other material, so I do not mind accommodating them. Recently, after a concert, I was reprimanded by a young woman who said she was a witch. She didn't like the story, "Barney McCabe," because the witch was portrayed in a bad light. That was a new one for me.

It becomes touchier if you are performing an adult show and children are in the audience. If I have a story or song that might be objectionable, I am careful how I introduce it. Giving the historical background and putting the tale in a cultural context will help the audience understand that it has been told for hundreds of years and was not created yesterday. The story is a treasured piece of our past. It is always a good idea to warn the audience if a story is gory or scary or sexual. Give them a chance to leave for a few minutes. Most people won't leave but they appreciate being warned.

Bill Mooney: I have a Halloween program. The stories that intrigue fifth graders terrify kindergartners. When I tell in schools, I have less-shivery stories for grades "K" through two. However, when I am hired to tell Halloween stories to a family audience, I explain that I will start out benignly and graduate to scarier stories. As the evening wears on, I continue to say, "The next story has witches and a lot of blood in it. If you feel this is inappropriate for your children, thanks for coming and I'll see you next year."

I recently told stories at a resort hotel in upstate New York. My closing story was very sweet, but I explained to the audience beforehand that it contained a couple of words that parents might have to define to their children under twelve. If they felt it was premature to explain these words, then this was the time to make their exit.

Gayle Ross: Elizabeth Ellis and I had a conversation about the list of topics that storytellers were having to leave alone in order to get work. It included everything I am. Creation tales that are not from the Bible, magic, witches, all of the things that are an inherent part of the Native American tradition of storytelling. I have experienced the phenomenon of telling to a large group of children in public school, beginning the introduction identifying a story as being about a ghost or a witch, and having the teachers immediately snatch specific children and take them from the room, because their parents have instructed that this be done. It was fairly unsettling. I honestly don't know what I would do if I was confronted with the idea that I could not use certain material. That has not happened to me yet. I have to admit that if it came up once I got there and was not brought up or made an issue when I was hired, I would probably do my best to skate gracefully through the day and get out of there. But if somebody called me up and told me this as a condition of being hired, I would say, "Sorry, you need to talk to somebody else. This is not my play." I could never willingly say, "Sure, I can come and do your school and I'll just leave those stories out." That would not work for me. I would not be able to do that.

Heather Forest: I am acutely aware when I am engaged to tell stories that I have been hired and I am in a service occupation. My responsibility is to serve the needs of my listeners and my sponsor, so I want to be aware on many different levels of what their expectations are. If I am in a community which finds references to the supernatural uncomfortable for their spiritual practice, then I want to know about that so that I am not insulting them with my presentation.

I don't feel that as a storyteller I can impose my values on my listeners, although my choice of stories tends to reflect my values. I do, on the other hand, try to be sensitive to the needs of the audience.

I have had an experience where I was told not to celebrate the imagination, because celebration of the imagination was part of new age theology, and visualization experiences would take children away from the Bible. I responded to that by saying that I understood that their spirituality was rooted in a fundamentalist interpretation of scripture and that I respect their right to their interpretation of scripture and their choice of educating their children in the way that they think is a healthy and fruitful way. However, they had invited me to tell stories, and that I felt that just telling stories to the children would be using their imaginations. But I was informed that this was different from talking about the imagination. So basically I told stories and didn't talk about the imagination because they didn't want to hear about it, but I was able to feel comfortable that I wasn't censoring my repertoire beyond reasonable requests, because, despite doing what I normally do, I would, by mentioning it or not, be helping children to use their imagination.

That was an awkward experience, but it opened my eyes to realize that there are many different viewpoints in the world and that I have to be respectful of the diversity in the world. I am sometimes dumbfounded by the requests that I should not tell stories about this or about that. Yet, with a wide enough repertoire, I have found that I have been able to be sensitive to the needs of my sponsors in a secular setting. For example, in a school setting I tend not to tell religious stories. Whereas in a religious setting, like a synagogue or a church, I might be more inclined to tell stories that would reflect the culture I have been invited to participate in. It's a feast for the mind, but one wants to serve the appropriate meal.

Milbre Burch: A few years ago I had a very strong reaction from a parent after I had told "Mr. Fox" in a school. Her child had been troubled by the story. That's legitimate. It's a troubling story. But, the mother was very frustrated in her attempt to get someone—the teacher, the principal, even the local police—to see how upset she was. And all of this by hearing the story second-hand from her child; there's an example of the power of storytelling. In the long run, the child felt better and eventually the mother calmed down. In the meantime, I had learned a lesson.

It made me realize that I have a lot of responsibility when I go to a school and do a concert, especially if it's a one-shot deal, in and out the same day. Now I only tell "Mr. Fox" in school settings with clearance ahead of time from a school representative.

I have been told not to mention "witches" in a variety of settings. I find this perfectly acceptable if I'm presenting to a group of mentally or emotionally challenged adults, some of whom are downright delusional. Otherwise, it seems to me that "not mentioning witches" is practically un-American. The horror of the witch trials both in the United States and in Europe foreshadowed the Holocaust fifty years ago, and the ethnic cleansing happening today. Talk about being forced to repeat mistakes we haven't learned from!

Olga Loya (a California storyteller who tells Latin American tales) once said in concert, "You can hardly tell a story from Latin America without mentioning the devil." So censoring certain images from stories advocates cutting whole pieces out of many cultural cloths. To what end? Making those cultures more acceptable? Excuse me? Coping with each other's cultural icons, rituals, and stories is all part of this great multicultural experiment that we call the United States.

Pleasant DeSpain: I have been censored from time to time in schools. When that happens, I see if I can compromise. I have found, so far, that I have been able to, when there has been a strong objection to a particular story. For example, one of the stories I tell is "The Boy Who Drew Cats," a Japanese tale. They don't want to hear about a demon rat in Christian schools.

That is surprising to me because good versus evil seems to be a central theme in most of these schools' curriculums. I, fortunately, have a large repertoire and have been able to substitute other stories. The thing is: I am their guest and being paid to give a program. I will do what I can to conform to their needs as long as it does not compromise my integrity. And when I am out doing my own programs, I tell what I want to tell in the way that I want to tell.

Carol Birch: A woman told me the other day that her husband said their son wasn't allowed to read any more fantasies. He was to read "real stuff with data." She actually said her husband wanted their son to become a great scientist. I told her to tell her husband that data changes, and that I thought without fantasy and invention their son could become a technician but never a "Great Scientist."

Reviews of Richard Kennedy's story "The Porcelain Man" judged it to be appropriate for preschool through second grade. I told it to third-graders at a school where three teachers went to their union representative to complain that I was inappropriately telling students about sexual matters. In one sense they were correct to notice that the story includes an awakening.

A girl "who had grown pale and dreamy from longing and too much obedience to her father," fashions a statue out of porcelain. The statue is naked and the embarrassed girl throws a blanket around it. When she touches it, the statue comes to life. He encircles her with his arms, says, "I love you," and kisses her. Who walks in but her father. He smashes a chair over the statue, shattering it to pieces. And then he drops to his knees, saying, "I've addled somebody's brains." This is one-thirtieth of the story, and the principal heard the story so she knew I hadn't spoken lasciviously to the children.

I wanted the principal to allow me to meet with the teachers, since I'd told this story to children many times without such a response, or I suggested she might want to discuss some issues of the story with the children.

Was the porcelain man really a man or a statue?

Why did the porcelain change from a broken vase to a male statue and then into a horse statue and finally end up a plate?

What other story can you think of in which a kiss awakens a girl from one level of life to another?

Another storyteller and educator suggested a worthwhile strategy to protect me from future attacks. The suggestion was to write out discussion questions and distribute them along with a synopsis of each story and photocopies of reviews of the books from which the stories come. The school then knows beforehand what you're going to tell. If they don't read them and object before, you are safe. They also see that you are not cavalier about your selection of stories and realize you've chosen a story that has been well-received by people who evaluate stories and care about children. While this may provide protection from accusations of telling "inappropriate stories," it feels stifling to me. I didn't become a teacher in elementary school because I didn't want to prepare lesson plans. And this leaves no room for spontaneity in my selection of stories. But if your bread and butter is school visits, it may be a useful strategy.

Whenever I tell witch stories, I think of Judith Black's experience. A newspaper reporter from somewhere in middle America called her to inquire about censorship issues. When he asked if she told stories about witches and she said no, he responded with: "Ah, censorship, huh?" But Judith told him she knew too many witches and she wouldn't want to offend them. The newsman laughed and said:

"Only in New England would you get this response!"

David Novak: Halloween and Christmas are the two times when you could run into trouble in schools.

It's Halloween time. I'm in a school. I say, "Can I do a ghost story in this school? Can I do a story that has gremlins in it or some other weird creature?" If there's an objection, I'll cut the story. I think it's more important that stories are being told to children, and that's where most of the censorship comes up—in the school setting. It's more important that stories be told than it is that *certain* kinds of stories are told. I'm not out to make sure the world appreciates a ghost story. I'm more interested in people being open to my stories.

WHAT ARE THE COPYRIGHT LAWS
CONCERNING STORYTELLING?

A lot of misinformation seems to circle around in the storytelling community about the copyright law. There's a good reason for that. The copyright law has gone through a number of changes over the past twenty-five years. We thought it would be a good idea to talk to a lawyer and ask him questions pertaining particularly to storytellers. Andy Norwood of the law firm Waller Lansden Dortch & Davis in Nashville, Tennessee, spoke at the 1994 National Storytelling Conference on the topic "Living Happily Ever After with the Copyright Act." In this section, Andy explains certain aspects of the copyright law in an easy-to-understand way. Following the interview with Andy, we have included portions of the Copyright Act that we think will be helpful.

[Editor's note: The information contained in this chapter is for illustrative and educational purposes only and is based on summaries of laws, court decisions, and hypothetical situations. Nothing in this chapter should be construed as legal advice on a specific situation. Moreover, the law constantly evolves and over time the information in this chapter may become inaccurate. Readers confronted with specific legal problems are therefore encouraged to seek advice from legal counsel. Neither Tennessee nor Alabama certifies specialists in intellectual property law, and Andy Norwood does not claim certification in any area.]

Andy Norwood: Understand that the underlying principle of the Copyright Act is not: "We want to protect people who create intellectual property." The underlying principle is: "We want you, because you have something valuable—that is, a piece of intellectual property—to share it with the rest of us. Here's our deal: If you will give it to us, so that we can all share it and build on it, we will give you as a *quid pro quo* a limited term of protection to reward you for sharing with us."

If you'll use that as your touchstone every time you think of the Copyright Act—if you'll go back and say, "OK, how does this affect the public good by getting me to share my idea with everybody"—it'll make things a lot clearer.

[If I hear a storyteller tell a folktale can I tell it the way he tells it?]

Well, maybe. Let's start with the basic presumption that it is a folktale in the public domain. Let's use "Johnny Appleseed" as an example. The question is whether or not the telling of that tale creates any property rights in that speaker so that he or she can prevent you from later telling "Johnny Appleseed." Under just the federal Copyright Act, the storyteller will not have any copyright in that story simply by virtue of telling it. That doesn't mean that the speaker couldn't pursue you legally under some other state law remedy, such as common law copyright, unjust enrichment, or unfair competition. But laying that aside for a minute, the issue of whether there is any copyright in that—just because the speaker got up and told it in a particular way—the answer is "no," there is no copyright.

[If I find a folktale in a copyrighted book, can I tell it?]

Understand, at its most basic, copyright does not protect an idea. It only protects the fixed form of expression of an idea. To the extent that there is a story about a man who wears a pot on his head and dances around the country planting appleseeds that later become apple orchards is not copyrightable. The particular way that you choose to tell that story—your fixed form of expression—is copyrightable. So while you can probably (under the Copyright Act, at least) tell the story you read (even though the book has a copyright), you must be very careful not to use the fixed form of expression that appears in that book.

Let me make it clear, we are only talking about copyright. There may be other remedies that come into play. I don't want people to have the idea that just because they are in a safe harbor under the Copyright Act that they can never be sued and sued successfully. Moreover, altering the fixed form of expression a little bit will not do. The standard under the Copyright Act is "substantially similar," not "identical."

[If I take that version of "Johnny Appleseed" and make it my own, can I copyright my version?]

Yes. Your fixed form of expression.

[What if you read a story in a copyrighted book, but you suspect that story is really from a traditional source. What must you do to prove that it is a folktale in the public domain? How do you protect yourself?]

Good old-fashioned legwork is the best. Many books now, especially the ones from the publishers that tend to specialize in this area, will contain bibliographies and statements about sources. You need to see if you can't find similar stories elsewhere.

The "Johnny Appleseed" story is a good one because it is unique. There's a specific set of facts. You're probably not going to be able to come up with a story from the Bible or Greek mythology that comes close to the basic plot lines of "Johnny Appleseed." As you start to search for the origins of stories, it's probably a matter of doing it once to learn how. After that, it'll begin to seem fairly easy. You'll learn which section of the library you need to go to. You'll learn exactly what book to look in. You may find three or four that are particularly good sources for you to find stories with plot lines similar to the one you're looking at. Even if you find a story in several sources, make sure it has been copied under a license in each source. A copyright owner has the right to tell forty other people "yes" and still sue if you use it without permission.

[If I'm not taking any pay for a performance, do I need to worry about permission to perform copyrighted material?]

Yes. The issue of whether you can use another person's copyrighted work under the Fair Use section of the Copyright Act is a very difficult and delicate question. There is not anything that says, for instance, if you only use three sentences then that's OK.

There is a list of purposes contained within the Fair Use section of the Copyright Act. It says that to the extent that you are using a copyrighted work for one of these purposes or a similar purpose, then there is a chance that what you are doing is a fair use.

The list that's specifically in the law is:
criticism,
comment,
news reporting,
teaching,
scholarship, and
research.
In addition to seeing whether you can jump over that first hurdle, there's a second hurdle—four factors that Congress actually listed in the Act that a court is

supposed to look to, at a minimum, to decide whether a particular use is fair.

One of those four factors is the one you just alluded to. That is, The Purpose and Character of the Use, including whether the use is of a commercial nature or is for non-profit educational purposes. It's helpful to understand that a lot of the Fair Use doctrine of the Copyright Act has to do with protecting teachers. We want teachers to be able to essentially photocopy things to help them teach. If a teacher is going make fifteen copies of a short story for fifteen members of his or her class, that's the genuine ideal the Fair Use section is there to protect.

The same thing goes for book reviews. We want critics at newspapers, magazines, radio and TV stations to feel free to say, "Norwood can't write a coherent sentence," and then quote a paragraph from my book showing that it makes no sense. We don't want that person to be subject to copyright infringement for having done that.

Just because you are telling your story someplace where they didn't charge admission doesn't mean that what you're doing is not of a commercial nature, or doesn't have a commercial purpose to it. It may be that you're telling the story at a festival where they've charged an admission fee and those funds go to support the festival. It may be that in so doing you're able to promote yourself into future fee-paying events. It may be that by doing that, you're able to promote your book or audio tape that you're selling on a little table outside the meeting hall. So, you can't just look at that and say, "Did I get a dollar for my five-minute talk?"

The second of the four factors is The Nature of the Copyrighted Work. What that basically comes down to is an analysis of two factors: one (there's a lot of litigation behind this and we probably don't want to go into it too deeply here), whether the

work is published or unpublished. There is more protection for works that have not been published. The thinking being that in addition to having the right to decide what to publish, a copyright owner also has the right to decide where and whether to publish. This also comes down more frequently on the side of the copyright holder where it is a creative work, which is entitled to more copyright protection than a factual work. A book of poetry gets more protection than a history book.

The third factor is The Amount and Substantiality of the Portion Used in Relation to Copyrighted Work as a Whole. I generally try to be a little more simple than that. They want to know, "What did you get?" and "How much of the good stuff did you take?" You're going to have what courts call the quantitative analysis. How many words of the whole story or the whole book did you take? And in the qualitative: Did you leave out the stuff that really didn't matter? Did you leave out the first paragraph and then take all the rest of it?

The last factor is the one the courts say is most important. That factor is The Effect of the Use on the Potential Market for Value of the Copyrighted Work. One thing to watch for here is the potential market for or value of the copyrighted work. Several courts have gone so far as to say, "We're looking at this to determine whether, if such a use were to become widespread, it would damage the market for or value of the copyrighted work." That's a pretty easy standard for the copyright holder to meet. The problem here is not just "I told the story three times, so that's three places the copyright holder could have told it." You also need to do an analysis of whether you're doing such a lousy job of telling the story that you're messing it up for the copyright holder.

[Let's talk about librarians for the moment. They have a lot more leeway with Fair Use—judging it by these four factors.]

Sure.

[What about a teacher—or a media specialist. If they take a story and tell it in the school, would this be OK, even though it is a copyrighted story?]

Yes, probably. Teachers are going to get a lot of leeway under this section of the Act. They're going to get a lot of opportunity to do what they want to. I think that the rule pretty much holds true with regard to librarians as well. We're talking about institutions where people are pursuing one of the worthiest goals we have, which is the education of our children. They're going to get a big break on using copyrighted material in that context. The idea being, "Well, copyright holders, show me where you really got hurt."

[Let's take this scenario one step further and suppose that the media specialist has worked up a program in which her students were all reciting copyrighted material. The school principal was so enthused about the program that he decided to open it to the public and charge admission at the door.]

Well, the section says, "… teaching, including multiple copies for classroom use." You've probably gone beyond teaching and copies for classroom use to "Play Production." It's very different if you sit in a class and read Our Town aloud among the students for two days to give them a flavor of what the play is like than if you actually stage it in the auditorium and sell $2.50 tickets and concessions. You've probably gone beyond teaching and beyond the scope of permissible fair use.

[Let's say I find a story and I know somehow that this story is still protected by a copyright. So I start my search, but this author or his estate is so obscure, so buried in the mists, that I can find no trace of it. And to hire someone to search it out is going to cost me more money than the story would ever give me in use value. What about that?]

Well, now you are not asking for copyright or legal advice. You're asking me for a business call. Obviously there are situations where hunting down a copyrighted piece and getting appropriate permissions will, in your mind, come down to a comparison of, "Is doing the story without permission really worth the risk?"

The advice I can give you is to tell you what the risks are under the Copyright Act. The Act provides civil and criminal penalties for copyright infringement. For the most part, storytellers aren't going to have to worry too much about the criminal infringement penalties. That's more for people who are bootlegging cassette tapes. They're the ones who are going to get fined and jail time. The civil penalties are stiff enough, nonetheless.

A copyright holder is entitled to recover his or her actual damages, which means the damages that I can prove that stemmed from what you did. It's hard, in most cases, to show exactly what damage you suffer because of copyright infringement. Recognizing that, the Congress has provided what are called "statutory damages." Per work infringed, a copyright holder may make an election to have the judge assess statutory damages. These are at the discretion of the judge, after the fact of liability for infringement has been established, and those damages run from $500 to $20,000 per work infringed.

Now those damages are only available where the copyright has been appropriately registered. In addition, the judge can assess court costs and attorneys' fees against the infringing party. The case that you put forward is one of willful infringement. "I know this is infringing. I know I shouldn't do it, but I'm going to go full-speed ahead and damn the torpedoes." In this case, the damages could be as high as

$100,000 per work infringed, plus costs and attorneys' fees.

[Are there any restrictions on my using material in which the copyright has lapsed? Writers like Robert Louis Stevenson or Edgar Allen Poe or Nathaniel Hawthorne.]

You are free to use anything in the public domain whether you are converting it to your own or taking their fixed form of expression and using it exactly as it appears.

[Is it safe to say that anything is in the public domain that was published seventy-five or more years ago?]

Generally.

There are a few things that might jump up and bite you. The Act has changed. We're dealing with two different laws in different periods of time, depending on where we are. The law now says that, generally, copyright is the life of the author plus fifty years.

There are some works where that doesn't apply. If you create what is called a work for hire, that is, a work that you do at the instigation of your employer as a part of your job, the copyright isn't tied to anybody's life. It runs from date of publication.

There was a time when the life of the author didn't matter. There was a copyright term from the time you registered it. There were renewal provisions. (You don't know it, but we're about to step into the murkiest, most tangled and complicated swamp in the great dismal that is the Copyright Act.) Generally, these terms total up to seventy-five years. There was a 28-year period, a second 28-year period, and then, on another amendment of the act, an additional 19-year period to make it fair.

That's why you hear the general rule of thumb that seventy-five years is as much copyright protection as anybody's going to have.

[What exactly is a work for hire? Is that when you write for a newspaper?]

Well, maybe.

It's simply a recognition by the Act that sometimes there are people other than the author who are entitled to be owners of the copyright.

The typical case is an employer who has an employee create what would otherwise be a copyrightable work in the line and scope of his employment. If I write a legal brief for my law firm to file in federal court, my law firm holds the copyright in that brief because that is a part of my job. It is copyrightable, but the copyright in the first instance belongs to my firm.

With a newspaper reporter, if that reporter is sitting at the city desk and somebody calls and says, "There's a fire on Main Street," and the reporter goes and does interviews with the arson investigator and the fire department and the people who lived in the building and writes that story, the copyright belongs to the newspaper.

On the other hand, if that person is a librarian who writes a twice-monthly book review on his own time and on his own schedule, it may be that the copyright in that belongs to that author.

[I have a daughter-in-law who is a jewelry designer. She works for a jewelry store. She designs there. Who owns the copyright?]

Well, assuming that there is any, and that's an open question, and assuming that is a part of her job, her employer would in the first instance own the copyright for those designs.

Let me tell you about another work for hire. There are two ends to this beast. The other end is a certain limited class of commissioned works which can become works for hire. However, it is a strict test and a lot of people are very confused about this.

To be a work for hire under this "specially commissioned" part of the test there has to be a written agreement between the person who creates the copyrightable work and the person who commissions it that says, "This is a work for hire."

At least one court has said (and I think it's going to become the dominant view) that this agreement has to be made in advance. In other words, there is no such thing as a retroactive commissioned work for hire. After that, assuming that you meet those two requirements, there is also a list of items that can be works for hire.

If the item is not listed, it cannot be a commissioned work for hire:

contribution to a collective work (like Encyclopedia Brittanica),

as part of a motion picture or audio-visual work,

translations,

supplementary work,

compilation,

instructional text,

tests,

answers to a test, or

an atlas.

[If my work is not a work for hire but I wish to sell it, I can still do that, can't I?]

Your copyright is as fully transferable as the title to your automobile. Maybe even to a greater extent. If you decide to sell your copyright to somebody, you can do so. If you decide to give someone an exclusive license to use your copyrighted material—even for the life of the copyright—you're free to do that. It is a piece of property. Visual artists have certain other, more extensive, rights.

[If I see a movie or a TV show or a play, and I condense that story into my own words, can I tell that story? Because I'm just telling the idea, right?]

There's no copyright on the idea. I've been following with some interest the litigation that's brewing out of Japan about whether the idea for *The Lion King* was stolen. My own personal take on that is you're going to have a hard time saying that the idea of a family where the son comes back

to avenge his father the king's murder by the uncle is an original idea. I don't think that line of reasoning is going to get you very far.

[If so, old Willie Shakespeare would have terrible trouble with Thomas Kyd's relatives over the plot of Hamlet.]

I think you have to stand up and take your medicine. You have to say, "You're darned right we ripped it off, your honor. And here's where—Hamlet." Of course, Hamlet is a public domain work.

[That's a hoot. So, basically, you're able to do that?]

Yes, there are certainly places where you can do that, but the question becomes: At what point does your attempt not to be substantially similar stop being a concern as far as copyright infringement is concerned and get you in trouble with state laws such as unfair competition?

[Let me be more specific. What if I saw an episode of "The Twilight Zone," can I lift the story from that episode and tell it for profit? It would be in my own words.]

You can, but you begin to run a risk. You run a risk that you're going to find somebody who is willing to pursue you, and who is litigious enough to do so, and who finds a lawyer who understands the intricacies of it to know that perhaps what you did was not copyright infringement, but it's worth pursuing you on the basis of other state law. He's going to say, "Your honor, it's just plain not fair!"

[Continuing with this line of questioning, what if I collect and tell someone else's true life story and I copyright my version? What are the rights to their own story? Let me further complicate it this question by asking: You and I are talking right now. I've called you on the phone. You're talking to me. I'm recording your words. Who owns the copyright on what you say?]

Which one of those disparate and complicated issues do you want to get into first?

[Let's start with the last question. Do you and all the other people interviewed in this book own the copyright on what you say? Who holds the copyright?]

Copyright in mere oral expression and utterances does not exist. To be a valid copyright, the copyrightable material (the property) must be fixed in a tangible medium of expression. Just saying it out into the air doesn't do the job.

[But it is being fixed right now by a tape recording.]

Merely recording your voice as your words go out into the air does not obtain copyright for you in *what you say.*

Now let me draw a couple of fine distinctions. I do have copyright in the way my voice sounds on your tape. So if you were to take this tape and begin to play it at seminars and conferences, while I might not have copyright in my expression (meaning the strings of words that I put together), I will have copyright in the sound of my voice as it is captured on that tape.

I got this question at the Storytelling Conference. Apparently there is a misconception out there among storytellers that if they just stick a Dictaphone under the lectern before they start speaking and turn it off when they're finished, that captures for them copyright in their story.

That's not true.

Some of them may have been told at some point that there is copyright in that (and there is), but it is the copyright in the sound of their voice as they tell it—not the story that was told.

[OK. Let's take this one step further. I go someplace where some storyteller is holding forth, and this storyteller has not written down that story. That story has not been "fixed" in some tangible medium of expression. I have a recorder with me. I record his story. I take it home. I transcribe it from the tape into my word processor. I change the story. Then I print it or I put it on an audio cassette. Does this storyteller have any recourse?]

Now wait. In all of those verbs, there was one where you said, "I change it." What do you change? Are you still telling the story of the son who revenges his father's death against the murderous uncle? Or do you change the word "black" to "gray" in an 800-word story and say, "I changed it."

Let's say you don't change it. Let's say you learn how to tell it word for word. Let's say you type it up. Copyright in the first instance belongs to the author at the time it is fixed in the tangible medium of expression. It does not have anything to do with when you register it or when you mail it in or when you do something silly like stick it in an envelope and mail it to yourself. That copyright will exist from the time you write it down.

[But how can you prove that?]

How can I prove you didn't? It is an interesting issue and one that I get at seminars constantly. And it's one that practically never comes up in the real world.

When you write down the story, at that point, you are the owner of copyright in that story if you are the author.

Now if it ever comes down to brass tacks, what's going to shake out is that you are not the author of that story. The author is the person who created it, and that is the person who told it at the storytelling conference where you nefariously went with your evil and wicked recording device, and thieved it away from its rightful owner.

Probably what is going to happen, if that storyteller is willing and able to pursue you, is he or she is going to get the copyright back, even if you take the time to record it, transcribe it, and register the copyright.

If you steal from one person, that's copyright infringement. If you steal from two people, that's plagiarism. If you steal from three people, that's literary deceit. If you steal from four or more people, that's masterful research.

[I love that.]

It's not a doctrine of the law.

[Let's go back to the first of these two questions. Can I collect and tell someone else's true life story and copyright my version? What are their rights to their own story?]

People's own name, image, likeness, and, if you will, story, are going to enjoy different protections outside of the Copyright Act. There is going to be a greater willingness on the part of courts to indulge those individuals against people who may be stealing from them. Furthermore, acting in this fashion would implicate privacy rights—a good topic for another day.

[But if I make a tape or a written version of that same story, is that story now mine?]

Well, you own copyright in your fixed form of the expression of that story. A lot of this will depend on the circumstances in which you got that story.

The easiest and most logical thing for people to do in the situation that you're talking about is to get a necessary permission. Even if it's not necessary, it's perfectly acceptable to have belts and suspenders.

[So if I want to tell someone's original story from, let's say, a copyrighted work, then I simply need to get permission. Is that it?]

Exactly. There are some tricks of the trade, if you will, that I can tell you to watch out for. But, yes, the easiest thing is to get permission. If the person denies you permission, don't do it.

You don't want to be in that situation anyway. Since my introduction to the storytelling community, I've heard there are some people out there who are notorious for never giving permission for anybody to do anything, ever.

But some of them are very willing and accessible and say, "Sure, send me fifty bucks and tell the story as many times as you want to." There is nothing as good as being on the side of God and the angels.

The best resource for anybody telling is to have their own mind and their own experience. That's my personal opinion—both as a listener to stories and as a copyright attorney.

The time, effort, incredible expense, and aggravation that I see people going through to get the rights to tell one four-minute story! If they had just turned that energy and attention to creating their own, they'd have a better story. Then maybe they could aggravate somebody else about permission to use it.

I am serious. You would not believe the length to which I have heard authors call my office, simply wail and moan because they had to have that story. Nothing else would do. "I've called the Copyright Clearance Center. I've called the publisher of the book and it's out of business. I've hunted down the estate in California and it's out of probate now. The widow's dead. I can't find the one son. Somebody thought he moved to Los Angeles." I'm thinking, how many phone calls and how many hours must you have expended trying to reach this one goal which, in my opinion (and I'm not an artist) is of questionable and dubious value once you get it?

I read a lot of legal publications, obviously, and I constantly read about people who have figured out these complicated, multi-state, tangled webs of conspiracy for criminal ends. And I think if that person had just turned half of that energy to a legitimate pursuit, there's no telling what they'd be worth.

One of the tricks of the trade to remember is when you go out and try to get the story that you absolutely have to have—

nothing else will do—it is the ultimate story that will cause the audience to burst into thunderous standing ovations and call you back for encores and you just have to have it—make sure that where you go to get permission is to the person who has the right to give the permission. Many, many times it is not the author. Especially if you found the story in a published source. You're always better off in the first instance to go to the publisher.

There is no incentive for the publisher to mislead you. If that publisher has the exclusive right to let you tell the story, under a contract with the author (or whoever owns the copyright), the publisher can allow you to tell the story and set the exact dollar amount. They will have a professional staff that can handle that, who will take your check, who will cut you the appropriate permission letter, and make sure everything is square with the author. Then, even if the author objects, there is not much he or she can do about it if the publisher has granted you permission.

On the other hand, many authors are ignorant, confused, or forgetful about what their publishing contract provides. They will tell you they have the right to grant a permission that they may not have. If the case comes down to it, and the publisher decides to sue you for copyright infringement, the publisher may well be able to sue you, proceed and prevail. And if you say, "But the author said I could." They will say, "Well, the author didn't have the right."

[Some storytellers think they have better luck when they go to the author first.]

It's fine to go to the author as long as the author is the one who holds the rights. If he doesn't, you're wasting your time.

Let's say you are the writer of a great book. If I look at the book, even if it says, Copyright, Bill Mooney, New Jersey, and gives your address and phone number and says, "For permissions call him," and I call; if you don't, in fact, own the copyright, you don't have the right to give me permission under the contract.

Now it may be that, in the real world, not every publisher is willing to risk ticking off its authors by saying, "Hey, you granted permission when you didn't have the right to grant it, and we're mad at you and we're going to pursue this person you granted the permission to." But there are at least a couple, because I have represented them.

In addition to that, the way for you to help yourself, as the person trying to obtain the permission, is to get the author to give you something in writing. Always do that just to be safe. In addition to getting them to say, "I give you permission to do thus and so," make them also say, "I have the right to give you permission to do thus and so."

There are people out there who will say, "Well, yeah, for my part of it, I'll let you tell that story all you want for twenty dollars. Send me a check."

You send them the check. Then you get a nasty letter from their publisher or their publisher's attorney saying, "Stop doing this."

And you say, "But I have permission from Joe."

And they say, "Well, that's fine, but you really need permission from us, too. What did you give him?"

"I gave him twenty bucks."

"Well, he owes us ten of that, and we're going to charge you a thousand." You can sue Joe, if you want. But if you do, it's nice to have something in writing.

[What about a story that's based on a newspaper article. Can I take it and tell it in my own words without permission?]

You're a lot safer telling stories based on true life actual events than you are trying to tell stories that are the product of someone else's imagination.

[Would that hold true for any historical event? You could use that event to make your own version of it?]

Sure. There's no copyright existing in the fact that in the 1860s there was a terrible battle near a shoe factory in Gettysburg, Pennsylvania. There is probably some copyright in phrases like, "Fourscore and seven years ago, our fathers brought forth …" Maybe that's a little bit silly and an extreme example, and presents me with a problem because there is no copyright in a U.S. government work, but that's the distinction. So, to the extent that you want to tell the story of the Battle of Gettysburg, have at it. Just use your own form of expression.

[So I can take all that has been written on the copyright law and use it in our book? Because it is written by the government?]

You can reproduce the Copyright Act one hundred percent, and they're happy for you to do so. It's a good source. I always beat this drum and everyone just nods at me like I was their senile old aunt, but it's a good thing to read.

Another thing about the government: Back in the 1930s, the WPA collected zillions of first-person accounts. There were hundreds of writers involved in interviewing projects during the Depression. All of that material is free for the taking and using.

[What would a simple permission form need to include? You just mentioned two things: Can I do it? and: Do you have the right to give me permission to do it?]

First and foremost, do you have the right?

The second thing is, grant me the right.

The third thing is, a term (how long you will have the right).

The fourth is the money, how much for how long.

It should be dated.

It should be signed, at a minimum, by the party giving the permission. Usually it is considered professional and courteous to have the person giving the permission sign it, send it to you, you counter-sign it, and send back a copy for them to keep.

It's also especially damning if they later come out of the woodwork screaming at you and you can go through the discovery processes to find the letter that they signed in their files.

[How do I go about obtaining a copyright?]

Copyright belongs in the first instance to the author who fixes the work in the tangible medium of expression (assuming it's not government work or work for hire or some other things we've discussed).

From the moment you write it down, you are the owner of the copyright. You have done everything you need to do to obtain the copyright. However, for your benefit, the U.S. government has created the Copyright Office.

The Copyright Office provides you certain benefits.

They will send you a nice shiny registration certificate, which is good for your ego.

They will record what is presumptively the date that you created the work and prevent others from being able to create it later and say, "See? I had it in 1997," when you can say, "I had it in 1995 and the government says so."

They will also provide you certain benefits under the Copyright Act.

You remember that we discussed earlier statutory damages. Unless you have registered your work with the U.S. Copyright Office within ninety days of first publication, you're not entitled to recover statutory damages. There are other benefits that are probably less important. Before you can file any suit for copyright infringement, you have to register for copyright protection.

[Can I find those forms at the library?]

It depends on your local library and how large your town is. If you come from Slapout, Alabama, you may have some trouble. If you're in Cincinnati, Ohio, your odds are pretty good.

You don't even have to go out in the weather and get wet if you don't want to. The Copyright Office maintains a forms hotline. You can call the hotline. It works just like an answering machine or voice mail. You just give them your address and phone number and tell them which copyright form you want. In about two weeks, a nice little book with tear-out forms and instructions arrives. You are also permitted to make photocopies of that work. There is no copyright. It is a U.S. government work.

Fill it out for as many different works as you have. Submit that to the copyright office, along with $20 and two copies of what they call the best edition of the work. If it's a book, you should send the book. If you're doing it at home on your laser printer and you're printing it out, print out two copies. Bind them the best you can.

(Editor's note: Taking Andy Norwood's advice, we have copied some salient sections of the copyright law that you might find interesting and useful. If the prose sometimes seems a little stiff, it is because we are quoting directly from the U.S. Government's Copyright Basics; hence the expressions "fixed," "tangible medium of expression," et cetera. If you wish to receive the booklets themselves from the Copyright Office, call their hotline: 202-707-9100. They are free.)

WHAT EXACTLY IS COPYRIGHT?

Copyright is the protection given to "original works of authorship" (a book, a story, a song, a painting, a sculpture, an audio- or videotape, etc.) that "are fixed in a tangible medium of expression" (very simply, there has to be a copy or a recording of the work).

The copyright law does not protect your ideas. It protects only the particular expression of your ideas. The copyright law states, "In no case does copyright protection for an original work of authorship extend to any idea, procedure, process, system, method of operation, concept, principle, or discovery, regardless of the form in which it is described, explained, illustrated, or embodied in such work." It is only the author's expression of an idea that is protected, not the idea itself.

A copyright is just that: a right to make a copy of a particular form of expression. The Copyright Act gives you (the owner of the copyright) the exclusive right to do and to authorize others to do the following:

• To reproduce the copyrighted work in copies or phonorecords;

• To prepare derivative works based upon the copyrighted work;

• To distribute copies or phonorecords of the copyrighted work to the public by sale or other transfer of ownership, or by rental, lease, or lending;

• To perform the copyrighted work publicly, in the case of literary, musical, dramatic, and choreographic works, pantomimes, and motion pictures and other audiovisual works, and

• To display the copyrighted work publicly, in the case of literary, musical, dramatic, and choreographic works, pantomimes, and pictorial, graphic, or sculptural works, including the individual images of a motion picture or other audiovisual work.

Copyright protection exists from the time the work is created in a fixed form.

Copyright is secured automatically when the work is created. A work is "created" when it is fixed in a copy or phonorecord for the first time. "Copies" are material objects from which a work can be read or visually perceived either directly or with the aid of a machine or device, such as books, manuscripts, sheet music, film, videotape, or microfilm. "Phonorecords" are material objects embodying "fixed" sounds (excluding motion picture soundtracks), such as audio tapes and phonograph disks. For example, a song (the "work") can be fixed in sheet music ("copies") or in phonograph disks ("phonorecords"), or both.

If a work is prepared over a period of time, the part of the work that is fixed on a particular date constitutes the created work as of that date.

The copyright immediately becomes the property of the author who created it. No publication or registration or other action in the Copyright Office is needed to acquire a copyright. However, even though registration is not required for protection, there are certain advantages when you do register.

» Registration establishes a public record of your copyright claim.
» If you register your work before or within five years of the publication date, that establishes evidence in court of the validity of your copyright.
» If you register within three months after publication of your work (or prior to an infringement of your work), statutory damages and attorney's fees will be available to you in court actions. Otherwise, only an award of actual damages and profits is available to you.

While it is not required, every copyrighted work should contain a copyright notice. The notice lets people know that a copyright is claimed and who the person is that claims it. There are three elements of the copyright notice. They should always be included together.

» The symbol ©, or the word "Copyright," or the abbreviation "Copr.";
» The year of first publication;
» The name of the owner of the copyright. (For example: ©1996 Bill Mooney and David Holt)

The copyright notice for sound recordings (such as audio tapes and phonograph disks known as "phonorecords") is different from that for other works. Sound recordings are defined as "works that result from the fixation of a series of musical, spoken or other sounds, but not including the sounds accompanying a motion picture or other audiovisual work." Copyright in a sound recording protects the particular series of sounds fixed in the recording against unauthorized reproduction, revision, and distribution. This copyright is distinct from copyright of the musical, literary, or dramatic work that is recorded on a phonorecord. Phonorecords may be records (such as CDs or LPs), audio tapes, cassettes, or disks. The notice should contain the following three elements appearing together on the phonorecord.

» The symbol℗;
» The year of first publication of the sound recording;
» The name of the owner of copyright in the sound recording, or an abbreviation by which the name can be recognized, or a generally known alternative designation of the owner. (For example: ℗ 1995 High Windy Audio)

WHAT WORKS ARE PROTECTED?
All original works of authorship in the following categories:

» literary works;
» musical works, including any accompanying words;

» dramatic works, including any accompanying music;
» pantomimes and choreographic works;
» pictorial, graphic, and sculptural works;
» motion pictures and other audiovisual works;
» sound recordings; and
» architectural works.

WHAT IS NOT PROTECTED BY COPYRIGHT?

1. Works that have not been fixed in a tangible form of expression. For example: choreographic works that have not been notated or recorded, or improvisational speeches or performances that have not been written or recorded.

2. Titles, names, short phrases, and slogans; familiar symbols or designs; mere variations of typographic ornamentation, lettering, or coloring; mere listings of ingredients or contents. For example, you cannot copyright the title of a book.

3. Ideas, procedures, methods, systems, processes, concepts, principles, discoveries, or devices, as distinguished from a description, explanation, or illustration.

4. Works consisting entirely of information that is common property and containing no original authorship. For example: standard calendars, height and weight charts, tape measures and rulers, and lists or tables taken from public documents or other common sources.

5. Works of the U.S. government, which include practically all works that are produced and distributed by the U.S. Printing Office. Taxpayers pay for the federal government, so they should be able to copy the work created by the government. For example, most of the information found in this chapter.

6. Works that fall into the public domain. For example, works that were not copyrighted before January 1, 1978, or those works whose copyright has expired.

WHO CAN CLAIM COPYRIGHT?

As we stated above, the copyright immediately becomes the property of the author who created it. Only the author or those deriving their rights through the author can rightfully claim copyright. (For example, Bill was commissioned by The Seeing Eye, an organization that trains guide dogs for blind people, to write and perform stories about its co-founder, Morris Frank. He held the copyright. However, The Seeing Eye wanted to own the copyright, so a financial arrangement was made wherein Bill sold them the copyright.)

In the case of works made for hire, the employer and not the employee is presumptively considered the author. Section 101 of the copyright statute defines a "work made for hire" as:

» a work prepared by an employee within the scope of his or her employment (for example, a newspaper reporter); or
» a work specially ordered or commissioned for use as a contribution to a collective work, as a part of a motion picture or other audiovisual work, as a translation, as a supplementary work, as a compilation, as an instructional text, as a test, as answer material for a test, or as an atlas, if the parties expressly agree in a written instrument signed by them that the work shall be considered a work made for hire …

The authors of a joint work (such as David and Bill in this book) are co-owners of the copyright in the work, unless there is an agreement to the contrary.

If your story is printed in a magazine or included in an anthology, you still own the copyright, even though there may be another copyright on the collection as a whole. (i.e. David Holt and Bill Mooney's anthology, *Ready-To-Tell Tales:* August House Publishers paid each storyteller a one-time use fee for his/her story, but the storytellers retained the ownership of their stories.)

If you merely own a book, a manuscript, painting, or any other copy or phonorecord, that does not mean you own the copyright to it. The law provides that transfer of ownership of any material object that embodies a protected work does not of itself convey any rights in the copyright. (For example, let's say you own one of Laura Simms's cassette tapes. You may play it, you may resell it, or you may choose to throw it at your cat, but that doesn't give you the right to make a copy of her cassette (reproduce it) or to tell the stories in the same way Laura told them on the cassette tape. You cannot copy the "fixed expression" of her creative effort. Many of Laura's stories are original. You cannot use them without her permission. Many of her stories are based on folktales that are in the public domain. You may tell the folktale, but not Laura's version without her permission. You must do your own research and find the source of the folktale. You must make sure it is in the public domain, and then create your own version of the folktale. If the folktale was not originally written in English, then you have to be sure that the translation is not copyrighted.

HOW LONG DOES COPYRIGHT PROTECTION LAST?

A copyright lasts for the life of the author, plus fifty years.

Older copyrights can last from twenty-eight to seventy-five years.

It is generally safe to say that anything written more than seventy-five years ago is no longer under copyright protection. Subtract seventy-five from the present year and that will give you the dividing line. We write this in 1996, so anything written prior to 1921 is probably in the public domain and no longer copyrighted.

Works Originally Created On or After January 1, 1978: A work that was created (this is, fixed in a tangible form for the first time) on or after January 1, 1978, is automatically protected from the moment of its creation, and is ordinarily given a term enduring for the author's life, plus an additional fifty years after the author's death. In the case of "a joint work prepared by two or more authors who did not work for hire," the term lasts for fifty years after the last surviving author's death. For works made for hire, and for anonymous and pseudonymous works (unless the author's identity is revealed in Copyright Office records), the duration of copyright will be seventy-five years from publication or one hundred years from creation, whichever is shorter.

Works Originally Created Before January 1, 1978 But Not Published or Registered by That Date: Works that were created but not published or registered for copyright before January 1, 1978, have been automatically brought under the statute and are now given Federal copyright protection. The duration of copyright in these works will generally be computed in the same way as for works created on or after January 1, 1978: the life-plus-50 or 75/100-year terms will apply to them as well. The law provides that in no case will the term of copyright for works in this category expire before December 31, 2002, and for works published on or before December 31, 2002, the term of copyright will not expire before December 31, 2027.

Works Originally Created and Published or Registered Before January 1, 1978: Before 1978, copyright was obtained either on the date a work was published or, if it was unpublished, on the date it was registered with the Copyright Office. In either case, the copyright was good for a term of 28 years from the date it was secured. During the last year of that 28-year term (that is, in its 28th year), the copyright was eligible for renewal for an additional 28 years.

The current copyright law has extended the renewal term from 28 to 47 years for copyrights that were in effect on January 1, 1978, making these works eligible for a total term of protection of 75 years. However, the copyright had to have been renewed in order to receive the 47-year protection. If the copyright was not secured for the second 28-year term, the work is now considered to be in the public domain.

Therefore, for storytellers' purposes, if the story or the translation of the story you are interested in using was published or registered more than 75 years ago, you can consider that story or its translation to be in the public domain.

WHAT DOES FAIR USE MEAN?

One of the rights accorded to the owner of copyright is the right to reproduce or to authorize others to reproduce the work in copies or phonorecords. This right is subject to certain limitations found in sections 107 through 118 of the copyright act. One of the more important limitations is the doctrine of "fair use."

Section 107 of the copyright law contains a list of the various purposes for which the reproduction of a particular work may be considered "fair," such as criticism, comment, news reporting, teaching, scholarship and research. Section 107 also sets out four factors to be considered in determining whether or not a particular use is fair:

» the purpose and character of the use, including whether such use is of commercial nature or is for nonprofit educational purposes;
» the nature of the copyrighted work;
» the amount and substantiality of the portion used in relation to the copyrighted work as a whole; and
» the effect of the use upon the potential market for or value of the copyrighted work.

The distinction between "fair use" and infringement may be unclear and not easily defined. There is no specific number of words, lines, or notes that may safely be taken without permission. Acknowledging the source of the copyrighted material does not substitute for obtaining permission.

The 1961 Report of the Register of Copyrights on the General Revision of the U.S. Copyright Law cites examples of activities that courts have regarded as fair use:

» quotation of excerpts in a review or criticism for purposes of illustration or comment;
» quotation of short passages in a scholarly or technical work, for illustration or clarification of the author's observations;
» use in a parody of some of the content of the work parodied; summary of an address or article, with brief quotations, in a news report;
» reproduction by a library of a portion of a work to replace part of a damaged copy;
» reproduction by a teacher or student of a small part of a work to illustrate a lesson;
» reproduction of a work in legislative or judicial proceedings or reports;
» incidental and fortuitous reproduction, in a newsreel or broadcast, of a work located in the scene of an event being reported.

Copyright protects the particular way an author has expressed himself; it does not extend to any ideas, systems, or factual information conveyed in the work.

The safest course is always to get permission from the copyright owner before using copyrighted material.

When it is impracticable to obtain permission, use of copyrighted material should be avoided unless the doctrine of "fair use" would clearly apply to the situation.

If you desire more information about what a library and archives may and may not do, we recommend looking over Section 108 of the Revised Copyright Act of 1976.

CITATION GUIDELINES

While in no way intended as a substitute for legal counsel, August House provides its authors with these guidelines for using and citing traditional material obtained from printed, oral, or recorded sources:

It's important to bear in mind that copyright infringement and plagiarism are two different issues. If you fail to adequately cite your sources, you may not be infringing on a copyright (if the work is in public domain or if your use falls within the definition of "fair use"), but you may be plagiarizing.

For August House, this is an important issue, since it jeopardizes the credibility of publisher, author, and book—and often translates directly to the bottom line in sales.

Likewise, merely citing a source doesn't insure that you haven't infringed on that source's copyright. In this case, you may not have plagiarized, but you may have appropriated.

For more information about copyright law and what it means to the storytelling community, see *Living Happily Ever After with the Copyright Act* by E. Andrew Norwood of Waller Lansden Dortch & Davis, prepared for the 1995 National Storytelling Conference.

How Citation Benefits You

Authors who work with traditional material protect themselves in two ways by conscientious citation:

» You protect yourself from claims of infringement by others by demonstrating that you are familiar with the original, public domain sources.
» You protect your work from being infringed upon by others by encouraging them to rely on original, public domain sources rather than only your specific version.

Good storytellers often add their own twists to traditional tales. If you want to protect your original contributions, you owe it to your readers to point them out—and to provide original sources so that they can create their own particular version.

Sourcing Guidelines

1. Wherever possible, attempt to find multiple versions of a tale. (Some of the standard reference books indexing tales by motif are the Motif Index of Folk-Literature by Stith Thompson; The Types of the Folktale by Antti Aarne and Stith Thompson; and The Storyteller's Sourcebook: A Subject, Title, and Motif-Index to Folklore Collections for Children by Margaret Read MacDonald.)

2. If relying on a single printed, oral, or recorded source, cite the source and request permission to reprint it. Get permission in writing and make sure the document reflects the title, approximate publication date, and publisher of your book. *If you change or adapt the story, get permission to do so* and indicate the extent of the alteration in your note.

If your single source is in the public domain, you do not need to get permission but you should provide full citation.

Be prepared to make a compelling argument to your editor for including single-source folktales.

3. If you have two sources, determine whether or not the later source relies on the first one.

(a) If so, you do not have two distinct sources, but one primary source and one derivative source. Follow the same steps as outlined in Paragraph 2 for the primary source.

(b) If not, cite the sources. Indicate in your source note in general terms any alteration or additions you have made in the story in making it your own. You probably don't need to get permission in this event, but your editor will help you make that determination.

4. If you have three or more sources, determine whether or not any of them relies on another.

(a) If all but one version derives from that source, again, you need to consider it the primary source. Follow the same steps outlined in Paragraph 2.

(b) If not, good for you. Follow steps for 3(b) above.

5. In citing printed sources, use the following bibliographic style:

Author, (Story Title, if in anthology or collection,) Book Title (Editor, if anthology). (City: Publisher, Date of Publication).

Follow the bibliographic data with further information about the story, about the culture from which it comes, other versions from other cultures, and other illuminating information. Be sure to disclose the extent to which you have changed the details of the tale.

6. In citing oral sources, include the following information: *(Informant), (Site of Collection), (Date of Collection).* Any further information about your informant—age, cultural background, attitude toward story—will be interesting to the reader.

7. Just because a storyteller or other oral informant gives you permission to include his or her story in your performance repertory doesn't automatically mean you have permission to use it in print or recorded form. Additional permission may be necessary. Please discuss these instances with your editor as soon as possible.

(If you wish to be more fully informed about the doctrine of fair use, call the Copyright Office hotline—202-707-9100—and ask for Circular #21—Reproduction of Copyrighted Works by Educators and Librarians.)

STORYTELLING RESOURCES
◆ ◆ ◆

TRADE ORGANIZATIONS

International Order of E.A.R.S., 12019 Donohoe Avenue, Louisville, KY 40243; 502/245-0643

Folk Alliance, 1001 Connecticut Avenue NW #501, Washington, DC 20036-5504; 202/835-3655

The National Story League, 259 East 41st Street, Norfolk, VA 23504

National Storytelling Association, P.O. Box 309, Jonesborough, TN 37659; 423/753-2171

AWARDS

American Library Association—Notable Books and Recordings, ALA/ALSC, 50 E. Huron Street, Chicago, IL 60611; (800)545-2433, ext 2163

Anne Izard Storyteller's Choice Awards, c/o Westchester Library System, 8 Westchester Plaza, Elmsford, NY 10523; 914/592-8214

Audiofile Earphones Awards, 37 Silver Street, Portland, ME 04112-0109; 207/774-7563

Parents' Choice Awards, P.O. Box 185, Newton, MA 02168; 617/965-5913

Storytelling World Awards, ETSU, Box 70647, Johnson City, TN 37614

REVIEW SOURCES

Audiofile, 37 Silver Street, P.O. Box 109, Portland, ME 04112-0109; 207/774-7563 (reviews audio products)

Blue Ribbon Storytelling, The Bulletin of the Center for Children's Books, 51 Gerty Drive, Champaign, IL 61820; 217/244-0324 (reviews audio and video products)

Booklist, American Library Association, 50 E. Huron Street, Chicago, IL 60611; 312/280-5750 (reviews audios and books)

Pass It On! The Newsletter of the Children's Music Network (CMN), P.O. Box 307, Monvale, NJ, 07645; 617/899-5053 (reviews audio products)

School Library Journal, 249 West 17th Street, New York, NY 10011 (reviews audios and books)

OTHER PERIODICALS OF INTEREST

Storytelling Magazine, National Storytelling Association, P.O. Box 309, Jonesborough, TN 37659; 423/753-2171

Storytelling World, ETSU Box 70647, Johnson City, TN 37614-0647; 423/929-4297

THE STORYTELLER'S BOOKSHELF
♦ ♦ ♦ ♦

The following is not intended to be a comprehensive listing of all the books recommended for storytellers. Indeed, one of the tasks of a storyteller is to constantly search for new sources and information. Rather, these selections are basic resources that form the backbone of a more comprehensive storyteller's library, and are recommended either because they include stories not widely available elsewhere, contain especially "tellable" versions of traditional tales, offer solid and valuable instructional information, or demonstrate a particularly innovative application for storytelling.

Barton, Bob. *Stories in the Classroom: Storytelling, Reading Aloud, and Role Playing With Children.* Portsmouth, New Hampshire: Heinemann, 1990.

————. *Tell Me Another.* Portsmouth, New Hampshire: Heinemann, 1986.

Bauer, Caroline Feller. *New Handbook for Storytellers.* Chicago: American Library Association, 1993.

Best-Loved Stories Told at the National Storytelling Festival. Jonesborough, Tennessee: National Storytelling Press, 1991.

Bettelheim, Bruno. *The Uses of Enchantment: The Meaning and Importance of Fairy Tales.* New York: Alfred A. Knopf, Inc., 1976.

Birch, Carol and Melissa A. Heckler, eds. *Who Says? Essays on Pivotal Issues in Contemporary Storytelling.* Little Rock: August House, 1996.

Blatt, Gloria T., editor. *Once Upon a Folktale: Capturing the Folklore Process with Children.* New York: Teachers College Press, 1993.

Brunvand, Jan Harold. *The Baby Train and Other Lusty Legends.* New York: W.W. Norton & Co., 1984.

————. *The Choking Doberman and Other "New" Urban Legends.* New York: W.W. Norton & Co., 1981.

————. *Curses, Broiled Again! The Hottest Urban Legends Going.* New York: W.W. Norton & Co., 1986.

————. *The Mexican Pet: More "New" Urban Legends and Some Old Favorites.* New York: W.W. Norton & Co., 1981.

————. *The Vanishing Hitchhiker: American Urban Legends and Their Meanings.* New York: W.W. Norton & Co., 1981.

Caduto, Michael J., and Joseph Bruchac. *Keepers of the Animals: Native American Stories and Wildlife Activities for Children.* Golden, Colorado: Fulcrum Publishing, 1991.

————. *Keepers of the Earth: Native American Stories and Environmental Activities for Children.* Golden, Colorado: Fulcrum Publishing, 1991.

Chase, Richard. *Grandfather Tales.* Boston: Houghton Mifflin Co., 1948.

————. *The Jack Tales.* Boston: Houghton Mifflin Co., 1943.

Chinen, Allen B. Once Upon a Midlife: Classic Stories and Mythic Tales to Illuminate the Middle Years. Los Angeles: Jeremy P. Tarcher, 1992.

Cole, Joanna, editor. *Best-Loved Folktales of the World.* New York: Anchor/Doubleday, 1982.

Cooper, Pamela J., and Rives Collins. *Look What Happened to Frog: Storytelling in Education.* Scottsdale, Arizona: Gorsuch Scarisbrick, 1992.

Cooper, Patsy. *When Stories Come to School.* New York: Teachers & Writers Collaborative, 1993.

Creeden, Sharon. *Fair Is Fair: World Folktales of Justice.* Little Rock: August House, 1994.

Crossen, Vicky L., and Jay C. Stailey. *Spinning Stories: An Introduction to Storytelling Skills.* Austin: Texas State University Press, 1988.

Davis, Donald. *Telling Your Own Stories.* Little Rock: August House, 1993.

Denman, Gregory. *Sit Tight, and I'll Swing You a Tail ... Using and Writing Stories with Young People.* Portsmouth, New Hampshire: Heinemann, 1991.

DeSpain, Pleasant. *Thirty-Three Multicultural Tales to Tell.* Little Rock: August House, 1993.

DeVos, Gail. *Tales, Rumors and Gossip: Exploring Contemporary Folk Literature in Grades 7-12.* Englewood, Colorado: Libraries Unlimited, Inc., 1996.

Egan, Kieran. *Teaching as Story Telling.* Chicago: University of Chicago Press, 1989.

Farrell, Catherine. *Storytelling: A Guide for Teachers.* New York: Scholastic Professional, 1993.

Gillard, Marni. *Storyteller Storyteacher: Discovering the Power of Storytelling for Teaching and Living.* York, Maine: Stenhouse Publishers, 1996.

Greene, Ellin. *Storytelling, Art and Technique, 3rd ed.* New Providence, New Jersey: R.R. Bowker, 1996.

Hamilton, Martha and Mitch Weiss. *Children Tell Stories: A Teaching Guide.* Katonah, New York: Richard C. Owen Publishers Inc., 1990.

Holt, David and Bill Mooney. *Ready-To-Tell Tales.* Little Rock: August House, 1994.

Jacobs, Joseph. *English Folk and Fairy Tales.* New York: G.P. Putnam's Sons, c.1988.

Lipman, Doug. *The Storytelling Coach: How to Listen, Praise, and Bring Out People's Best.* Little Rock: August House, 1995.

Lurie, Alison. *Don't Tell the Grown-Ups: Why Kids Love the Books They Do.* New York: Avon Books, 1991.

MacDonald, Margaret Read. *Look Back and See: Twenty Lively Tales for Gentle Tellers.* New York: The H.W. Wilson Co., 1986.

————. *The Storyteller's Sourcebook: A Subject, Title, and Motif-Index to Folklore Collections for Children*. Detroit: Neal-Schuman/Gale Research, 1982.

————. *The Storyteller's Start-Up Book: Finding, Learning, Performing and Using Folktales*. Little Rock: August House, 1993.

————. *Twenty Tellable Tales: Audience Participation Stories for the Beginning Storyteller*. New York: The H.W. Wilson Co., 1986.

————. *When the Lights Go Out: Twenty Scary Tales to Tell*. New York: The H.W. Wilson Co., 1988.

Manheim, Ralph, translator. *Grimms' Tales for Young and Old*. New York: Anchor/Doubleday, 1977.

May, Rollo. *The Cry For Myth*. New York: W.W. Norton & Co.: 1991.

Miller, Teresa. *Joining In: An Anthology of Audience Participation Stories and How to Tell Them*. Cambridge, Massachusetts: Yellow Moon Press, 1988.

Mooney, Bill and David Holt, eds. *The Storyteller's Guide*. Little Rock: August House, 1996.

Moore, Robin. *Awakening the Hidden Storyteller: How to Build a Storytelling Tradition in Your Family*. Boston: Shambhala Publications Inc., 1992.

More Best-Loved Stories Told at the National Storytelling Festival. Jonesborough, Tennessee: National Storytelling Press, 1992.

National Directory of Storytelling. Jonesborough, Tennessee: National Storytelling Association, annual.

Pellowski, Anne. *The World of Storytelling*. New York: The H.W. Wilson, 1990.

Rosen, Betty. *And None of It Was Nonsense: The Power of Storytelling in School*. Portsmouth, New Hampshire: Heinemann Educational Books, Inc., 1988.

Ross, Ramon Royal. *Storyteller, 3rd Ed.* Little Rock: August House, 1996.

Sawyer, Ruth. *The Way of the Storyteller*. New York: Viking Press, 1942.

Schram, Peninnah. *Jewish Stories One Generation Tells Another*. Northvale, New Jersey: Jason Aronson Inc., 1987.

Sherman, Josepha. *Once Upon a Galaxy: The Ancient Stories Behind Star Wars, Superman, and Other Popular Fantasies*. Little Rock: August House, 1994.

Sierra, Judy and Robert Kaminski. *Twice Upon a Time: Stories to Tell, Retell, Act Out, and Write About*. New York: The H.W. Wilson Co., 1989.

Smith, Jimmy Neil. *Homespun: Tales from America's Favorite Storytellers*. New York: Crown Publishing Group, 1988.

Tales as Tools: The Power of Story in the Classroom. Jonesborough, Tennessee: The National Storytelling Press, 1994.

Thompson, Stith. *Motif-Index of Folk-Literature*. Bloomington: Indiana University, 1966.

Trousdale, Ann M., Sue A. Woestehoff, and Marni Schwartz. *Give a Listen: Stories of Storytelling in School*. Chicago: National Council of Teachers of English, 1994.

Williams, Michael. *The Storyteller's Companion to the Bible* (multi-volume set). Nashville: Abingdon Press, 1991.

Wolkstein, Diane. *The Magic Orange Tree and Other Haitian Folktales*. New York: Schocken Books, 1980.

Young, Richard and Judy Dockrey Young. *Favorite Scary Stories of American Children* (2 vols.). Little Rock: August House, 1990.

Young, Richard and Judy Dockrey Young. *The Scary Story Reader*. Little Rock: August House, 1993.

PUBLISHERS, IMPRINTS, AND SERIES

August House Publishers, Inc. Little Rock, Arkansas. (Imprints include August House Little-Folk, August House Audio, and the American Folklore Series.)

The **Folktales of the World** series, edited by Richard M. Dorson. Chicago: University of Chicago Press.

Libraries Unlimited. Littleton, Colorado.

Linnet Books. Hamden, Connecticut.

The National Storytelling Press. Jonesborough, Tennessee.

Oryx Multicultural Folktale Series. Phoenix: Oryx Press.

The Pantheon Fairy Tale and Folklore Library series. New York: Pantheon Books.

Yellow Moon Press. Cambridge, Massachusetts.

CONTRIBUTORS

◆ ◆ ◆ ◆

CAROL BIRCH, an award-winning recording artist, is chairperson of the Anne Izard Story-teller's Choice Award committee, a children's librarian with the Chappaqua (N.Y.) Library, and an instructor of Storytelling and Children's Literature. She is also the author of *Who Says? Essays on Pivotal Issues in Contemporary Storytelling.*

JUDITH BLACK has recorded seven tapes of stories and songs for adults and children. She has been on the faculty of Leslie College's Art Institute for fifteen years and has led numerous storytelling workshops.

CONNIE REGAN-BLAKE, a former member of the storytelling duo the FOLKTELLERS, was a founding member of the National Storytelling Association and has served as chair of the board and artistic director of the national festival. Most recently, she has performed with the Kandin-sky Trio in a unique collaboration of new chamber music and traditional storytelling.

ROBERTA SIMPSON BROWN currently teaches at Southern Middle School in Louisville, Ken-tucky. She is the author of *The Walking Trees and Other Scary Stories* and *The Queen of the Cold-Blooded Tales.*

JOSEPH BRUCHAC is a storyteller and writer. Many of his stories are based on his Abenaki Indian and European ancestry. He has written several books, including *The Faithful Hunter* and *Hoop Snakes.*

MILBRE BURCH has told stories from Maui to Martha's Vineyard. She lives with her husband and two daughters in Pasadena, California.

LEN CABRAL co-founded the Sidewalk Storytellers, a children's theater company, and Spell-binders, the Rhode Island storytelling collective. He has served on the board of the Rhode Island Council of the Arts and as regional advisor to the board of the National Storytelling Association.

VIRGINIA CALLAWAY heads High Windy Audio, an independent record label specializing in storytelling and folk music. She founded the company in 1987 to promote storytelling on the retail level with the hope that one day every child would have a storytelling tape.

DONALD DAVIS grew up in the Appalachian Mountains in a family and community where telling stories was a part of everyday life. The author of five books for adults and a children's picture book, *Jack and the Animals*, he lives on Ocracoke Island, off the North Carolina coast.

PLEASANT DESPAIN is recognized as a pioneer of the storytelling renaissance. After living in Seattle for more than twenty years, where he was known as "Seattle's Resident Storyteller," he now lives in Tucson, Arizona. He is the author of six books.

GAY DUCEY is a free-lance storyteller, who performs throughout the United States, and teaches storytelling at the University of California at Berkeley and at Santa Rosa Junior College. She is the former chairperson of the National Storytelling Association and is also the founder and director of the Bay Area Storytelling Festival.

ELIZABETH ELLIS grew up in the Appalachian Mountains of Tennessee and Kentucky. In 1969, she began working for the Dallas Public Library, where she was a children's librarian for ten years before becoming a professional storyteller. She is working on a book about personal storytelling style based on several theories and techniques she has developed through the years.

DIANE FERLATTE is a native of New Orleans and now lives in California. Her audio tapes have received awards from Parents' Choice and The American Library Association. She performed at the John F. Kennedy Center for the Performing Arts in Washington, D.C., in *Salute to Children*, as part of President Bill Clinton's inauguration.

HEATHER FOREST offers a blend of original music, folk guitar, poetry, and prose to storytelling audiences. *Wonder Tales Around the World*, her first full-length collection, won the Storytelling World Anthology Award in 1996. Her work appears in six anthologies, and most recently, she authored *A Big Quiet House*, a children's picture book. She lives in Huntington, New York.

MARNI GILLARD is a full-time storyteller who taught middle schoolers for twenty years. She is the author of *Storyteller, Storyteacher* and co-editor of *Give a Listen: Stories of Storytelling in School*. She is currently the Northeast Region's representative of the National Storytelling Association's Board of Directors.

JACKSON GILLMAN is called a Stand-Up Chameleon. He incorporates mime, dance, song, and sign language into his nationally-known storytelling programs. He has produced a number of audio cassettes, as well as videos of his anti-drug program, *Hard Knocks*, and Rudyard Kipling's *Just So Stories*.

ELLIN GREENE, a former storytelling specialist at The New York Public Library, currently teaches a course in storytelling at Rutgers—The State University of New Jersey. The author of several books, she has served on the board of the National Storytelling Association and twice presented at the National Storytelling Festival.

BILL HARLEY has learned his craft in thousands of performances over the past decade. Familiar to many adults as a regular commentator on NPR's *All Things Considered*, Bill has appeared at festivals, schools, and educational conferences. Every one of his ten recordings for children has won a national award. Harley is also the author of two children's books.

BETH HORNER is a former children's librarian and creative drama instructor and has been telling stories professionally for more than ten years. She has produced a six-part storytelling series for radio.

GWENDOLYN JONES recently retired from Trenton State College, Trenton, New Jersey, where she taught children's literature and storytelling, creative arts, and teacher training courses. In 1982 she founded the Garden State Storytellers' League, an affiliate of the National Story League.

FLORA JOY, a professor at East Tennessee State University, is the founder and editor of the journal *Storytelling World*. She has published twenty books and numerous articles. She has taught from elementary through college levels.

SUSAN KLEIN has been featured at dozens of storytelling festivals, including the National Storytelling Festival. She resides on Martha's Vineyard, where she was born and reared. Susan founded the Festival of Storytelling on Martha's Vineyard in 1988 and still directs the event annually the last weekend of June. Susan is the author of *Through a Ruby Window*.

CHUCK LARKIN is a bluegrass storyteller, who also gives workshops on joke telling, musical instruments such as the jaw harp, bones, spoons and the musical saw. He has performed through out the United States at festivals and libraries.

GWENDA LEDBETTER grew up on Virginia's Eastern Shore where storytelling was part of the conversation. A teacher, she has recorded tales of growing up on the coast.

SYD LIEBERMAN is a storyteller and award-winning recording artist based in Evanston, Illinois. A teacher with more than twenty years of classroom experience, he received the Golden Apple Award for excellence in teaching and is also the author of *Streets and Alleys: Stories with a Chicago Accent.*

DOUG LIPMAN, a storyteller, musician, and Parents' Choice Award-winning recording artist, is the author of *The Storytelling Coach* and has appeared at the National Storytelling Festival and the National Jewish Storytelling Festival. He lives outside Boston.

MARGARET READ MacDONALD is the children's librarian at the Bothell Public Library near Seattle, Washington. She received her doctorate in folklore from Indiana University, producing *The Storyteller's Sourcebook: A Subject, Title and Motif-Index to Folklore Collections for Children.*

JIM MAY was awarded a Chicago Emmy Award in 1989 for his performance in a television version of "A Bell for Shorty," an original story that appeared on WTTW-TV. His book, *The Farm on Nippersink Creek* is a collection of stories based on his childhood in the rural Midwest.

RAFE MARTIN is an award-winning author and storyteller. His work has been featured in *Time, Newsweek, U.S. News & World Report*, and the *New York Times Book Review.*

BARBARA McBRIDE-SMITH is a full-time school librarian in Oklahoma. She also travels extensively across the United States as a storyteller and workshop presenter.

ROBIN MOORE has been a professional storyteller since 1981 and has presented more than five thousand programs at schools, libraries, and festivals. He served as a combat soldier in Vietnam, earned a journalism degree from Pennsylvania State University, and worked as a newspaper reporter and magazine editor.

ANDY NORWOOD, a lawyer specializing in copyrights for the Nashville, Tennessee, firm of Lansden Dortch & Davis, spoke at the 1994 National Storytelling Conference on "Living Happily Ever After with the Copyright Act."

BOBBY NORFOLK began his career as a National Park Service Ranger presenting first-person historical narratives for tours at the Gateway Arch in St. Louis. A multi-award winning storyteller, he founded The Bobby Norfolk Comedy Revue in the mid-1970s and opened for such entertainers as Roberta Flack and B.B. King.

SHERRY DESENFANTS NORFOLK, a professional storyteller, is youth services coordinator for the Dekalb County Public Library in Georgia. She is married to storyteller Bobby Norfolk.

DAVID NOVAK has been telling stories professionally since 1978. He has produced programs for The Lincoln Center Institute in New York and the Los Angeles Music Center on Tour. He works in Celebration, Florida, at the Disney Institute.

JAY O'CALLAHAN tours the world, performing at festivals and in theaters. His stories have been heard on NPR, The Voice of America, and "Mister Rogers' Neighborhood." He was recently honored by the New England Reading Association with its Special Recognition Award for his significant contribution to literacy education. He lives in Marshfield, Massachusetts.

MICHAEL PARENT tells stories that reflect his growing up in a bilingual family. Along with Julien Olivier, he co-authored *Of Kings and Fools*, a collection of Franco-American folktales. He now lives in Charlottesville, Virginia.

MAGGI PEIRCE, a native of Northern Ireland, has lived in the United States since 1964. In 1974, she received the prestigious Eisteddfod Award from Southeastern Massachusetts University for her dedication to traditional music and song. In 1988, she received a finalist award from the Massachusetts Arts and Humanities Artists Foundation for excellence in storytelling.

GAYLE ROSS is a direct descendant of Chief John Ross, Principal Chief of the Cherokee Nation during the infamous Trail of Tears. Since 1979, she has traveled the country telling Native American stories at schools, libraries, colleges, and festivals.

STEVE SANFIELD, an award-winning author, poet, and storyteller is the founder and artistic director of the Sierra Storytelling Festival. He has written more than twenty books, his latest are *The Great Turtle Drive* and *The Girl Who Wanted a Song*.

PENINNAH SCHRAM has been telling stories professionally since 1970. She is the founding director of the Jewish Storytelling Center in New York City.

LAURA SIMMS founded the Storytelling Center of Oneonta at Oneonta, New York, in 1977, and in 1985, she co-founded the New York City Storytelling Center.

JON SPELMAN, a solo theater performer, narrative artist, monologist, and storyteller, travels throughout the United States with almost twenty hours of performance material for children, families, and adults.

JAY STAILEY is principal of Carver Elementary School in Baytown, Texas. He teaches reading specialization for undergraduates in the College of Education at the University of Houston in Clear Lake, Texas. He is also the chairperson of the National Storytelling Association Board of Directors.

FRAN STALLINGS grew up in a traditional storytelling family. Although trained as a biologist with a doctorate in research, she has been a traveling storyteller since 1978. She has worked intensively with thousands of students through State Arts Council of Oklahoma residencies.

ED STIVENDER is known for his unique renditions of fairy tales with a comic twist and his comic portrayal of St. Francis. He is the author of *Raised Catholic (Can You Tell?)* and *Still Catholic After All These Fears*. He lives in Germantown, Pennsylvania.

JACKIE TORRENCE has performed at the Lincoln Center, the Kennedy Center, the Chicago Blues Festival, and the National Storytelling Festival. She has won numerous awards and commissions.

MARK WAGLER is a teacher in Madison, Wisconsin. A professional storyteller and folklorist, The founder of *I Wonder: The Journal for Elementary School Scientists and It Figures! The Journal for Elementary School Mathematics,* he is the first president of the Northlands Storytelling Network.

JIM WEISS is a storyteller and award-winning recording artist. His fifteen recordings are published by his own label, Greathall Productions, and have received seventeen national awards. A native of Highland Park, Illinois, he presently lives in northern California with his wife, Randy, and their daughter.

RANDY WEISS teaches in Benicia Middle School, forty-five minutes north of San Francisco. She is a partner in Greathall Productions and is married to Jim Weiss.

KATHRYN WINDHAM is a nationally-known storyteller and a frequent commentator on NPR's *All Things Considered.* For years, she was an award-winning reporter for the *Selma (Alabama) Times-Journal.* She is the author of numerous ghost story collections. Kathryn co-founded the Alabama Tale Telling Festival.

DIANE WOLKSTEIN has told stories since 1967 at the Hans Christian Andersen statue in New York City's Central Park. Diane is the author of many award-winning books of folklore for adults and children, including *Inanna: Queen of Heaven and Earth* (with Samuel Noah Kramer).